The Clean Tech Revolution

The Clean Tech Revolution

The Next Big Growth and Investment Opportunity

RON PERNICK and CLINT WILDER

An *Imprint of* HarperCollins*Publishers*

Note to the Reader

Ron Pernick is cofounder and principal and Clint Wilder is contributing editor of Clean Edge, Inc., a research and publishing firm focused on clean technologies. Clean Edge has worked with many entities in the clean-technology sector since the company's launch in 2001. Companies, organizations, and firms covered in this book that Clean Edge has worked with (at the time of completing the book manuscript) include the California Energy Commission, the City of San Francisco, Cleantech Venture Network, ClearEdge Power, the Energy Foundation, Energy Innovations, Environmental Entrepreneurs (E2), Global Environment Fund, Miasolé, NASDAQ, Nth Power, Pacific Growth Equities, Piper Jaffray, Sharp, Solaicx, Solaria, and Stoel Rives.

While the information in this book is believed to be accurate, it is not intended to be used as a guide to investing, and the authors make no guarantees that any investments based on the information contained herein will benefit you in specific applications, owing to the risk that is involved in investing of almost any kind. Thus, neither the publisher nor the authors assume liability for any losses that may be sustained by the use of the advice described in this book, and any such liability is hereby expressly disclaimed.

HarperCollins books may be purchased for educational, business, or sales promotional use. For information, please write: Special Markets Department, HarperCollins Publishers, 10 East 53rd Street, New York, NY 10022.

FIRST EDITION

Designed by Level C

Printed on acid-free paper

Library of Congress Cataloging-in-Publication Data is available upon request.

ISBN 978-0-06-089623-2

06 07 08 09 10 DT/RRD 10 9 8 7 6 5 4 3 2 1

This book is dedicated to our wives, Dena Shehab and
Ellie Barrett Wilder. Without their support, love, understanding,
and guidance, this book would never have been possible.

CONTENTS

I find out what the world needs, then I proceed to invent . . .

—Thomas A. Edison

ABBREVIATIONS

AMR: automated meter reading

BIPV: building-integrated photovoltaics

BPL: broadband over power line

CIGS: copper, indium, gallium, selenium

CNG: compressed natural gas

CO_2: carbon dioxide

CPV: concentrating photovoltaics

ETF: exchange-traded fund

EV: electric vehicle

FCV: fuel-cell vehicle

FFV: flex-fuel vehicle

GHG: greenhouse gas

GMO: genetically modified organism

GPS: global positioning system

GW: gigawatt (equal to 1,000 megawatts)

HEV: hybrid electric vehicle

HVAC: heating, ventilating, and air-conditioning

IGCC: integrated gasification controlled cycle, or coal gasification

IPO: initial public offering (of stock)

kW: kilowatt (equal to 1,000 watts)

kWh: kilowatt-hour

LED: light-emitting diode

LEED: Leadership in Energy and Environmental Design (Green Building Rating System)

LEV: low-emission vehicle

LOHAS: lifestyles of health and sustainability

mpg: miles per gallon

mph: miles per hour

MW: megawatt (equal to 1 million watts)

MWH: megawatt-hour

NIMBY syndrome: "not in my backyard" syndrome

NiMH: nickel–metal hydride

PHEV: plug-in hybrid electric vehicle

PLA: polylactic acid

PTC: production tax credit

PV: photovoltaic

REC: renewable energy certificate or credit

RFS: renewable fuel standard

RPS: renewable portfolio standard

SUV: sport utility vehicle

VC: venture capital

W: watt

Introduction

THE CLEAN-TECH OPPORTUNITY

In New York City, hiply dressed residents of the Solaire, a luxury apartment building in lower Manhattan, head home after a day of office work and mocha grandes. They step into a Cesar Pelli & Associates–designed "green building" that uses 35% less electricity and 50% less water than comparable structures, thanks to solar photovoltaic panels, energy efficiency, and recycling.

Half a world away, a group of engineers from New Hampshire is testing water-purification devices in a small village in Bangladesh. The mobile devices, dubbed Slingshots, are a product from inventor Dean Kamen of DEKA Research and Development Corp., best known as the creator of the Segway scooter. Powered by a small amount of biofuel such as wood or cow manure, the Slingshot harnesses its own waste heat to use 50 times less energy than traditional purification systems.

In another small town—Elkin, North Carolina—textile mill workers are turning out fibers for carpeting from Atlanta-based Interface Engineering, one of the world's largest suppliers of commercial flooring materials. The Terratex brand fabric is a combination of 100% recycled polyester and so-called bio-based fibers, derived from corn, rice, and beet plants. Some of the carpet fibers are not only recyclable but also fully compostable and biodegradable.

Welcome to the future—today. Following on the heels of the computer, Internet, and biotech revolutions, "clean tech" is bringing unprecedented opportunities for wealth creation, high-growth career development, and innovative solutions to a range of global problems. It is becoming the cornerstone of corporate, investment, and government strategies to profit in the next decade and to guarantee economic competitiveness for years to come.

At a time when the U.S. economy sputters in fits and starts and faces unprecedented challenges from high energy prices, depleted natural resources, volatile sources of foreign oil, record deficits, and unprecedented environmental and security challenges, clean tech offers the promise to be the next big engine of business and economic growth. Companies, investors, entrepreneurs, job seekers, and governments have a choice to either embrace and lead in this brave new world of clean-tech innovation or risk falling behind a host of competitors.

At stake: trillions of dollars in economic opportunity and prosperity for the companies and individuals at the forefront of this next great growth and investment opportunity.

WHAT IS THE CLEAN TECH REVOLUTION?

For most people the concept of clean technology, or clean tech, is relatively new. *Clean tech* refers to any product, service, or process that delivers value using limited or zero nonrenewable resources and/or creates significantly less waste than conventional offerings. Clean technology comprises a diverse range of products and services, from solar power systems to hybrid electric vehicles (HEVs), that

- Harness renewable materials and energy sources or reduce the use of natural resources by using them more efficiently and productively
- Cut or eliminate pollution and toxic wastes
- Deliver equal or superior performance compared with conventional offerings
- Provide investors, companies, and customers with the promise of increased returns, reduced costs, and lower prices
- Create quality jobs in management, production, and deployment

Clean tech covers four main sectors: energy, transportation, water, and materials. It includes relatively well-known technologies such as solar photovoltaics, wind power, biofuels, bio-based plastics, advanced lithium-ion batteries, and large-scale reverse-osmosis water desalination. It also includes such emerging technologies as tidal power, silicon-based fuel cells, distributed hydrogen generation, plug-in hybrid vehicles, and nanotechnology-based materials.

In the 1970s, clean tech was considered "alternative," the province of back-to-the-land lifestyle advocates, altruistic environmentalists, and lab scientists on research grants—and for good reason: It was in an early stage of development, it was too expensive, it didn't have widespread political support, and very few large, established companies were embracing the sector. Even at the start of the twenty-first century, the term *clean tech* wasn't yet in the financial or business community's lexicon. If you had done a Web search on *clean technology* or *clean tech* in 2000, you'd have received only a few relevant results. If you did a similar Web search on the topic today, you'd find more than 500,000 relevant hits, reflecting today's reality—clean technology is everywhere.

Throughout the world, in trends large and small, we're seeing the beginning of a revolution that is changing the places where we live and work, the products we manufacture and purchase, and the development plans of cities, regional governments, and nations around the globe. One need look no further than the daily headlines to see clean tech taking hold. Portland, Oregon, recently became the first city in the United States to require all gasoline sold within city limits to contain at least 10% ethanol. California passed landmark legislation to cap and reduce greenhouse gas (GHG) emissions and to install nearly 1 million solar roofs over the next decade. Gas-guzzling sport utility vehicle (SUV) proprietor Ford has seen its fortunes plummet as those of hybrid-leader Toyota rise. Entrepreneurs have raised venture capital (VC) to develop everything from a high-performance, battery-powered, $92,000 electric sports car to solar cells based on nanotechnology.

The revolution is not coming; it's here today. Consider these facts:

- **State mandates in the United States**. More than half of the American people live in states that have mandated that their utilities generate a specified percentage of electricity (in many cases up to 20% or 25%) from renewable sources such as solar, wind, biomass, and geothermal by a specific target year. Two recent states to join the club, Colorado and Washington, did so by 2004 and 2006 ballot measures that each state's voters approved by comfortable margins.

- **Leadership in the European Union.** Wind farms in Denmark, many of them offshore, now generate about 20% of the nation's electricity, proving many doubters wrong about the viability of clean, renewable energy. Germany and Spain rank first and second, respectively, in world wind-power production, creating thousands of jobs in the process.
- **Clean power options.** Hundreds of investor-owned utilities, municipal utilities, and electric cooperatives in every region of the United States offer the option of green power to customers who can choose to receive electricity from renewable sources. While most of these utilities charge a small green surcharge, that charge is sometimes locked in for a fixed period, providing a hedge against spikes in the price of natural gas. In some regions, green-power customers have at times seen their electric rates drop below those of their neighbors who are paying for conventional power.
- **A solar boom.** The solar PV (photovoltaic) industry reached more than 1 gigawatt (GW, or 1,000 megawatts [MW]) of total manufacturing output in 2004, approximately 1.5 GW in 2005, and more than 2 GW in 2006, making the solar manufacturing and installation industry worth nearly $16 billion. And it is projected to continue to expand by more than 30% each year for the foreseeable future. Sharp, the leading manufacturer of solar PV modules, believes in a bright future for the technology. The company has expanded its manufacturing capacity from 54 MW in 2000 to a planned 710 MW in 2007.
- **A hybrid takeoff.** Since 2003, hybrid cars have gone from a tiny speck on the automotive landscape to one of the U.S. vehicle market's fastest-growing segments. Toyota doubled its flagship hybrid car's allocation in North America in 2005, to 100,000, and started building hybrids on U.S. assembly lines in 2006. By the end of 2006 there were some 15 hybrid models on showroom floors, including hybrid models for such popular vehicles as the Honda Civic and Accord and the Toyota Camry.

- **Clean extreme makeover.** Since 2000, more than 730 buildings comprising 5% of all new commercial structures in the United States have been certified as green buildings by the U.S. Green Building Council, and nearly 5,800 more are in the pipeline. For example, Ford's 600-acre Rouge Factory complex in Dearborn, Michigan, the world's largest integrated industrial facility when it was completed by Henry Ford in 1928, has undergone a complete "greening." Ford workers assemble trucks under a 10-acre roof with grasses and plants growing on it; the insulation cuts energy costs by nearly 10%.
- **Bio big business.** Bio-based materials are moving from the organic food co-op to the shelves of major chains such as Wal-Mart and Sam's Club. Cargill, via its NatureWorks unit, is manufacturing bio-based materials using renewable resources such as maize instead of petrochemicals. The material uses up to 50% less energy to produce and is compostable. DuPont has also been aggressively pursuing the biopolymers market, launching a new manufacturing facility in 2007 to produce a patented biomaterial based on fermented and purified sugars. Agribusiness giant Archer Daniels Midland (ADM) is building a plant in Clinton, Iowa, that will produce 45,000 tons of natural, corn-based plastics annually after it opens in 2008.

The list goes on and on.

WHAT IS DRIVING THE REVOLUTION?

So how did clean tech go from the stuff of back-to-the-earth utopian dreams to its current revolution among the inner circles of corporate boardrooms, on Wall Street trading floors, and in government offices around the globe?

We've identified six major forces—what we call the six C's—that are pushing clean tech into the mainstream and driving the rapid growth, expansion, and economic necessity of clean tech across the globe: *costs*, *capital*, *competition*, *China*, *consumers*, and *climate*. These six forces are aligning to catalyze the growth and expansion of clean-energy solutions for transportation fuels and electricity generation; clean sources of water for drinking, irrigation, and manufacturing; and clean, environmentally benign materials for buildings and industrial processes. Together they are creating dynamic, lucrative business and investment opportunities for established companies, entrepreneurs, and investors of all types.

> **Costs.** Perhaps the most powerful force driving today's clean-tech growth is simple economics. As a general trend, clean-energy costs are falling as the costs of fossil fuel energy are going up. The future of clean tech is going to be, in many ways, about scaling up manufacturing and driving down costs.

As recently as a decade ago, most clean technologies were not ready for prime time and were often prohibitively more expensive than their conventional counterparts. Now, that's changing. Recent advances in core technology and manufacturing processes have significantly improved performance, reliability, scalability, and cost. At the same time that clean-energy technologies are getting cheaper, the costs of products and services driven by conventional fossil fuels are rising dramatically. The convergence of these two cost trends is starting to make clean tech competitive economically.

In conventional fossil-fuel power such as coal and natural gas (which together provide approximately 60% of the world's electricity), the generating technologies are mature, stable, and already widely deployed. Notwithstanding incremental technical improvements in generation and transmission efficiency, the turbines powered by burning coal and natural gas still function essentially the same way they have for decades—so their *technology* costs are relatively steady and predictable. What determines the price of conventional power is the cost of *fuel*. Since the 1970s, the costs of fossil fuels, while certainly experiencing directional gyrations, have nearly always moved in the same general direction over the long term: up.

With solar, wind, small-scale hydroelectric, geothermal, and even the nascent technology of ocean tide- and wave-generated electricity, the price-determining formula is just the opposite. There is no cost of "fuel"—the sun, the breeze, the heat of the earth, the tides and waves arrive free of charge daily. "Coal, natural gas, and oil costs move in directions that can be hard to predict," says Mark Little, former vice president of power generation at General Electric's energy unit, now director of GE Global Research. "But we can make one projection that we know will be accurate: The price of wind will always be zero. And that is a fundamental of our industry."

All of the costs involved in clean tech are in the technology used to harness and deliver the energy. And over time, as their markets expand, efficiencies improve, and production volumes ramp up to create economies of scale, the costs of new technologies consistently go down. The clearest and most well-known example of the theory of declining tech costs comes from the high-tech industry. The multimillion-dollar room-sized computers of the late 1950s have progressed, in less than a half century, to today's sub-$1,000 laptops and iPods, which boast more computing power and data storage capacity than their gargantuan ancestors.

Moore's Law, the famous axiom of Intel cofounder Gordon Moore, states that the number of transistors on a semiconductor chip of silicon (the same base material of PV cells that deliver solar energy) will double every 18 months. In other words, the same-size chip will deliver twice the computing power at essentially the same cost—the direct cause of the falling high-tech technology cost trends we all know. A number of experts believe that clean-energy sources, such as solar, could be experiencing a kind of Moore's Law of their own, establishing a long-term trend of declining costs for clean tech.

It's not just the downward directions of clean-energy costs that contrast with that of fossil-fuel costs—it's their smoothness as well. With some notable exceptions, such as a current temporary blip in solar costs due to a global shortage of silicon for PV cells and for wind turbines due to rising steel prices and very high demand, clean-energy costs are notably less volatile than their conventional counterparts. It's a lot easier to plan your future energy budget when it's not subject to the vagaries of the world commodity markets of oil and gas described above.

One of the great advantages of most clean-energy technologies is price stability. Once you pay for a solar PV array on your rooftop or install a wind farm, there are no costs for fuels. You need to pay for your capital expenditure up front and amortize it over a 10- or 20-year loan, but beyond that, your pricing is generally stable and fixed. For a small but growing number of green-power customers—individuals and organizations that purchase a percentage or all of their electricity from clean-energy sources—the ability to lock in a consistent fuel charge for up to 10 years is a great business plum. It converts a variable budget line item into a fixed cost. Even if the initial green-power charge is a bit higher, many companies, government agencies, college campuses, and even military bases think it's worth it.

Capital. An unprecedented influx of capital is changing the clean-tech landscape, with billions of dollars, euros, yen, and yuan pouring in from a myriad of public and private sector sources.

Where there's money, technology expansion is sure to follow. Capital, in the form of corporate investments, VC, government grants, project finance, debt equity, and the public stock markets, is critical to the growth of any emerging sector. It provides the means to develop new technologies, build management teams, create new distribution channels, and effectively market products and services. In fact, all the major technology expansions, from biotech to the computer revolution, owe their success to an influx of capital from a range of sources. Clean tech will be no exception.

Since the 1970s, investments in clean technology have moved from primarily government research and development (R&D) projects to major multinationals, well-heeled venture capitalists, and savvy individual investors. While governments still have a significant role to play, this shift is changing the investment landscape and bringing clean technology to the commercial forefront. A number of leading companies, for example, are embracing clean-tech initiatives and investing billions of dollars in their efforts: General Electric (GE), the world's largest diversified manufacturer, plans to invest up to $1.5 billion a year in clean-tech R&D by 2010 as part of its "Ecomagination" business strategy. BP recently launched an alternative-energy unit that will spend up to $8 billion over 10 years to further the company's activities in solar, wind, and hydrogen. Spain-based energy giants Iberdrola and Acciona are both poised to spend billions of dollars building out their clean-energy portfolios, primarily wind power, over the coming years. In 2006, Toyota is reported to have spent an astounding $8 billion in R&D, much of it for hybrid and fuel-cell development. Sanyo, the fourth largest solar cell manufacturer in the world behind Sharp, Q-Cells, and Kyocera, has said it will invest $350 million over 5 years to expand its solar operations as well.

In 2005, investment banker and Wall Street icon Goldman Sachs acquired Zilkha Renewable Energy, one of the world's leading wind-energy developers. Renamed Horizon Wind Energy, the development firm had 1,350 MW of wind-power capacity planned by the end of 2007 (1 MW of wind electricity, or 1,000 watts (W), is enough to power about 750 homes). The acquisition positioned the white-shoe Goldman Sachs firm as one of the leading players in the world of wind-farm development and finance and firmly established a new era of "big-money" wind power in the United States and abroad. The deal placed Wall Street's stamp of approval on the wind-power industry, further legitimizing the wind-energy investments of huge electric utilities such as American Electric Power, FPL Energy, TXU, and Xcel Energy. Goldman Sachs, which is branching out into other clean-energy investments, now has approximately 20 full-time investment professionals putting about $2 billion of capital to work into such companies as First Solar, GridPoint, Iogen, and SunEdison.

Venture capitalists and investors are also taking note of the clean-tech opportunity. In fact, many of the same entrepreneurs and investors who fueled the high-tech and Internet revolutions are now leading the charge in clean tech. They are getting involved in clean tech because it is built on many of the same concepts that influenced the growth of computers and the Internet. In 2006, clean-energy investments represented more than 9% of total venture investing in the United States—up from less than 1% in 1999—and all of clean-tech investing, comprising clean energy, water, and materials, represented more than $2.9 billion of venture investments in North America. Clean tech is now one of the largest VC investment sectors, and Cleantech Capital Group, a Michigan-based research firm, predicts it will account for $10 billion in venture dollars in North America between 2006 and 2009, compared with $6.4 billion in the previous 3-year period—a 56% increase.

Kleiner Perkins Caufield & Byers, best known for its investments in Amazon.com, Google, and Netscape, has created a $200 million Greentech investment fund. Even the Carlyle Group, one of the world's largest private equity firms, is roaring into clean tech. Reviled by political activists for its close ties to two Bush administrations, global military contractors, and oil and gas interests in the Middle East, Carlyle nonetheless sees potential for big returns in the clean-energy sectors of solar, wind, geothermal, and biomass. As clean-tech evangelist and Technology Partners general partner Ira Ehrenpreis likes to point out: "Energy-tech investing is *all* about the green, and this has nothing to do with the environment!" To the high-tech inventors, visionaries, and bankrollers jumping on board the clean tech revolution, financial returns come first.

Capital is also flowing into clean tech–focused companies through many existing and emerging retail investment products and offerings. Individuals can now invest in a handful of index-based exchange-traded funds (ETFs) and mutual funds. The first ETF representing the clean-energy sector, the PowerShares WilderHill Clean Energy Portfolio based on the ECO Index, had more than $700 million in assets in early 2007. (WilderHill founder Robert Wilder is not related to coauthor Clint Wilder.) Other indexes have followed WilderHill's lead: the NASDAQ Clean Edge U.S. Index (CLEN) and its liquid series (CELS), the Ardour family of "alternative" energy indexes (which include the Ardour North America [AGINA] Index), and the Cleantech Capital Group's Cleantech Index (CTIUS). By early 2007, additional ETFs had been created based on the CELS and CTIUS indexes. Investors can also invest directly in the stocks of pure-play companies focused primarily on clean technology and large multinationals with clean-tech initiatives.

A number of mutual funds also offer investors opportunities in the clean energy and clean-tech sector. These include the New Alternatives Fund (NALFX), which is focused primarily on clean energy, and broader socially responsible investing mutual funds that have stakes in clean-tech companies, such as the Winslow Green Growth Fund (WGGFX). Another trend is the advent of "green banks," such as ShoreBank in Chicago and New Resource Bank in San Francisco, that support green and socially responsible businesses and plan to begin offering customers high-yield, interest-bearing online banking accounts.

There's also a major transition in capital that's funding clean-tech growth in developing nations. In these emerging economies, most of the funding in clean energy and clean technology has traditionally come from national governments or international government-financed agencies such as the World Bank, particularly its Global Environment Facility (GEF). They are still heavily involved and will continue to be for years to come.

But today, big international banks and investment houses, among them Goldman Sachs, Morgan Stanley, Citigroup, Australia's Macquarie Bank and ANZ, Belgium's Fortis and Dexia, and RBC Royal Bank of Canada, are becoming aggressive funders of clean-energy and clean-water projects in developing countries.

Competition. Governments are competing aggressively in the high-stakes race to dominate in the clean-tech sector and build the jobs of the future.

From small cities to urban metropolises and from states to nations, governments at every level are competing to be leaders in the clean tech revolution. A number of factors are driving this competitive field, not the least of which is the need to build regional economies and develop high-paying regional jobs. Equally important, the competition for limited global energy and water resources is driving the clean-tech imperative to reduce the geopolitical and terrorist risks posed by dependence on resources from politically volatile regions such as the Middle East and West Africa.

Governments, via tax incentives, standards, subsidies, and other tools, can make or break the growth of any labor- and capital-intensive industrial sector. In energy, government policy has played a key role in bolstering and supporting oil, coal, natural gas, and nuclear power with extensive subsidies and tax incentives. Even in an era of record-breaking oil industry profits, Big Oil continues to receive billions in tax subsidies annually. Government policies determine issues ranging from how utilities operate to the efficiency of vehicles to the distribution of water. The clean tech revolution, in many ways, rests on the advent of long-term consistent government policies and the bolstering of subsidies for solar, wind, and other emerging sectors.

For clean tech to thrive, governments at a range of levels must embrace and support fledgling clean-tech industries with supportive policies and incentives. In cities as diverse as Bonn, Abu Dhabi, and Sacramento, forward-thinking governments are shifting regulatory and financial support away from older, polluting technologies to more efficient technologies that create jobs, reduce pollution, and make regions and countries more economically competitive. In China, the central government is advocating three times more renewable energy by 2020 than its target for nuclear power. Japan embarked on a 10-year program in the 1990s to fund and nurture the growth of its solar PV industry, and that industry is now flourishing without any significant subsidies. Iceland is aiming to be one of the first fossil fuel–free economies—leveraging naturally occurring resources such as geothermal energy and building out a hydrogen-based economy. Germany is spending heavily to build out its solar and biodiesel industries. Sweden's prime minister, Göran Persson, has announced the ambitious intention for his country to be oil free by 2020. At least eleven other developing nations ranging from Cambodia to Turkey have some sort of national policies in place to promote, incentivize, or directly fund clean-energy development.

Across the globe, many regional and national governments are pushing initiatives that could result (and in some cases already are resulting) in more than 20% of their energy coming from renewable sources. A shift of unprecedented proportions is afoot—although clearly, much more will need to be done to put clean technologies squarely in a leadership position.

In the United States, the Republican and Democratic governors of New York, Pennsylvania, California, Montana, New Mexico, and other states are calling for massive investments in clean energy and clean technology. California recently increased its renewable portfolio standard by accelerating its 20% renewable energy target to 2010 (7 years earlier than initially targeted) and calling for 33% of California's electricity to come from clean-energy sources by 2020. Its landmark greenhouse-gas reduction legislation, signed by Governor Arnold Schwarzenegger in September 2006, is the first-ever such bill in the United States requiring major industrial emitters to cut GHG emissions 25% by 2020. Although traditional industries such as oil, cement, and some manufacturers said the bill would hurt business, venture capitalists, investors, and entrepreneurs lobbied hard to pass it. The state's Climate Action Team, formed by Schwarzenegger in 2005, predicts that the legislation will create up to 83,000 new jobs worth $4 billion in personal income by 2020.

Unfortunately, even as local governments are acting, the administration of President George W. Bush has fallen far behind other nations in pursuing aggressive clean-tech initiatives and providing long-term guidance and incentives. While Japan and Germany have been championing clean tech for some time, the U.S. federal government has basically been missing in action. Once the U.S. federal government finally gets on board, in an aggressive way, it will augment significant developments already in place at the state level and around the globe.

China. Clean tech is being driven by the inexorable demands being placed on the earth not only by mature economies but also by the explosive demand for resources in China, India, and other developing nations. Their expanding energy needs are driving major growth in clean-energy, transportation, building, and water-delivery technologies.

China is emblematic of the resource constraint issues facing our planet—it is currently the earth's number-one consumer of coal, burning more of it each year than the United States, India, and Russia combined. It is now the second largest consumer of oil on the planet behind the United States, recently eclipsing Japan, and also the world's largest consumer of steel, meat, and grain. With a projected migration of more than 400 million people from rural areas to cities by 2020 (equal in size to three New York Cities per year), China will not be able to sustain its growth if it doesn't widely embrace clean technology.

The Chinese government is starting to understand this and in 2006 committed to investing up to $180 billion over 15 years to meet nationally mandated targets for clean energy. China is planning to have 60 GW of renewable energy (not including large hydroelectric) by 2010 and 120 GW by 2020. If the country meets these national mandates, clean-energy sources will represent upward of 10% of total generating capacity by 2020.

And it isn't just China that is embracing clean tech. Across the globe, developing nations in Asia, Africa, and South America view clean-energy sources such as wind, solar, and biofuels not as niche novelties or environmentalist-motivated "alternatives" but as a critical, urgent, and growing piece of a diversified energy mix needed to fuel their rapidly developing economies and middle classes. With the hypercharged economies of China and India both growing 5% to 9% annually, there's a palpable feeling of wanting to deploy and use any energy source they can get their hands on. There's less of a perceived conflict between established energy sources and newer, cleaner options. Wind, solar, small hydroelectric, biogas, biofuels—we need all of those, these nations seem to say. As much as possible, as soon as possible, and above all, as cheaply as possible.

This adds up to unprecedented opportunity for clean-tech manufacturers and investors in meeting the power and water needs of billions of people. The profit opportunity to serve the emerging markets in China and countless other nations is expanding for both large corporations and emerging start-ups. That's why today the world's leading wind, solar, and other clean-tech providers are already moving into the Chinese market via joint ventures with local companies and other avenues.

Tapping these markets won't be easy, but the growing, energy-hungry middle classes of developing nations require massive new water and energy infrastructure projects, be they wind farms off the Indian coast, ethanol plants in China, or desalination facilities in Algeria. And rural communities, which still represent nearly 50% of the global population, are in desperate need of finding creative ways to meet the resource needs of their residents. In India, some 56% of the population's 700 million rural residents lack reliable access to electric power. The nation wants to deliver electricity to all of them by 2012—*50% of it* from renewable sources including wind, solar, and biogas.

China, emblematic of this mounting and critical need for clean and efficient energy, transportation, water, and materials, offers up a unique opportunity for investors and innovators. The nation will be one of the largest consumers of clean technologies and a potentially inexpensive manufacturing base for export to other nations.

Consumers. Savvy consumers are demanding cleaner products and services that use resources efficiently, reduce costs, and embrace quality over quantity.

Without consumer demand, no market would materialize. Today, high energy prices, polluted ecosystems, and growing awareness of climate change and the geopolitical costs associated with fossil fuels are driving a shift in consumer attitudes and consumer demand for clean-tech products and services. That's forcing companies that sell to consumers—from appliance makers to auto manufacturers—to produce cleaner, more efficient products and market them aggressively.

Companies such as organic food purveyor Whole Foods Market, the fastest-growing grocery chain in the United States, have proven that huge shifts in mainstream consumer perception, behavior, and spending are possible. The demographic sector known as LOHAS—lifestyles of health and sustainability—has swelled to 50 million people, or one sixth of the U.S. population, according to the Natural Marketing Institute. Even more significantly, those consumers spend more than $220 billion annually on a wide range of products and services, including yoga, organic foods and cosmetics, acupuncture, ecotourism, and organic cotton clothing, according to the *LOHAS Journal*. Even if that figure is inflated, when mainstream retailers like Safeway and Wal-Mart Stores start embracing organic foods as they have, it's clear that there's a shift going on that makes consumer markets ripe for clean tech if it's marketed effectively.

In fact, there is already some indication of a significant and expanding consumer interest in clean-tech products and services. Not unlike the explosive growth of the organic foods market, clean technologies such as solar, wind, and biofuels are seeing annual growth rates exceeding 30%. The number of EnergyStar homes, so designated by standards of the U.S. Environmental Protection Agency because they are equipped with the most efficient heating and air-conditioning systems and appliances, have gone from zero in 1995 to more than 130,000 in 2004, comprising up to 40% market share of new homes in some regions. Who is driving this demand and growth? Both early adopters, who installed the first solar PV system in their neighborhood or purchased an early model Toyota Prius, and mainstream customers, who are installing high-efficiency water heaters, buying higher-mileage cars, insulating their homes with recycled denim, and demanding efficient EnergyStar appliances and windows.

In clean tech, broad, growing mass consumer markets are already coming into being for hybrid cars in the United States (where hybrid sales nearly tripled between 2004 and 2006), solar hot-water heaters and electric scooters in China, and energy-efficient appliances and lighting in Europe, Asia, and the United States. Whether it's efficient compact-fluorescent or light-emitting diode (LED) lightbulbs at Sears and

Home Depot or ethanol from Wal-Mart's 400 filling stations at its Sam's Club stores, clean-tech products are squarely in the consumer mainstream.

Another factor impacting the consumer trend is the newly minted consumer classes of the developing world. Fueled by their nations' boom economies, these consumers won't just be buying clothes and gadgets—they'll be using energy at a modern, consumer-driven pace that their parents and grandparents scarcely could have imagined. Economists estimate that the Chinese middle class, already more than 100 million people strong, will reach 200 million by 2010. The same trend is occurring in India and, to a lesser extent, in other developing nations. That's both a driver and an opportunity for clean tech, with hybrid cars, energy-efficient appliances, and renewable energy-powered homes and apartments already gaining significant traction in rapidly developing nations.

Climate. The debate around climate change has gone from question mark to peer-reviewed certainty, and smart businesses are taking heed.

Alarm is growing about the climate-change consequences caused by our continued dependence on carbon-intensive, GHG-emitting energy and transportation sources and manufacturing processes. Scientific data and research overwhelmingly support this growing concern. Eleven of the hottest years on record occurred between 1995 and 2006; the United States and Japan both recorded the highest number of extreme weather events in the form of hurricanes and typhoons in 2005. The devastation of Hurricane Katrina in particular brought the issue of the effect of warming oceans on storm severity to the forefront of public attention.

NASA released a report in 2006 showing that the Greenland ice belt is melting far faster than earlier believed and could cause considerable global sea-level flooding. The National Academy of Sciences delivered a 155-page report to the U.S. Congress in 2006 supporting the human–climate change connection. A panel of climate scientists reported that the "recent warmth is unprecedented for at least the last 400 years and potentially the last several millennia" and that "human activities are responsible for much of the recent warming." And with insurance giants such as Swiss Re and Munich

Re thinking twice about climate impact on the issuance of their policies (try getting an insurance policy for an oil rig in the Gulf of Mexico), the climate issue is coming front and center for companies, governments, and individuals. Human impact on climate is clear and concise—we are adding more carbon dioxide (CO_2) into the atmosphere now than at any other time in recorded history.

That's driving clean-tech investment and deployment and becoming an increasingly important factor in assessing investment risk factors. Global companies from DuPont to Wal-Mart are investing heavily to promote energy efficiency and clean tech in their operations to reduce their GHG contributions. Government and private carbon trading schemes, in which companies earn financial credits for cutting CO_2 emissions and pay penalties if they don't, are creating further economic incentives for companies to operate more efficiently and run clean. Forward-looking U.S. companies and investment managers, even without their government's participation in the Kyoto Protocol to the United Nations Framework Convention on Climate Change, are joining their European and Japanese competitors to reduce their production of CO_2. They believe, as we do, that future carbon regulation is inevitable and are following a fundamental principle of business innovation: Be proactive, not reactive.

For businesses and investors, the climate-change issue works as a two-pronged driver. The increased regulation of CO_2 and other GHGs will pump up worldwide demand for technologies that deliver energy or power transportation with reduced or zero amounts of GHGs, growing the markets for those technologies. At the same time, investors will increasingly assess companies in all industries on their downside risk from carbon emissions and their upside potential from reducing them. A growing number of leading investment banks, such as Innovest Strategic Value Advisors and Sanford C. Bernstein, have begun rating stocks in terms of carbon risk and establishing funds of potential winners.

"As an investor, do you believe that we're going to take climate change seriously in terms of legislation?" asks Mark Trexler, president of Trexler Climate + Energy Services, a firm in Portland, Oregon, that advises companies and utilities on carbon-reduction strategies. "If you do, then figure it in to your investment decisions. If you're right, you'll be way ahead in the long run. To completely ignore it, in terms of investment decisions, would be a terrible thing."

These powerful global forces—the six Cs—have put clean tech onto center stage and awakened a diverse range of stakeholders across the world. The clean tech revolution is not about environmental do-goodism and is not a rejection of business and technology. Instead, it embraces capital, business, and technological innovation and provides a viable new path for a world that's reaching resource limits and dealing with unprecedented challenges. Governments, investors, companies, and entrepreneurs that seize the opportunity of clean technology are positioned to reap significant benefits and profits.

From Beijing to Berlin, from San Francisco to Bangalore, the clean tech revolution is well under way. It will determine which regions lead and prosper and which regions are left drowning in their own effluents, choking on their own emissions, and struggling to compete in a world that is leaner, greener, and less reliant on fossil fuels.

WHO STANDS TO WIN?

Is it too late to participate in the clean tech revolution? Have all the big players cornered the market? Has all of the smart capital been invested? Have all of the best innovations been developed? Certainly not. Although the rapid pace of change in clean-tech developments and breakthroughs rivals that of other tech sectors, the infrastructure challenges of energy, materials, and water mean that the clean tech revolution will be a lengthy one compared with the almost instant revolution of personal computers, the Internet, and Wi-Fi. We won't simply wake up one day and find that an entire city has switched from coal to wind power. So it's far from being too late to get started. The clean tech revolution is, despite decades of development to date, still in the early to middle stages of transforming the world's largest markets.

Take the energy industry. It took coal nearly 100 years to bypass traditional energy sources (such as the burning of wood) as the world's primary energy source. It then took oil nearly 100 years to surpass coal usage. Natural gas has been more than 100 years in development and now represents about 20% of global primary energy use. Similarly, it will take new renewables, such as wind, solar, and biofuels, 10, 20, or 30 years or more to catch up with coal, oil, and natural gas. That's the reality of clean tech and one of the reasons why long-term thinking is so crucial.

But herein lies the opportunity. The clean tech revolution is actually already 30 to 50 years in the making; the first conversion of sunlight to electricity in a solar PV cell, for example, took place at Bell Labs in 1954. Moving forward, clean technology will exhibit both disruptive sudden advances and more deliberate, incremental change. In a world of increasingly constrained natural resources, it's hard to conjure up a sector that offers more promising long-term returns and rewards.

Unlike the Internet, which went through a rapid boom-and-bust cycle—a classic bubble—the transition to new energy, transportation, advanced materials, and water technologies will look more like a long boom. To be sure, there will be periods of high growth spurts and then retrenchment. There will be occasional irrational exuberance. But with the right combination of policy, capital, and technology, the exploding global market for clean tech will not abate anytime soon.

Consider some of these facts: According to Clean Edge research, the global biofuels market (manufacturing costs and wholesale pricing of ethanol and biodiesel) will grow from $20.5 billion in 2006 to $80.9 billion by 2016. Wind power (new-installation capital costs) will expand from $17.9 billion in 2006 to $60.8 billion in 2016. The solar PV industry (including modules, system components, and installation) will grow from $15.6 billion in 2006 to $69.3 billion by 2016. And the fuel-cell and distributed-hydrogen market will grow from $1.4 billion (primarily for research contracts and demonstration and test units) to $15.6 billion by 2016.

In total, the four clean-energy sectors tracked by Clean Edge amounted to $55.4 billion in 2006, larger than the international music industry. We project that the wind, solar, hydrogen, and biofuels markets will grow fourfold to more than $226 billion by 2016.

With cities, states, and nations around the globe planning to generate at least 20% to 30% of their total energy from renewables such as wind, solar, and biofuels by 2030, investments in clean energy are likely to continue to rise—rewarding investors and companies that get on board now.

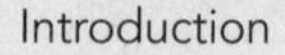

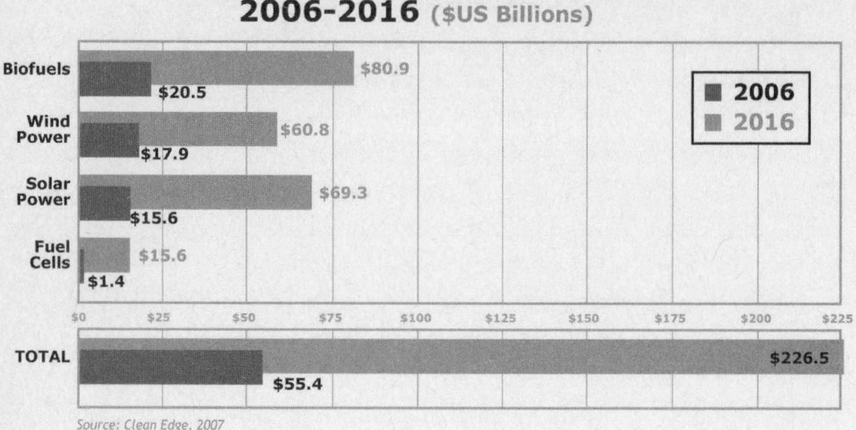

HOW TO PROFIT: THE EIGHT MAJOR CLEAN TECHNOLOGIES

In *The Clean Tech Revolution* we show how clean technologies offer entrepreneurs, individual investors, recent college and business school graduates, corporate executives, policy makers, and others the opportunity to profit financially while providing solutions to some of the greatest issues facing humankind. Our book will help you spot the winners among technologies, companies, and regions likely to reap the greatest benefits from clean tech—and show you why the time to act is now.

In the following chapters we highlight the eight major clean technologies that we believe offer investors the best opportunity. In narrowing down the list, we needed to exclude some emerging clean technologies, but we believe the following list offers the greatest near- to midterm opportunity. These are the top eight technologies and sectors that we'll cover in detail:

- **Solar energy.** The solar-power market offers perhaps one of the greatest opportunities among its clean-tech peers. Not only is the worldwide solar market growing by 30% to 50% per year, but the same technologies that enabled the semiconductor and computer revolution are now being leveraged in the solar market. Savvy venture capitalists, companies, and industry experts believe that solar power will be cost-competitive with conventional retail electricity rates before 2020. The solar industry, we believe, will be dominated by those that can significantly lower costs for solar PV modules, drive down installation costs, and integrate solar PV into everything from building rooftops to utility infrastructure.

- **Wind power.** Wind energy has been expanding rapidly since the mid-1990s—right up there with solar. From 1995 to 2006, global cumulative installed wind-power capacity expanded fifteenfold, from less than 5,000 MW to more than 74,000 MW. While investing in some of the current wind giants such as GE, Denmark's Vestas Wind Systems, and Spain's Gamesa could offer lucrative opportunities, there are other emerging avenues for entrepreneurs. The advent of smaller-scale community wind projects could enable local farmers, developers, and financiers to reap profits. And the market for new materials for turbines and control systems for wind farms is still relatively untapped. As nations such as Germany and Denmark get upward of 15% of their electricity from wind, and other nations and regions push to reach similar targets, the wind industry is the current champion of new renewables.

- **Biofuels and biomaterials.** Today, Brazil gets more than 30% of its automobile fuels from sugar cane–based ethanol. In the United States, ethanol is nearly a 5-billion-gallon-a-year industry, on target to reach 7.5 billion gallons (about 5% of total gasoline consumption) around 2010. One of the greatest opportunities will lie in distilling fuels and creating materials from cellulosic nonfood crops such as switchgrass and jatropha. Entrepreneurs and companies that can crack the cellulosic ethanol code, along with those that develop new methods of refining and distributing biofuels, are poised to profit from the mass adoption of biofuels and biomaterials.

- **Green buildings.** Today's green buildings use some 30% less energy than their comparably sized nongreen counterparts (some save much more), and they're generally brighter, healthier, and more aesthetically pleasing. Often built with little or no additional up-front cost, green offices, for instance, pay back not only in energy savings but also in greater employee retention, attendance, and productivity. Green buildings of all stripes, including houses, apartment buildings, schools, and condominiums, are using advanced lighting, new building materials, efficient appliances, and energy-management systems to reinvent the buildings we call home.

- **Personal transportation.** Clean transportation is changing the means of mobility for consumers and workers across the globe. It includes today's HEVs as well as plug-in hybrids and the revival of electric-vehicle technology in high-powered, innovative, and even sexy designs. Imagine a car that can get the equivalent of 100 miles per gallon (mpg) from a gallon of conventional gasoline. The technologies to make this a reality already exist—and offer individuals, forward-thinking companies, and entrepreneurs unprecedented opportunity. And we're not talking just about cars but also about more efficient and less polluting motorcycles, scooters, and mopeds.

- **Smart grid.** In the future our electric grid, which is woefully outdated, will start to look a lot more like the Internet. Homes and businesses will no longer be just energy consumers but also energy producers. This two-way flow of electrons will transform the electric utility industry. Already, some companies such as Itron are deploying smart meters that enable utilities to better track and monitor consumption and performance, and companies such as CURRENT Communications are working to communicate, monitor, and manage the flow of electrons. New interconnect standards—regulations that guide how utilities access, quantify, and pay for distributed-energy sources—are also changing the utility landscape. The smart grid, while still a relatively new concept, offers one of the brightest opportunities in the clean-tech marketplace as it works to transform decades-old utility infrastructure.

- **Mobile applications.** The need for portable, lightweight, long-lasting sources of power spans four huge areas: consumer devices for today's untethered masses; the military; remote, rural villages in developing nations; and disaster recovery zones, from the U.S. Gulf Coast to the Indian Ocean. Often overlooked by casual observers of clean tech, these areas represent huge opportunities for the deployment and growth of high-efficiency solar panels, portable fuel cells, nanotechnology-based advancements in batteries, and many other clean technologies. In many areas the U.S. military is at the leading edge of investing in and deploying a range of these technologies. The Pentagon's vast funding arsenal clearly spells big business opportunities in mobile clean tech.

- **Water filtration.** Although the earth has plenty of water, clean and potable water is becoming increasingly scarce. And while energy security is currently capturing the media's attention and attracting significant pools of capital, water will not be far behind. In places such as Israel and Singapore, new forms of desalination technology are converting saltwater to tap water. Nanotechnologies are being used to filter and purify water once deemed unusable. Although water technologies are the traditional domain of big business such as GE and Siemens, a number of smaller players are also competing in the effort to provide the world with clean water. With an estimated 1 billion people on the planet without access to clean water and the increasing threat of "water shocks"—abrupt water shortages due to pollution, rapid water-table depletion, or natural disasters—the ability to deploy clean technologies to enable water filtration and purification is likely to expand considerably in the coming decades.

After our review of the top eight clean technologies, we follow with a chapter titled "Create Your Own Silicon Valley" that examines the paths that city and regional governments around the globe can take toward the payoffs from clean-tech leadership: business development, job growth, and improved quality of life. We wrap up the book with a chapter that highlights successful clean-tech marketing examples and looks at both the hurdles and opportunities in moving clean tech into a mass market embraced by millions of mainstream consumers worldwide.

In each technology chapter, we also provide a list of 10 companies or organizations that are likely to be at the forefront of clean-tech activities, as well as *Clean-Tech Consumer* sidebars that present brief snapshots of particular products and services most likely to show up in your home, office, or car now or in coming years. Throughout the book, we also highlight breakthrough technology and business-model opportunities for entrepreneurs and "intrapreneurs" (those leading entrepreneurial initiatives within large companies).

WHAT'S NOT CLEAN TECH: NUCLEAR AND COAL

At first blush, the notion that a technology producing radioactive waste could ever be considered "clean" sounds ludicrous. But global warming's threat to the planet has cast this debate in a new light. Nuclear generation's lack of GHG emissions has brought new supporters on board. We, however, are not among them. There is a long list of reasons why we do not consider nuclear power clean with current technology: radioactive waste disposal and storage challenges; proliferation of nuclear material in a world that lived through the terrorist attacks in the United States on September 11, 2001; and the security threat of nuclear power stations as inviting terrorist targets. In addition, nuclear plants use vast amounts of carbon-intensive energy and materials such as cement in their construction. They also require large amounts of water in their cooling operations, which can further constrain development and operation. France, long considered a model for the success of nuclear power, experienced brownouts in the drought-prone summer of 2005 because French nuclear plants couldn't get enough water to run at peak capacity.

But our number one argument against nuclear power is found right on the bottom line: Multibillion-dollar nuclear plants are simply not cost-effective compared with other energy sources. No utility in the United States has completed a nuclear plant ordered since 1973, and money has been one of the biggest reasons why. Nuclear advocates talk about the low price per kilowatt-hour of nuclear energy once a plant's up and running, but that doesn't include life-cycle costs such as decommissioning and accident liability insurance. A new nuclear plant costs around $1.5 billion, according to industry estimates. Most outside estimates place the tab at closer to $2 billion to $5 billion (not including government subsidies and incentives). Insurance costs are so prohibitive that the U.S. government has to foot the bill for any accident costs above $10.9 billion. The nuclear industry simply wouldn't exist without extensive government subsidies.

There's also the issue of scale. The U.S. Department of Energy's Energy Information Administration projects that the world will need 14 terawatts (14,000 GW) of new energy sources between now and 2050 to keep up with growing demand. It would require 14,000 one-GW nuclear power plants to cover the projected gap in global new energy demands. There are currently fewer than 450 nuclear plants operating in the world today, roughly 100 of them in the United States. This estimate is admittedly a hypothetical, all-or-nothing game scenario, but even a fraction of that number means a hugely expensive proposition with a publicly unacceptable level of nuclear proliferation.

So until safeguards are in place, nuclear containment is achievable, realistic waste solutions are deployed, and costs are accurately calculated and accounted for, we strongly disagree with current political efforts in the United States and elsewhere to "revive" the nuclear power industry. That verb is not lost on Amory Lovins, longtime energy-efficiency and clean-energy guru whose consulting clients include Wal-Mart and the Pentagon. "Paying new subsidies to the nuclear power industry is like defibrillating a corpse," says Lovins, cofounder and CEO of the Rocky Mountain Institute in Snowmass, Colorado.

The other conventional energy source that aspires to be clean, but doesn't make the cut, is "clean coal." A number of proponents and innovators are working to develop new forms of burning coal with reduced pollutants and GHG emissions. However, at present, we believe that *clean coal* is an oxymoron for a myriad of reasons, including the sheer number of coal mine–related deaths and the fact that coal-fired plants, even some cleaner ones, are major contributors to serious illnesses such as asthma, heart disease, and mercury poisoning. A more accurate label would be *cleaner* coal, but we remain skeptical on whether its technologies can really put a significant dent in carbon emissions. Sure, clean coal is better than dirty coal, but it's a long way from sharing the clean-tech label with wind, solar, small-scale hydroelectric, and other emissions-free energy sources.

That said, there is one clean-coal technology that seems to offer some future hope, with an increasing chorus of diverse interest groups calling for it: integrated gasification controlled cycle, much better known by its initials IGCC, or simply coal gasification. This process essentially breaks coal down into gaseous components, including natural gas, a cleaner-burning fossil fuel, and CO_2. That enables the easier use of carbon sequestration, a promising but still widely developmental technique of capturing CO_2 and storing it underground or underwater—that is, out of the earth's atmosphere. The technique remains expensive and unproven on a large scale, and we believe it is years away from deployment.

The best way to "clean up" coal is to replace as much coal-fired power as possible with electricity from wind, solar, biomass, geothermal, tidal, and other renewable clean-tech sources and to make both clean and nonclean power generation as efficient as possible.

WHAT WE MEAN BY INVESTING

In *The Clean Tech Revolution* we talk about investing in the broadest terms—and highlight opportunities for everyone from individual investors to corporate managers to politicians to recent college graduates. When we refer to investing opportunities, we are referring not only to the investment of money or capital but also to the investment of time, vision, energy, and talent. Our focus includes:

- **Individuals.** We highlight potential sectors for investing in clean-tech stocks and mutual funds as well as opportunities in emerging clean-tech markets for career growth for current workers and new graduates. We also look at how consumers can purchase clean-tech products and services that can improve their lives and save them money.
- **Venture capitalists and entrepreneurs.** We track investor commitments to innovative, early-stage companies and look at some of the emerging companies that are on track to transform the energy, transportation, water, and materials markets.
- **Corporations.** We delve into the investments in clean-tech research, development, and deployment being made by some of the world's largest multinationals and explain how their commitments to clean technology are reconfiguring the business landscape.
- **Governments.** We show how governments at the regional, state, and national level can focus their time and money to become clean-tech revolutionaries—in the process creating jobs, building robust economies, and positioning themselves for the future.

What we do not do in this book, however, is make investment recommendations in specific stocks and securities. Instead, our mission is to shine a light on areas of emerging opportunity; highlight key technologies, companies, and players; and map out areas of potential entrepreneurial breakthroughs. We believe this approach serves our readers best—by looking out over the next 2, 5, and 10 years at trends that have the power to dramatically shift the business, economic, and political landscape.

CLEAN TECH NOW

The Clean Tech Revolution explains how major trends in clean tech will continue to unfold and grow, offering readers vast new opportunities for investment, employment, and lifestyle choices. We will explain why clean tech, over and above the arguments for environmental protection and climate-change mitigation, is an economic imperative. Nations, companies, and investors who dismiss or disregard these trends run a strong risk of falling behind their competitors in attracting top talent and generating profits in the global marketplace.

So let's get started on a closer look at the clean tech revolution and how you, your business, and your government can participate. A world facing unstable energy prices, resource shortages, and environmental challenges can't afford to wait, and the most innovative and visionary companies, investors, and governments are already on board. It's time for you to join them.

1

SOLAR ENERGY

Scaling Up Manufacturing and Driving Down Costs

Above the tree-lined streets of Pasadena, California, in the sleek, open-air offices of high-tech start-up incubator Idealab, a team of researchers is huddled around a strange-looking device that concentrates the light of the sun and generates on-site electricity. Bill Gross, Idealab's founder and the CEO of upstart concentrating-solar PV company Energy Innovations, beams with the nerdy excitement of a computer programmer who's just created a nifty chunk of code or a biologist who's uncovered a new genome. "The economic potential for solar is enormous," says Gross. "Within a decade, solar will reach price parity with other energy sources." His vision is to replicate Idealab's rooftop, where a dozen solar-concentrator demo units track the sun from dawn to dusk. He wants Energy Innovations units sprouting on commercial and industrial roofs around the world, providing low-cost, efficient, distributed electric power from the sun.

Gross, whose Idealab hatched such Internet winners and losers as City-search, eToys, Overture, and Tickets.com, is now in a race to develop his solar technology and bring it to market before other firms, such as Practical Instruments, SolFocus, and Solaria. He firmly believes that the future belongs to those who can help solve two of our world's most pressing issues, energy and water—global access to clean, reliable, and abundant sources of each. His solar technology company—which aims to use relatively inexpensive mirrors to reflect the light of the sun onto expensive high-efficiency solar cells—raised more than $40 million in 2005 and 2006, with hopes of putting its first commercial products onto rooftops in 2007.

Energy Innovations represents just one of the many technological developments taking place in the rapidly expanding solar industry. These developments include everything from incremental improvements in the most abundant form of solar electricity—silicon-based solar PV—to new nonsilicon forms of solar electric generation, including nanotechnology-based innovations and CIGS (copper, indium, gallium, selenium). The variety of emerging solar electric technologies and applications demonstrates the richness of opportunity in an industry expanding by more than 30% per year since the mid-1990s.

What does this mean for investors, entrepreneurs, and others who want a piece of the growing solar pie? The solar business, once the domain of back-to-the-earth zealots and government and corporate research labs, is now being embraced by nimble, visionary entrepreneurs with access to capital, skilled management, and business acumen. Also joining the race are established multinationals such as Applied Materials, GE, and Sharp—companies that are basing their future, at least in part, on corporate spoils in the solar industry.

RAPID FIRE

Part of the growing interest in solar power has to do with the sector's astounding growth rate. In 2000, the total annual manufacturing output of all solar companies was about 300 MW. In 2005, solar industry manufacturing output rose almost fivefold to more than 1,500 MW of solar PV modules and surpassed 2,000 MW in 2006. That's enough electricity-generating capacity to serve two cities the size of Atlanta for an entire year.

The entry of multinationals and large, well-funded, publicly traded solar companies into the space provides opportunities for individual and institutional investors to put money into some of the more promising companies and developments. In 2005 and 2006, for example, solar companies such as SunPower and China's Suntech Power Holdings had successful initial public offerings on U.S. stock exchanges and global giants such as Applied Materials joined longtime corporate solar stalwarts such as BP and Sharp.

Although current solar power costs can be prohibitive in some regions, solar systems can make a great deal of sense in regions that have high-utility costs, offer solar subsidies, or are blessed with a preponderance of sunny days—offering opportunities to a new class of systems integrators and financiers. As we discuss below, some companies are packaging systems and financing in such a way that solar can cost less for the customer from first day of use—including builders of new homes who are integrating solar systems into mortgages and firms that have developed unique financing options.

The solar landscape is filling up with a range of new companies and business models, offering opportunities for qualified entrepreneurs, managers, and workers to join current efforts in solar manufacturing, financing, installation, systems integration, and elsewhere along the solar value chain.

Solar's challenges, however, are many. They include entrenched interests that support fossil fuels over clean energy, shortsighted rather than long-term policies and incentives that disrupt growth, nonuniformity among utility districts that makes consistent standards and protocols nearly impossible, and cost barriers that have kept solar from reaching cost parity with retail electric rates. But like any high-growth technology innovation story, solar is in a unique position to overcome many of these challenges and change the world in ways unimaginable.

BRINGING SOLAR DOWN TO EARTH

Invented at Bell Labs in the 1950s and commercialized in the 1970s, solar PV has moved from a niche industry powering space satellites to a mainstream business with such well-known multinational players as BP, GE, Sharp, and Shell and pure-play efforts such as Evergreen Solar, First Solar, Q-Cells, SunPower, and Suntech Power. Since the mid-1990s, the industry has looked eerily similar to the consumer electronics revolution that preceded it—with annual growth rates in the 30% to 60% range.

Solar is becoming big business, representing more than $11 billion in global sales in 2005, more than $15 billion in 2006, and a projected $60 billion–plus in 2016, according to Clean Edge research. In 2005, venture capitalists poured more than $150 million into deals based in North America, such as Advent Solar, HelioVolt, Energy Innovations, Miasolé, and Nanosolar. Nearly $1 billion was raised via initial public offerings (IPOs) in Europe and the United States for SunPower, Suntech Power, and

Q-Cells; those companies' IPOs represented three of the largest technology offerings of 2005.

Piper Jaffray clean-energy analyst Jesse Pichel highlights what the excitement is about. "Our investment partners like solar because it leverages advances made in the semiconductor space," he says. "Our investors understand semiconductors—and are therefore more comfortable with solar than many other emerging energy sectors."

Because of the nature of the solar business, it is the *electronics* giants in the solar industry, such as Sharp, Sanyo, and SunPower, that are likely to be the big winners, rather than the energy giants such as Shell and BP. And as highlighted below, it will likely be the domain of new nimble start-ups that are leveraging lessons learned from earlier semiconductor manufacturing revolutions.

THE SOLAR "EXPERIENCE CURVE"

Even though there is no such thing as a subsidy-free energy source (oil, natural gas, coal, and nuclear are all heavily subsidized), solar still must reduce its overall cost to become truly competitive. And that's exactly what's been happening. As cumulative global output from solar soared from 5 MW in 1979 to more than 2,000 MW in 2006, the wholesale price of a solar PV module dropped from $32 per watt to about $3 per watt—roughly a 50% drop per decade.

And solar, we believe, is poised to reach significantly lower costs and prices in coming years. Technology advances, market growth, increased competition, and economies of scale in manufacturing are all playing a big part in this transformation. Solar PV manufacturing has benefited from fairly constant, decades-long progress in fabrication technology, which has shrunk solar cell weight and thickness while harnessing sunlight more efficiently.

Dr. Richard Swanson, who founded PV cell maker SunPower in 1985 while teaching electrical engineering at Stanford University, is one of the solar industry's most respected experts on declining technology costs. The costs of PV modules, says Swanson, have moved in a "classic experience curve," where product costs fall in direct correlation to increased worldwide production volume. Prices fall about 18%, reckons Swanson, for every doubling of cumulative production volume.

In the late 1990s, his company's innovations and growth caught the attention of Cypress Semiconductor CEO and noted chip industry maverick T.J. Rodgers. Cypress bought a majority interest in SunPower in 2002, signifying a major confluence of high tech and clean tech. SunPower is now public, its IPO rekindling memories of the earlier high-tech heydays when its share value jumped 41% on its first day of trading in November 2005.

HIGH-VOLUME, LOW-COST MANUFACTURING

Suppose you could accelerate the learning curve and drive down costs even more rapidly than occurs in the classic "experience curve"? One person who's explored this concept is former Hewlett-Packard (HP) executive Marvin Keshner. He wrote a report with coauthor Rajiv Arya for the U.S. Department of Energy's National Renewable Energy Lab (NREL) in 2004 entitled "Study of Potential Cost Reductions Resulting from Super-Large-Scale Manufacturing of PV Modules." The authors reported on the concept of a massive solar production facility that could enable the production and installation of $1-per-peak-watt solar systems; the average cost for solar in 2006 was roughly $6 to $8 per peak watt installed. Some of the innovations they envisioned include the use of materials optimized for a 25- to 30-year operating life, driving down costs by minimizing transportation and handling expenses and eliminating intermediaries, automating factory processes to reduce breakage and increase yields, developing modular lines that can be rotated for planned downtime and maintenance, and dramatically scaling up the size of solar manufacturing facilities. Today, Keshner is heading up a new solar venture that is working to drive down costs by implementing many of the recommendations outlined in his report.

It's not surprising that an HP executive would take up an interest in solar. Indeed, many of the same companies and entrepreneurs that innovated and built profitable integrated-circuit, flat-panel, and disk-drive manufacturing businesses are poised to win in next-generation solar. They're applying to the solar industry the same expertise they've gained in applying conductive materials onto substrates and in ramping up low-cost, high-volume, continuous-flow, semiconductor-based manufacturing processes.

In fact, many current and emerging clean technologies take advantage of manufacturing breakthroughs perfected in the computer and high-tech industries. As in the high-tech revolution before it, semiconductor-based chips and circuits also lay at the heart of grid innovation and energy delivery. Semiconductors—silicon-based devices such as microprocessor chips and transistors—have shaped our modern era by enabling the mass manufacturing of computers, radios, TVs, and other consumer electronics. But something equally striking is happening at the intersection of semiconductors and energy—increasingly semiconductors are *becoming* the energy source. The first semiconductor revolution enabled the proliferation of computers and consumer electronics, while the second semiconductor revolution is literally powering our homes, cars, and a range of other consumer products.

In the heart of Silicon Valley, Miasolé in Santa Clara, California, is one example of a company applying manufacturing breakthroughs from the disk-drive space to the solar industry. Miasolé founder and CEO David Pearce and his team are leveraging a unique form of sputtering technology that they originally developed and applied to high-volume coating processes for the production of hard disks for the data-storage industry. Now the company is using the same process to enable low-cost manufacturing of thin-film solar technologies. Since 2005, Miasolé has raised more than $51 million from such seasoned investors as Kleiner Perkins Caufield & Byers to help deliver on its plan.

HIGH STAKES

Keshner and Pearce, of course, aren't alone in working to adapt technologies from traditional semiconductor manufacturing and applying them to a new era of low-cost, large-scale solar production. The list of innovators is long, and the stakes are high.

Large electronics companies such as Sharp, for instance, have understood the connection between semiconductors and energy for decades. The Japan-based company, a leader in consumer electronics and flat-panel displays, committed itself to being a leader in solar power in the 1960s. Today, it is the world's leading manufacturer of solar PV modules, representing more than a quarter of global solar PV output, with annual revenues of more than $1 billion from that business. The company's president,

Katsuhiko Machida, predicts that the cost of generating solar power could fall by half between 2006 and 2010, and he's targeting approximately 20% of the company's revenue from its solar division by the end of the decade.

Q-Cells, the German solar cell manufacturer, provides another interesting example. The company, based in Thalheim, Germany, went from zero manufacturing output in 2000 to being the world's second largest manufacturer of solar cells in 2006. Q-Cells planned to manufacture about 250 MW of solar cells in 2007.

Solaria, a concentrating solar company in Fremont, California, is taking fabrication technologies used in contract semiconductor manufacturing and applying them to concentrated solar power. The company raised $22 million in series B financing in 2006 from venture capitalists and strategic investors, including Q-Cells. The company aims to drive down the cost of solar modules by replacing silicon with an inexpensive concentrating layer. Unlike some of its competitors that are working on high-concentration solar developments (up to approximately 500 times concentration), the company is focused on low concentration of two to three times. The company's products require no moving parts and have a form factor nearly identical to today's flat solar panels.

And as mentioned earlier, the leading semiconductor equipment manufacturer for the chip industry, Applied Materials in Santa Clara, California, is now taking aim at the solar industry. What this all means is that the same technologies that have driven down computer chip and PC costs since the 1980s are now being used to drive down solar-cell and module costs. The industry will increasingly become a commodity-driven business, which means it will likely be won by those companies, like electronics manufacturers, who know how to thrive in a competitive commodity environment. And in the same way that the computer industry spawned value-added resellers who provided add-on services, the solar business offers big opportunities for its share of systems integrators and value-added systems packagers.

BREAKTHROUGH OPPORTUNITY

The $2-Watt Solar Photovoltaics System

It goes without saying that one of the biggest opportunities for solar entrepreneurs is getting the cost of solar to cost parity with conventional retail electricity. While the big players such as Sharp and Kyocera continue to drive down costs, it may be one of the new entrants to really rock the boat with breakthrough technology and significantly lower pricing. Players such as Miasolé, Nanosolar, HelioVolt, and Q-Cells could be the first to deliver a truly low cost solar cell or module. Watch out for a current or emerging player that can bring the cost of an entire solar PV system to around $2 per peak watt—the equivalent of $5,000 for an average-sized 2.5-kW (2.5-kilowatt) residential rooftop system, for example. Systems priced at this level would provide electricity at less than 10 cents per kilowatt-hour (kWh), beating out most customers' retail utility rates throughout the United States. Someone, we believe, is likely to break this price barrier by 2015—paving the way for a low-cost, ubiquitous, solar future.

SYSTEMS THINKING

It's important to note the distinction between the cost of a PV module (approximately $3 to $4) and the retail price actually paid for a full solar PV system for a home or business, known in the industry as the *installed* price. Installed price includes the cost of inverters that change the sun's direct current (DC) to usable alternating current (AC), other integration components, racks to mount the modules, and installation and connection service fees. The installed price is typically at least double the wholesale solar module price.

That's $6 to $8 per watt in the United States today, without any subsidies, which translates to approximately 18 to 36 cents per kilowatt-hour (depending on the application, finance charges, and other variables)—still very expensive compared with most utility rates of less than 10 cents per kilowatt-hour.

On a direct-cost basis, solar compares favorably only in specific circum-

stances: in countries and regions with extremely high utility costs, such as Japan and San Diego; in states with generous solar rebates, such as New Jersey and California; and at high-demand times, such as hot summer afternoons when utilities must draw on their expensive "peaker" plants to keep power-hungry air conditioners running. The good news for solar is that those sultry afternoon hours also provide the most sunlight, making PV an attractive option for peak demand. Remember, however, that it's the sun's light, not its heat, that is converted to electrons in the photovoltaic process. Solar modules are actually less efficient at very high temperatures, so a rooftop system on a clear 70-degree day in Seattle produces more power than the same-size system broiling under 110 degrees in Phoenix.

To be competitive with conventional grid power in most markets, solar PV has to be available for $2 to $2.50 per watt installed, which would generate power at 5 to 12 cents per kilowatt-hour. Ever-higher spikes in natural gas and coal-fired power, of course, would lower the comparative bar for solar and accelerate the crossover point. But even without fossil-fuel price jumps, SunPower's Swanson and others see solar PV prices falling by the same rate—50% per decade—as they have since the mid-1980s. And solar power costs may soon decrease even further because of advanced technology development. On the technology front, a raft of start-ups in Silicon Valley and elsewhere, many well funded by the leading lights of venture capital, are working on innovative tech breakthroughs to make solar cells lighter, thinner, faster to manufacture, and, above all, cheaper.

Companies that are working to drive solar prices down with potentially disruptive, nonsilicon technologies include Konarka, Miasolé, Nanosolar, and Nanosys. Instead of silicon, these photovoltaic materials include nanostructured titanium dioxide (Konarka); CIGS (Miasolé and Nanosolar); and nanocomposites, which refer to multiple materials reengineered at the molecular, or nanotechnology, level (Nanosys). All of these aim to disrupt the cost structure, conventional size, and customary manufacturing methods of traditional solar cells.

Others, such as First Solar, are using cadmium telluride technology, while still others, including United Solar Ovonic, are pursuing innovations in silicon-based thin-film technologies. And the larger players are involved as well, including the likes of Shell, Sharp, and even Honda. Instead of building wafer-sized solar cells, these firms are variously sputtering, printing, or stamping flexible, lightweight solar cell architectures on foil and polymer substrates, often in a continuous, roll-to-roll manufacturing process. As a result, solar cells can literally be peeled off a polymer roll rather than produced as the traditional hard, brittle, crystalline panels.

SILICON SPEED BUMP?

But even as clean energy leverages technology advances and market growth into lower costs, there's another economic fundamental that can have the opposite effect: a shortage, and resultant cost increase, of the raw material needed to produce the product. Since 2004, solar PV has experienced just that, with a worldwide shortfall of PV-grade silicon that's made it difficult, and more expensive, for manufacturers to keep up with soaring worldwide demand. Japan and Germany, in particular, are to solar PV what China and India are to oil—fast-growing markets putting a crimp on supplies for the rest of the world.

The good news is that the world has plenty of silicon—it's the second most common element in the earth's crust, trailing only oxygen. There's no shortage of sand, feldspar, quartz, and other minerals that serve as the raw materials for what the solar PV industry calls silicon feedstock. For many years, with the size of the solar power business a mere blip compared with the global semiconductor industry, PV manufacturers were able to rely on scrap silicon from high tech's wafer-fabrication facilities. By 2008, however, the solar industry is projected to surpass the high-tech semiconductor industry as the largest consumer of raw silicon feedstock—a truly historic milestone in solar's growth history.

To address the current shortage, silicon manufacturers are ramping up production of solar-specific feedstock. The world's largest polycrystalline silicon producer is Hemlock Semiconductor, a joint venture of Dow Corning and two Japanese manufacturers. Hemlock is increasing capacity at its plant outside Saginaw, Michigan, by 50% in a $500 million expansion that's adding 150 full-time and 400 contractor jobs in the economically depressed region. With producers such as Hemlock gearing up, solar industry executives figure the current supply shortfall will last only 2 to 3 years, with traditional cost decline trends returning after that.

Solar Grade Silicon, based in Moses Lake, Washington, a division of Norway-based REC, was the first silicon manufacturer to focus exclusively on the solar industry. It's currently in the process of doubling its manufacturing capacity from 6,500 metric tons to 13,000 metric tons annually. Other companies that are also ramping up silicon production for the solar industry include Wacker Chemie AG, based in Munich, and Tokuyama, a chemical group based in Japan.

We believe the shortage of silicon will dissipate, if not disappear, sometime before 2010. At that point, we believe that silicon suppliers will have begun to bring enough silicon feedstock online to meet the needs of both the global solar PV and computer-chip industries. In addition, new technologies that reduce the need for silicon or replace silicon altogether will offer relief. There will be some turbulence on the road ahead as solar PV and silicon feedstock manufacturers provide each other with the right market signals as they both ramp up production, but we expect the resumption of lower costs as the silicon market normalizes.

BREAKTHROUGH OPPORTUNITY

Concentration

A number of players are competing to develop solar PV systems that get more power out of the sun by concentrating its solar rays. The technology is called concentrating PV (CPV). It's a diverse group, including those using low-scale concentration, such as Solaria and Stellaris, and others going for high-scale concentration, such as Concentrix, Energy Innovations, Practical Instruments, and SolFocus. It also includes a number of companies that aren't using PV at all—but are concentrating the sun to heat oil and turn turbines to create electricity. These include players such as Stirling Energy Systems and Solargenix (now a subsidiary of Spain-based Acciona), pursuing a long-term opportunity for desert-based, utility-scale solar. One issue for high-concentration players: The technologies require moving parts, which adds complexity and the potential for breakdowns. But for investors and businesses, the solar concentration market is clearly heating up.

THE INSTALLATION GAME

One company riding the wave of falling solar energy prices to impressive growth is PowerLight in Berkeley, California. PowerLight, acquired by SunPower in 2007 for $332.5 million, is the leading systems integrator and installer of commercial and industrial systems in the United States. PowerLight president Dan Shugar, an intense, hyperactive guy who gets his full money's worth out of a swivel chair, can easily rattle off the firm's annual revenue totals for the past several years. From its first million in 1996 to $92 million in 2004, PowerLight has parlayed dozens of large commercial solar systems integration projects to a spot in the *Inc.* 500 Hall of Fame. PowerLight shares that honor, for being listed for 5 straight years among the nation's fastest-growing privately held companies, with the likes of Microsoft and Oracle.

PowerLight isn't shy about cheerleading. In its corporate office in a renovated former Heinz ketchup factory near the shores of San Francisco Bay, shiny blue crystalline photovoltaic modules are everywhere—wall decorations, cubicle partitions, tabletops. Venues where PowerLight rooftop PV systems silently crank out electrons include U.S. Navy bases in Pearl Harbor and San Diego, several Napa Valley wineries, FedEx's California air hub in Oakland, San Francisco's Moscone Convention Center, several Lowe's home improvement stores, a resort hotel on Hawaii's Kona coast, and the Las Vegas Valley Water District. In 2005, PowerLight completed what was then the world's largest solar PV generating plant, the 62-acre, 10-MW Bavaria Solarpark in southern Germany. All told, PowerLight systems produce about 100 MW of energy; Shugar proudly points out that that's more than three times the world's entire solar PV production in 1990, the year he started in the business.

Solar power can't yet compete with centralized wind or fossil-fuel grid power on a straight cents-per–kilowatt-hour basis, so PowerLight customers, like all users of solar, must take a long-term payback view. "Our customers are essentially financing a power plant with all the fuel up front," says Shugar. "You have to be willing to look at life-cycle costing. Being super short-term focused won't get it done."

Alameda County, California, is the home of progressive-minded cities Berkeley and Oakland and the nation's first major wind farms (dating to the 1970s) at Altamont Pass, but county officials approach capital energy projects as soberly as any local government under a twenty-first-century budget squeeze. Matt Muniz, energy program manager for the county, says projects must meet a specific annual investment hurdle rate over a 25-year project life, including debt service and interest. "It's all based on how much power we can generate that we don't have to buy," he says. The county compares its project investment against a forecast of 2.5% annual increases in electric rates from utility PG&E (where Shugar once worked in solar R&D), which Muniz admits is conservative; PG&E's base rate jumped 6% in January 2006.

Solar PV systems from PowerLight generate electricity for seven Alameda County facilities, including the roof of an Oakland courthouse and the offices of county emergency services and environmental health services. The first and by far the largest project is the 3-acre solar array on the roof of Santa Rita Jail, a sprawling facility used by author Tom Wolfe as the site of key character Conrad Hensley's incarceration (and escape, when an earthquake destroys the prison) in his 1998 best seller *A Man in Full*. The real-life Santa Rita houses 4,200 inmates and 500 prison employees near the suburb of Dublin, and its 1.18-MW installation is one of the largest solar roofs in the United States.

When Muniz and his colleagues first considered solar power for the jail in 2000, the economics didn't work. Average electric rates from utility PG&E were less than 7 cents per kilowatt-hour, so in the first 500-kW phase of the project, PowerLight offered energy-efficiency improvements, such as a better water chiller for air-conditioning, to augment its solar generation. The following year brought the infamous summer of rolling blackouts and Enron market manipulation as California's deregulation energy crisis hit, and utility rates nearly doubled. "We took another look at the economics," says Muniz, "and in phase two we didn't need the efficiency measures to get the payback." Phase two added another 180 kW, and the final phase (three, completed in 2002) brought an additional 500 kW.

PV panels now generate as much as half of the jail's peak power on bright summer afternoons. Throughout the year, solar contributes an average of 20% of the daytime juice and 12% overall, since solar panels can't harness any sun after dark. "I was hoping we might get something from the light of a full moon," Muniz jokes, "but I guess the technology isn't quite advanced enough yet."

BREAKTHROUGH OPPORTUNITY

Integrated Photovoltaics

For solar to become truly ubiquitous like computers, cell phones, and the Internet, it will have to be embedded into everything from portable electronic devices to roof tiles to glass. Consider it the ultimate disappearing act, with solar cells integrated into daily products and services. A number of players are already doing this for the home-building industry, including Sharp and PowerLight, which both offer residential solar roof tiles. Perhaps the largest opportunity right now is among roofers and builders in California, where they can take advantage of the state's Million Solar Roofs incentives along with federal tax credits to bring down costs. Homebuilders such as Clarum Homes, Centex, Grupe Company, and Lennar are starting to build entire developments with solar BIPV (building-integrated photovoltaics). Increasingly, BIPV could become a standard option on new homes not just in California but also around the United States.

THE POWER OF FINANCE

Breakthroughs aren't happening only at the technology level.

In the electric power business you've got Con Edison, Commonwealth Edison, Detroit Edison—why not a SunEdison, the utility that delivers 100% solar power? Indeed there is one, but the "utility" actually generates its power right on the roof of your retail location or product warehouse. SunEdison LLC, based in Baltimore, is one of several clean-tech companies building a growing business on innovative finance techniques. SunEdison secures investor financing for each project, builds the solar PV array and assumes the payback risks, then sells the power to the customer under the roof for a fixed rate—usually at or below current utility rates. Like PowerLight, SunEdison requires a long commitment—a 10- or 20-year contract. Customers, including a Whole Foods Market store in Edgewater, New Jersey, and three Staples distribution centers in New Jersey and California, typically save about 5% on their annual energy bills and earn renewable energy credits.

SunEdison's model took top honors in the 2004 Harvard Business School business plan competition's social enterprise track, and the following year it attracted even better and more lucrative attention. In June 2005, Goldman Sachs and Hudson United Bank combined to form SunEdison's $60 million SunE Solar Fund I, projected to finance 25 solar roof projects across the United States. The fund covers construction loans, senior term loans, and partnership equity.

To make the numbers work, SunEdison typically operates in states with generous solar rebate programs for commercial projects: California, Connecticut, Hawaii, Illinois, Massachusetts, Nevada, New Jersey, Oregon, and Rhode Island. But that's starting to change; the firm typifies the solar industry's gradual transition from subsidy dependence to more of a bottom-line focus. In an effort to reduce costs by up to 20% from economies of scale, SunEdison raised its minimum PV array size to 500 kW, after an earlier increase from 100 to 280 kW. The firm also benefits from its exclusive relationship with BP Solar, the solar unit of the global energy conglomerate that likes to say its initials stand for *Beyond* (instead of its original name *British*) *Petroleum*. Unlike other small PV firms, SunEdison receives a guaranteed supply of panels from its very large partner. In 2006, the company also shored up its installation capabilities by acquiring Sacramento-based systems integrator and installer Team Solar. SunEdison's model, along with others such as that of MMA Renewable Ventures, solves the significant issue of up-front capital costs for solar power.

"The next five to seven years," says young SunEdison founder and CEO Jigar Shah, "are going to be all about costs. Rebates will be tight—a state like New Jersey has a fixed amount of money to devote to clean energy, and more and more projects will be competing for it. It's becoming a zero-sum game, and the lowest-cost providers will win." SunEdison is truly putting that model to the test with its largest project—one of the largest solar PV projects in the world, in fact. It's an 18-MW solar "farm" covering several square miles in the Nevada desert outside Las Vegas, and the customer is the U.S. military.

BREAKTHROUGH OPPORTUNITY

Sell Electrons, Not Systems

Photovoltaics (PV) modules represent about half the cost of a solar PV system. So-called balance-of-system components such as inverters and racking, along with installation, make up the remaining cost for putting in a system. To cover the considerable up-front costs of solar—as well as capture the tax benefits for those willing to take the risk—a number of innovators such as SunEdison and MMA Renewable Ventures are pulling together financing and systems packaging to lower the end cost for business owners. Instead of selling entire systems to end users, they sell or lease electrons. Their financial models are interesting and complex—and offer a unique opportunity to entrepreneurs and bankers. We believe there's an opportunity for both new national and regional players to compete in this emerging financing market—making solar more affordable for companies and building owners.

DRIVING EFFICIENCY

As the solar industry drives down costs across the value chain, it also needs to focus on another key issue: efficiency. Cell efficiency refers to how much sunlight a solar PV cell converts into electricity—so, for example, a 15% efficient cell can convert about 15% of the sunlight hitting its surface into electricity. Today's average silicon-based solar cell gets around 17% efficiency. In October 2006, SunPower, a leader in the quest to increase cell and module efficiency, said it reached 22% efficiency at the cell level. But what if a solar cell could get to 50% efficiency? This would mean you could more than double or triple the amount of electricity coming out of today's average solar modules—using the same square footage of solar material.

In the race for solar cell efficiency breakthroughs, as in many areas of clean tech, the U.S. military is at the forefront of pushing technological boundaries. In 2005, the Pentagon's DARPA (Defense Advanced Research Projects Agency) announced a $30 million program to more than double the efficiency of solar cells. Dubbed the Very High Efficiency Solar Cell (VHESC) program, the effort is targeting a new breed of solar cells with efficiency rates more than double those of conventional current solar cells. The best commercially available solar cells today have efficiency rates of around 20%. The VHESC program is targeting efficiency rates closer to 50%.

This could make accessible the holy grail in distributed PV: low-cost, lightweight, extremely efficient solar cells. VHESC team coleader Dr. Alan Barnett, former CEO of AstroPower (a solar company that went from boom to bust and was eventually acquired by GE) and now a professor at the University of Delaware, explains the significance. "Our soldiers carry more mission-critical electronic devices than ever before—which requires a huge amount of energy in the form of batteries," he says. "The first shipment of batteries sent into Iraq needed to be flown in on three cargo planes and weighed more than five hundred forty tons," or the equivalent of more than 200 Hummer H3s. This can be a logistical nightmare. The military aims to figure out how to significantly lighten the load of soldiers by reducing the need for conventional batteries while meeting the needs of the modern soldier.

The VHESC consortium, led by the University of Delaware, is also receiving support from such corporations as DuPont, BP Solar, and Corning and involves more than 10 other universities and laboratories, including NREL, Massachusetts Institute of Technology (MIT), Harvard, Yale, and Carnegie Mellon. The programs could see total project funding of more than $50 million from its military and corporate donors. If successful, the program could enable a new class of integrated solar-powered devices for military use. This means that rather than carrying backup batteries for their myriad communication devices, global positioning system (GPS) equipment, and night-vision goggles, soldiers would carry devices powered by the sun. Others have talked about this vision before, but the project's unique approach to ultra-high-efficiency solar cells sets this effort apart.

Barnett says this represents the *largest single government investment to date* in solar research and could translate into some significant commercial applications. "You could charge your entire laptop in just one hour—all from the power of the sun," he explains.

But the military isn't waiting around for 50% efficient cells to get into solar procurement. In Hawaii, the U.S. Army is deploying 7 MW of solar energy to power thousands of military homes in a new development on Oahu. The system is designed to reduce use of fossil fuels by 30% for an entire complex of 7,894 new and renovated homes. The army development is currently the largest known planned residential solar project of its kind. And as we point out in chapter 7 ("Mobile Technologies: Powering a World on the Go"), the military is using solar technology to provide power to soldiers in the field.

Taking a page from the military's book, NASA and other space agencies have also been some of the earliest investors in emerging clean technologies. The thriving global solar power industry, now valued at nearly $15 billion annually, arguably has the space industry to thank for its existence. NASA was one of the first large-scale customers of solar cells for the deployment of solar-powered satellites, starting back in the 1960s. Solar cells cost hundreds of dollars per watt back then, compared with less than $4 per watt today. Investing in the developing technology for use in outer space, NASA helped bring solar PV prices out of the stratosphere and down to earth, putting the solar industry on a path to the mainstream corporate and investment opportunity that it is today.

THE BIG BUSINESS OF SMALL

While there is no single definition for nanotechnology, most scientists and technologists who work in the sector agree that nanotechnology is generally the manipulation of matter at a very tiny scale—from 1 to 100 nanometers. To put this scale in perspective: an average human hair is 50,000 to 100,000 nanometers wide and a sheet of paper is about 100,000 nanometers thick. In other words, you could stack a thousand nanodevices side by side to equal the thickness of either paper or a human hair. Using advances in nanotechnology, solar scientists are creating materials at the molecular level that could enable similar advances as those seen in the chip industry—lower costs, higher efficiency, and increasingly smaller devices.

Nanotechnology and clean tech are in many ways a natural fit. Many of the large corporations that are active in clean tech are also active in nanotech. Nanotech could end up enabling many next-generation clean technologies such as advanced batteries, water-desalination and water-filtration membranes, building insulation, and of course, solar power. "I strongly believe that nanotech holds the ability to push a number of clean technologies' costs, in particular solar, down dramatically," says Scott Mize, a nanotech entrepreneur, advisor, author, and speaker. "In a lot of areas it is the missing ingredient in getting clean-energy technologies over the line. Nanotech—and remember that most semiconductor technologies today are now nanotechnologies—could enable a new breed of low-cost energy sources and more."

Nanosolar, whose name bespeaks its mission, is pairing nanotech innovations with advanced thin films to embed solar cells into roof tiles and achieve other tech breakthroughs to make solar power cheaper and easier to deploy.

The company, based in Palo Alto, California, is attempting to dramatically scale up manufacturing processes while significantly lowering prices. The company plans to do this without using traditional silicon, the raw feedstock that enables the manufacturing of semiconductor chips and conventional solar PV cells. Instead, it is using a promising, yet still unproven, thin-film technology, CIGS, along with novel nanoparticles and patented process technologies. Nanosolar's "photovoltaic ink" can be sprayed or coated onto flexible materials in a continuous-flow process similar to that used by a printing press.

"We're aiming to mass-manufacture solar cells with one hundred times the throughput of conventional cell production, one fifth the cost, and with similar efficiency," explains Nanosolar CEO Martin Roscheisen. "Our goal is to create materials that can be integrated into rooftops and deployed in large-scale ground-mounted plants."

The company has become one of the solar industry's hottest VC plays, lining up more than $100 million in funding. In June 2006 the company announced plans to build a 430-MW-capacity manufacturing line in the San Francisco Bay Area. Roscheisen predicts that Nanosolar's products will be priced competitively with grid-based electricity by 2010. Google cofounders Sergey Brin and Larry Page were early investors in the company, along with such VC stalwarts as Mohr Davidow Ventures and Benchmark Capital, the Sand Hill Road firm that funded eBay and other Internet blockbusters.

Nanosolar's fortunes, along with those of others working in thin-film and nano-based solar technologies, will not be without challenges. No one has yet figured out how to mass-manufacture CIGS technology, for example, though many are very close to achieving this feat. Nanosolar's initial products will have warranties in the 15-year range, rather than the silicon-based solar PV industry's average 25-year warranties, and the company's conversion efficiency levels will likely lag behind those of the crystal silicon leaders.

But the move toward "tiny" technology in the solar industry is well under way. Other companies such as Altairnano, DayStar Technologies, HelioVolt, Konarka, Miasolé, and XsunX are developing nano-scale technologies to embed solar PV into everything from rooftops and glass to electronic devices.

The reduction of matter and the integration of nanotechnologies into products could also eventually have a significant impact on the issue of manufacturing waste, with the promise of reducing or even eliminating it. Nanotechnology could be the ultimate goal of a green materials revolution—the replacement of today's "heating, beating, and treating" approach (which not only is materials intensive but also results in significant pollution) with the building of finished materials and products atom by atom. If achieved, this could change the course of modern technology.

BREAKTHROUGH OPPORTUNITY

Utility-Scale Solar

While nanotechnology might enable low-cost solar, the solar-power industry's size and reach will be anything but small. In recent years we've begun to see multimegawatt solar photovoltaics (PV) installations—with some in development as large as 20 MW. And in California's Mojave Desert, there is approximately 300 MW of solar generation provided to utilities from solar thermal concentrators that have been up and running since the 1980s. Combine these larger solar PV and concentrating thermal systems with tens of thousands of smaller distributed PV systems that sit on rooftops, and all of a sudden you have a resource that can be deployed effectively by mainstream utilities in the multimegawatts, especially to provide peak power on sunny, high-demand electricity days. Until recently, most utilities set up roadblocks to the implementation of solar, but that's shifting as government policies, incentives, technology costs, constrained fossil fuel supplies, and other dynamics change. PG&E in Northern California and Austin Energy in

Austin, Texas, are both examples of utilities that are starting to embrace solar power. We believe the embrace of solar by utilities will be one of the big stories in coming years and will provide "utility-size" market opportunities for the solar industry.

THE DEVELOPING WORLD: LIGHTING UP WITH SOLAR

When Nigeria comes up in a conversation about energy, it's usually as an oil-producing nation where political unrest is threatening supplies and helping drive up the price of crude for the entire world. But several hundred miles north of the heavily guarded oil ports near Lagos, in three villages on the desert grasslands of Jigawa State near the Niger border, a very different energy story is unfolding. Here, photovoltaic panels from the Solar Electric Light Fund (SELF) have not only replaced diesel generators and kerosene stoves to provide electricity for basic necessities such as lighting and cooking but are also helping the communities improve and transform. They've brought things that didn't exist before: automated water pumping, free schools with evening adult-education classes and Internet connections, and health clinics with refrigerated vaccines. Perhaps most significantly, they're powering small businesses clustered under one solar roof in micro-enterprise buildings—tailors, barber shops, radio repair, and an oil expeller production shop that crushes peanuts and sells the oil for cooking.

"We've really evolved from simply lighting homes to a village empowerment model, using solar power to enable income generation," says Bob Freling, executive director of SELF, a nonprofit based in Washington, D.C., that finances and manages rural solar projects in Nigeria and 14 other developing countries. Jigawa's governor is looking to expand the model to 30 more villages, and when former president Bill Clinton's Global Initiative development group sought the purchase of carbon offsets to make its 2005 New York City conference "carbon-neutral," it chose the Nigeria project (to the tune of $10,000) for its twin achievements of clean-energy use and increased economic opportunity.

Providing solar energy to rural, off-grid villages in the developing world is a challenging but promising growth opportunity for small entrepreneurial companies in the United States and other countries. For more than two decades, Soluz, an innovative company in the Boston suburb of North Chelmsford, Massachusetts, has delivered more than 10,000 clean, distributed electricity systems, usually with solar PV panels, to rural communities in the Dominican Republic and Honduras. Since founder Richard Hansen first flew to Latin America with a solar panel under his arm in 1984, the company has learned that providing clean energy to developing nations requires nothing if not flexibility. "When we started, we used to talk about ourselves as a PV company," says Soluz vice president John Rogers. "Now we use the term REDCO—renewable energy delivery company. It's a proxy for a number of technologies. Customers in these countries aren't motivated by the greenness of it—they just want a high-quality product at a good price."

For Soluz, whose revenue grew 80% in Honduras in 2005, that means providing clean-energy technology on a cash, credit, or lease basis—what Rogers calls "micro-rental." "That makes sense for rural areas," he says. "You can get their costs down to what they'd otherwise pay for kerosene and batteries."

But make no mistake, it's a very challenging business. Lack of infrastructure in remote areas may create the opportunity for off-grid technologies such as solar power, but it also has a major downside. "It's not just a matter of whether the on-site technology can work," says Navigant Consulting managing consultant Shannon Graham. "Is the infrastructure there to support it, in terms of repair, maintenance, parts? I knew of providers in Mexico who would literally fly in to a rural airstrip from Mexico City, drop off and install PV panels, fly out, and never come back. You really have to decide up front if you're doing a development model or a true business model."

One outfit making a pretty good go of it is SELCO India (Solar Electric Light Company). Based in Bangalore, SELCO India operates 25 solar PV sales and service centers serving both rural and urban markets in the states of Karnataka, Kerala, and Andhra Pradesh. Since 1995, SELCO India has installed more than 35,000 solar PV systems, most of them just 50 to 75 W, enough to power three to seven efficient lightbulbs, a radio, and a small TV for a couple of hours. The company is profitable, with yearly revenue of about $3 million. Cofounder and managing director Harish Hande returned to his native country to start SELCO after getting his doctorate in energy engineering, with a solar power specialty, from the University of Massachusetts Lowell. Hande served as the in-country project manager for the Tsunami Solar Light Fund raised to help rebuild the ravaged infrastructure of Sri Lanka with solar power after the 2004 disaster.

A key part of SELCO's business is helping customers line up financing with partners such as micro-credit provider Grameen Shakti. More than 90% of SELCO's customers use financing with a SELCO partner; the customer typically puts 10% to 25% down and repays a three- to five-year loan at 5% to 14% interest.

Although SELCO's original market was mainly rural, in recent years companies and residents in booming Bangalore have used the company's PV panels for supplemental power because of the area's notoriously unreliable centralized power grid, accounting for some 40% of SELCO's sales. "That's where people have more money, and that helps grow the company it can do more rural work," says Navigant's Graham.

Exemplifying public–private partnerships, SELCO receives financing m the PV Market Transformation Initiative (PVMTI), a 12-year, $25 llion program to seed solar service companies like SELCO in India, ıya, and Morocco. Administered and funded by the World Bank's Inter- ional Finance Corporation and the Global Environment Facility, PVMTI focuses on nurturing and growing replicable business models for the selling and servicing of solar PV equipment in those countries.

Throughout rural areas in developing nations, solar and other distributed clean-energy technologies are often the simplest and cheapest electrification option, compared with the expense of building new central power plants, installing a massive grid infrastructure, and running wires from the power grid. Off-grid solar photovoltaic panels are the fastest-growing source of electricity in rural areas of East Africa. Two percent of the rural residents of Kenya use solar power, the highest penetration rate in the world and equal to the rate of rural Kenyans who are connected to the nation's power grid. Nationwide, 20,000 solar home systems are sold annually by more than 50 vendors in Nairobi and some 500 providers in smaller towns. In Brazil, the federal Luz para Todos ("light for all") program aims to electrify 2.5 million rural homes by the end of 2008, 10% of them with clean energy.

The marriage of efficiency and clean energy is particularly critical in remote rural areas. "You can't stop people from wanting TVs and refrigerators, but you can make them run better," says Kristin Peterson, cofounder and chief development officer of Inveneo, a San Francisco nonprofit that provides computers with Internet and voice-over-Internet Protocol (VoIP) capability—and the solar PV panels to power them—to villages and schools in Uganda, Afghanistan, and other countries. Inveneo's engineering VP Bob Marsh, who built a computer in the late 1970s that's now in the Smithsonian Institution, developed a computer and communications system that uses only 20 W—one tenth the power of a standard desktop computer and less than half the juice of a laptop. The system usually runs on solar but can also be fired up by a small generator run by villagers or schoolkids taking turns pedaling a stationary bicycle. High tech powered by low tech, if you will, but clean tech nonetheless.

SEEING THE LIGHT

Solar electricity, we believe, will continue to show considerable growth in the years and decades ahead. We expect that silicon-based solar PV technologies will continue to dominate the market for some time, with the advent of nonsilicon and concentrating solar approaches beginning to gain share by the end of the decade. Most important, whether the approach is silicon or nonsilicon, we see a significant scaling up of manufacturing and driving down costs—bringing solar to cost parity with conventional retail electricity in many regions by 2015. We consider solar a shining example of what we call the "semiconductorization of energy"—in which energy technologies are increasingly based on fabrication technologies used in the earlier semiconductor chip revolution. By leveraging many of the same manufacturing techniques used in transistors and chips, solar will see significant cost improvements via economies of scale in production. And like the computer revolution that preceded it, we see significant opportunity for "value-added resellers," or those who integrate, package, and help finance solar systems.

The sector is ripe for change and will be rife with turbulence. There will be mergers, acquisitions, and consolidation in the industry as solar becomes the domain of large, well-funded multinationals and a few stellar newcomers. For every winning start-up there will be dozens of lesser-known failures. But for now, the solar industry provides one of the best opportunities for a Google or Microsoft of the energy sector to emerge.

Continuous cost reductions, manufacturing scalability, technological innovations, and solar's ability to work in a range of embedded applications mean that the solar industry holds bright promise for the future.

THE CLEAN-TECH CONSUMER

Solar mortgage: Increasingly, home buyers will have the option of purchasing a new house with the solar cells already on it, as roof tiles or exterior wall material. Then solar power is embedded not only in the house but in the mortgage as well. That means your electricity cost is part of the home price and mortgage, rather than an add-on expense up front. And if the sun shines enough, monthly electric bills go away too. Says solar industry pioneer Dr. Donald Aitken of the Union of Concerned Scientists: "Why should you own your home but rent your electricity?" His idea could catch on. With programs like California's 2006 Million Solar Roofs initiative offering $3 billion in rebates and incentives over 11 years, BIPV will be a common feature of new home construction.

Mighty fine lighting: How about a solar-powered lantern that costs around 45 bucks and lasts up to 30 years? Dubbed "the new electric lamp" by *Time* magazine in 2006, the MightyLight from U.S.–India joint venture Cosmos Ignite Innovations is just that. It has replaced polluting, dangerous, and nonrenewable fuel–burning kerosene lamps for thousands of people in India, Pakistan, Afghanistan, Guatemala, and Rwanda. The key component is the most efficient lighting technology on the market, the solid-state light-emitting diode (LED). Cosmos Ignite focuses on poor, needy areas with both direct sales and grant-funded distribution, but anyone can order a MightyLight online.

TEN TO WATCH

Applied Materials
Santa Clara, California
www.appliedmaterials.com
NASDAQ: AMAT

What's Applied Materials, the leading equipment manufacturer in the semiconductor industry, doing in solar? In late 2006 the company announced plans to enter the solar industry. As part of its activities, the company acquired Applied Films, a firm that, among other things, has a thin-film solar manufacturing equipment business. Charlie Gay, a solar industry veteran most recently at SunPower, was recently brought on to help guide Applied Materials in its solar ramp-up—and the company's venture arm has begun investing in a number of clean-energy concerns, including silicon wafer manufacturer Solaicx. As the solar industry expands, Applied Materials is positioning itself to do for solar what it did for the computer industry.

Miasolé
Santa Clara, California
www.miasolé.com

The founders of Miasolé initially developed their technology for a very different market: disk storage. Now they're applying their "sputtering" technology to develop low-cost, high-efficient solar cells. With funding from the likes of Netscape and Yahoo backer Kleiner Perkins, Miasolé is in a strong position to take lessons learned from the high-tech industry and apply them to clean tech.

MMA Renewable Ventures
San Francisco, California
www.mmarenewableventures.com

The solar power industry is full of technology innovators. MMA, like another company on this list, SunEdison, stands out for its innovations in project finance. Once a VC firm, MMA decided to invest in on-site solar

PV projects instead of companies. For clients ranging from a museum in Bridgeport, Connecticut, to a Napa Valley winery, MMA builds an on-site PV system with third-party investor financing and sells the electricity to the client in a power purchase agreement. MMA raised a $100 million fund from institutional investors in 2006 to finance such projects. Formerly Renewable Ventures, the company added MMA to its name after its 2006 acquisition by real estate financier Municipal Mortgage & Equity LLC (NYSE: MMA), better known as MuniMae.

Nanosolar

Palo Alto, California
www.nanosolar.com

In mid-2006 Nanosolar announced plans to develop a 430-MW solar production facility in the San Francisco Bay Area—based on a new form of nanotechnology that basically lets you "print" solar cells. It's audacious by any standards, considering that Sharp took more than 30 years to reach the 400-MW milestone and that the second-largest solar PV manufacturer, Q-Cells, took about 6 years to reach 200-MW production capacity. But the company has some big backers and a unique technology platform, so it could potentially deliver on a next-generation solar solution.

Q-Cells

Thalheim, Germany
www.q-cells.com
Munich Stock Exchange: QCE

The German solar cell manufacturer raised nearly $300 million in its 2005 IPO and was the ninth-fastest growing company in Europe that year. Q-Cells is helping drive down costs of traditional crystalline silicon cells with large-scale manufacturing improvements and greater generating efficiencies from the cells themselves.

REC
Høvik, Norway
www.scanwafer.com
Oslo Stock Exchange: REC.OL

A diversified solar company, REC does everything from solar-grade silicon production to wafer, cell, and module manufacturing. It operates three groups, REC Silicon, REC Wafer, and REC Solar. The company went public on the Oslo Stock Exchange in 2006 and is well positioned because of its diversified approach. While others scramble to gain access to silicon feedstock in a constrained environment, REC can rely on its own supply. It also provides silicon to the largest solar player in the world, Sharp; the company recently signed a deal worth nearly U.S. $500 million through 2012 to supply silicon to the company.

Sharp
Osaka, Japan
www.sharp.co.jp
Tokyo Stock Exchange: 6753

The granddaddy of solar, Sharp currently dominates the global solar market. It not only pumps out around 25% of total worldwide solar cell and module supply but also commands an impressive lead in the growing U.S. market. Sharp will have to fight to stay ahead as the market transforms, but we see it staying a dominant force in the industry. What other multinational's president is stating that solar could generate up to 20% of his firm's total revenue by 2010?

SunEdison
Baltimore, Maryland
www.sunedison.com

An innovative player in solar systems packaging and finance, SunEdison seems to be making all the right moves. It received $60 million in funds from a number of banks, including Goldman Sachs, in 2005. It has been on a buying spree acquiring installation and systems integration capabilities. We believe others are likely to replicate and improve on SunEdison's model, so the company must figure out how to stay ahead of the curve. But for now, SunEdison is impressive for developing a unique model and delivering on its strategy.

SunPower

Sunnyvale, California
www.sunpowercorp.com
NASDAQ: SPWR

Acquired by chip industry pioneer Cypress Semiconductor in 2002 and then spun off in a successful IPO in 2005, SunPower is emerging as a leading player in low-cost, high-volume solar cell production. Its Manila manufacturing facility currently produces 25 MW of solar panels yearly, with the capability to expand to 100 MW; $50 million from its IPO cash haul should help. Industry watchers have hailed SunPower's $332.5 million acquisition of top solar project developer PowerLight as a strong combination.

Suntech Power

Wuxi, Jiangsu Province, China
www.suntech-power.com
New York Stock Exchange: STP

China could very well be the next big solar market, following in the footsteps of Japan, Germany, and California. Chinese manufacturers such as Suntech Power, who are known for driving down manufacturing costs, won't only ship their wares abroad but will also provide cells, modules, and services to the millions of people without access to reliable grid electricity in China. Suntech Power, which was the first major Chinese solar company to go public on a U.S. exchange, is well positioned to reap the benefits of a growing domestic and international market for its products.

2

WIND POWER

Exploiting Big Finance, Large Projects, and Emerging Niches

After years of anticipation, a tipping point in energy pricing had arrived. The place was the state of Colorado; the time, November 2005. That was when, for the first time in the United States, more than 33,000 retail customers—homeowners and businesses—began paying less for electricity generated by wind turbines than other customers buying conventional power from the burning of natural gas and coal. Why was wind power cheaper? Because of a spike in natural gas prices after Hurricanes Katrina and Rita roared through the Gulf of Mexico's drilling rigs and pipelines, electric utility Xcel Energy raised the fuel surcharge for its conventional power customers to a rate 27% higher than the surcharge for customers of Xcel's wind-power program, Windsource. Ratepayers who chose the clean energy generated from the 77 Xcel-owned turbines on northeastern Colorado wind farms Ponnequin (whose Web site regales visitors with the old show tune "They Call the Wind Maria") and Peetz Table started saving an average of 10 bucks a month.

"No longer an environmentalist's pipe dream," wrote the *Denver Post* in an editorial, "wind is an energy source worthy of a bigger role in meeting a growing state's electrical power needs." The marketplace response was swift. Xcel saw as many customers sign up for Windsource on the day it announced the new fuel surcharge as it normally did in 2 months. Windsource quickly sold out—Xcel was selling 100% of the power its wind farms could produce—and a waiting list of 1,100 customers began. Said a headline on one local news station's Web site: "No Wind for You."

Two months later, the trend spread southeast to Austin, Texas. Along with their holiday credit card bills in January 2006, customers of municipal utility Austin Energy's conventional power mix from coal, natural gas, and nuclear plants had to swallow a fuel surcharge that kicked their rates higher than those paid by customers buying power from west Texas wind farms through Austin's GreenChoice green-power program. It wasn't a big difference, but the lower rate for clean energy, like a fixed-rate mortgage, was locked in for up to 10 years.

As with Xcel, demand for Austin Energy's cheaper green power exceeded its supply; the utility chose to hold a raffle in early 2006 to divvy up the last of the available GreenChoice accounts. "One or two years ago, there were some instances where we started seeing the price of wind power dip below natural gas on the spot market," Roger Duncan, deputy general manager of Austin Energy and a former Austin city council member, said at the time. "Now it's just consistently cheaper." Although the trend was temporary in Colorado—as natural gas prices eased and Xcel raised its rates, Windsource returned to costing a bit more—it was still a historic moment and, we believe, a portent of trends to come.

Some thirty years since the first big push for power from the sun and the wind in the 1970s, the long-awaited crossover point between the costs of clean energy and fossil fuels had finally arrived. Xcel, the largest buyer of wind power among U.S. utilities, intended to more than double its wind use in 2007 to 2.3 GW. Of all widely available renewable sources of electricity, utility-scale wind power is the most cost-competitive with conventional coal, natural gas, or nuclear generation today. And that's a key reason why wind energy, with some exceptions, is and will continue to be the domain of large, global players worldwide.

In this chapter we'll explore the exploding growth of the wind industry in North America, Europe, and Asia. For the foreseeable future, most of the large-scale business and investment opportunities will come from the big players—the large turbine manufacturers such as GE, Denmark's Vestas, Spain's Gamesa, Japan's Mitsubishi, Germany's Siemens, and India's Suzlon Energy; big utilities such as FPL Energy, Xcel, and Iberdrola; and powerful global financiers such as Goldman Sachs (parent of its own wind-farm developer, Horizon Wind Energy), Morgan Stanley, Deutsche Bank, Dutch insurance giant AEGON, and Spain's largest bank, Santander Central Hispano. It's a game of big capital costs, big project finance deals, and big industrial companies supplying the necessary equipment. Those factors will only be enhanced by the coming growth of carbon credits, with large utilities around the world looking for the carbon-trading payoff from adding more emissions-free power to their electricity mix. With the world's biggest names in manufacturing, finance, and electric power dominating the industry, wind power has clearly transformed from its alternative roots to an important and growing segment of mainstream power generation worldwide.

Although such global giants are the best place to look for investments and career opportunities in utility-scale wind, there continue to be potentially lucrative niche opportunities for start-ups and smaller players in smaller-scale projects. We'll highlight those opportunities throughout the chapter as well, including on-site microturbines, small community-based wind farms, innovations in components such as gearboxes and turbine blades, and small turbines integrated *within* a building's design.

BIG PLAYERS, BIG GROWTH

By almost any measure, wind is booming. Take overall market size. The global wind-power industry from $11.8 billion in 2005 to $17.9 billion in 2006, according to Clean Edge research, and we project that the market will more than triple to $60.8 billion by 2016. In the United States in 2006, wind was the second-largest source of new generating capacity, trailing only natural gas. More than 2.4 GW of new capacity was installed, a 27% increase that brought total U.S. wind to 11.6 GW, enough to power about 2.9 million homes, according to the American Wind Energy Association (AWEA) trade group. North of the border, Canada nearly doubled its wind-power capacity in 2006, adding 657 new MW—about U.S. $800 million of new investment—for a total of more than 1.3 GW. The demand of about 406,000 Canadian homes is met by wind generation, says the Canadian Wind Energy Association. In 2006 Canada's largest wind farm, the 189-MW Prince Wind Energy Project, opened with 126 turbines sprawling over 120,000 acres near Sault Ste. Marie, Ontario.

Big players are enjoying healthy growth. GE Energy, the dominant player in the U.S. wind-turbine industry supplying some two-thirds of the domestic market, was to garner nearly $3 billion in wind-turbine revenue in 2006, a fourfold increase since just 2002. Horizon Wind Energy in Houston, acquired (as Zilkha Renewable Energy) by Goldman Sachs in

2005, has become one of the nation's most aggressive developers of wind farms in the Northeast, Midwest, Texas, and other regions. India's Suzlon Energy has crashed the party of European companies that comprise, along with GE and Mitsubishi, the world's top 10 wind-turbine manufacturers. Its growth has made founder Tulsi Tanti and his three brothers billionaires since the company went public in 2005.

Investors and entrepreneurs would also do well to note specific countries, states, and regions where wind is growing fastest, often aiding depressed rural economies with lease revenue for siting turbines on agricultural land—wind *farms*, indeed. Local regions now compete for such sites in what has been dubbed the PIMBY syndrome—"put it in my backyard" syndrome (though skeptics might counter that such backyards are cornfields or cow pastures, not million-dollar ocean views). Oil industry icon Texas surprised many by passing California in 2006 as the king of wind, the U.S. state with the most wind generation. A big boost was the completion of FPL Energy's 735-MW Horse Hollow wind farm near Abilene, at the time the largest onshore wind farm in the world. And the Lone Star State is poised for much more, with a consortium of companies, including Airtricity, FPL Energy, Horizon, and PPM Energy, pledging in late 2006 to invest a total of $10 billion in new Texas wind farms before 2016. The Midwest is a boom region as well, with Iowa and Minnesota ranking third and fourth in generating capacity among U.S. states at the end of 2006.

Europe accounts for about 75% of the world's installed wind-energy capacity, with more than 40 GW. As it does in solar power, Germany leads the world in wind production, with more than 18 GW—33% more than the United States. But the hottest current growth market in the European Union is Spain, which has vaulted past Denmark and the United States to become the world's second largest wind user, with more than 10 GW (although the Danes still lead the world in the percentage of their power consistently generated by wind—about 20%). Spanish companies Acciona, Endesa (Spain's largest utility, 10% owned by Acciona), Gamesa, and Iberdrola are moving aggressively in wind markets around the world, as well as in their hot domestic market. Gamesa employs some 300 workers in Pennsylvania, for example, while Iberdrola in 2006 acquired three U.S. wind developers, Community Energy in Wayne, Pennsylvania, and MREC Partners and Midwest Renewable Energy Projects, both in Joice, Iowa.

Other European growth markets for wind include the Netherlands, Italy, Portugal, and the United Kingdom, where Shell WindEnergy, Germany's E.ON, and Denmark's CORE are seeking to build the world's first 1,000-MW offshore wind farm in the Thames River estuary in Kent. The controversial project, approved in late 2006, could meet 25% of the power needs of metropolitan London. Construction is also proceeding on Europe's largest onshore wind farm, ScottishPower's Whitelee project near Glasgow. Its 140 turbines will generate 322 MW within 3 years.

In the United States, however, there's one factor that looms larger than any other in the continued growth of the wind industry: the federal production tax credit (PTC) for wind. Government policy and subsidy decisions always play a decisive role in the growth (or lack thereof) of a particular energy sector, but the direct effect of the PTC on the wind-power industry in the United States has been even more pronounced than other policies. That's because the PTC, a 1.9-cents-per-kilowatt credit that's critical to making wind cost competitive with traditional energy sources, has had a checkered history of on-again, off-again legislative approval. It's a critical issue that investors and business planners must follow closely, because PTC expirations every couple of years or so have turned graphs of new U.S. wind installations into designs for a roller-coaster track. Growth shot up in 1999, 2001, 2003, and 2005, and hurtled downward in 2000, 2002, and 2004. Both 2005 and 2006 were boom years, thanks to Congress's extension of the PTC through the end of 2008. Industry groups, especially the influential AWEA, are pushing hard for a long-term (five-year) extension so that U.S. growth can follow the world market's steady upward curve instead of the yearly peak-and-valley model that has business planners from the likes of GE, FPL Energy, and Xcel Energy tearing their hair out.

BREAKTHROUGH OPPORTUNITY

Community Wind

Financiers, including high-net-worth individuals, have a growing opportunity to participate in the wind-power industry via small, community-based wind projects. Usually generating less than 10 MW (with most producing 5 or 6 MW), these small wind farms are sprouting in more than 30 states around the United States but particularly on the cornfields and prairies of the upper Midwest. Many investors can expect very impressive after-tax returns of 12% to 15% for 5 to 10 years, according to Ted Bernhard, a corporate and securities lawyer and founder of the energy ventures group at Stoel Rives in Portland, Oregon, one of the nation's top law firms in clean-energy projects. Community wind projects also carry a low risk factor; deals are usually structured so that investors commit to participate in what's essentially debt financing but don't put up the money until the turbines go online. "They don't have to cough up a dollar until the project starts producing power," says Bernhard. Such projects are the offspring of the Public Utilities Regulatory Pricing Act of 1978, which requires utilities to buy clean energy from community projects at the "avoided cost" of what they would have otherwise paid for the electricity from a conventional power plant of their own. That, along with other federal and state policy incentives for wind, makes community wind an increasingly attractive investment with a built-in market.

ASIA: WINDS OF CHANGE

Wind isn't taking hold just in the United States and Europe. Both India and China are looking to wind farms to supply a significant chunk of their rapidly growing power needs. India, now tapping its legendary monsoon winds for electricity, is one of the world's fastest-growing markets for wind power. Indian wind-farm generation surged 42% in 2006 to overtake industry pioneer Denmark as the number four market behind Germany, Spain, and the United States, according to the Brussels-based Global Wind Energy Council. India added 1.8 GW of wind in 2006 for an installed capacity of 6.27 GW, and in November 2006, the nation hosted the annual World Wind Energy Conference for the first time in New Delhi. Suzlon Energy, based in Pune in the state of Maharashtra, is one of the world's most consistently profitable wind-turbine makers. Suzlon founder Tulsi Tanti, dubbed "Wind Man" in a June 2006 *Forbes* cover story, holds a 70% stake in the company along with his three brothers.

In China, companies from Europe, the United States, and Australia are moving aggressively to capitalize as the nation moves from 2.6 GW of wind in 2006 to more than 30 GW—enough to power some 30 million average Chinese homes—by 2020. Joint ventures with local partners is the name of the game. Acciona, for example, is building some 500 wind turbines a year for the Asian market in Nantong, Jiangsu Province, in a joint venture between state-owned enterprise China Aerospace and Technology Corporation and Acciona's wind-energy unit, EHN. Seizing the China opportunity has helped boost the stock price and financial analysts' outlook for Acciona, which was slipping behind Spanish competitors such as Gamesa in the European wind market. The joint venture's shared initial investment of €24 million could lead to annual revenue of €400 million, the companies say.

"The challenge of China is an opportunity as well," says Josu Arlaban Gabeiras, finance director of Acciona. "The country is taking the opportunity to diversify its energy mix and develop the renewable sector from scratch. The potential is massive. The keys are showing that you have know-how and a good track record, and showing that you have come here to stay." What about the risks of sharing tech trade secrets in a country renowned for piracy, a very real fear that has some global clean-tech giants such as German wind-turbine maker Enercon staying away? "Sure, we were afraid of handing over our technology, so we looked for a well-established local partner," says Gabeiras. "Business is riskier here, so make it a controlled and shared risk. If it fails, it will be a failure on both sides."

Roaring 40's is a wind-farm development joint venture between Australia's Hydro Tasmania and Hong Kong's CLP Power Asia. Taking its name from the powerful gusts that roar across the Pacific along the fortieth parallel and sweep over Tasmania, Roaring 40's built several wind farms in Australia and New Zealand and is now muscling into China, India, and Thailand to do the same. It considers these growing economies a key piece of its ambitious plan to build a 1,000-MW portfolio of wind and hydroelectric power throughout south Asia and Oceania by 2010. Roaring 40's commissioned its first China project in October 2006, the 49-MW Shuangliao Wind Farm (running fifty-eight 850-kW Gamesa turbines) in Jilin Province, a joint venture with China Datong. "We've always said we're in China for the long term," says Roaring 40's communications director Josh Bradshaw. "That means a lot to them. This is a strategic decision for our business. We want to be the leading renewable energy developer in Asia for the next thirty to forty years."

SUPERSIZE IT

In the previous chapter, we explored the opportunities created by solar PV engineers seeking cost-effectiveness breakthroughs down to the nanotech level. Wind-turbine manufacturers are also looking at nanotech advancements for their blade and tower materials. Nanocomposites could help address the industry challenge posed by worldwide steel shortages, while offering improved strength and durability of turbine blades, gears, and other components. But in a bit of irony, the industry is often looking to molecule-sized breakthroughs to aid its quest for ever-larger turbines. In recent years—with some notable exceptions—bigger has become better. Advances in metallurgy, materials science, and manufacturing at very large companies such as GE, Mitsubishi, NRG, and Vestas have all contributed to this trend. Since construction costs are relatively comparable regardless of the size of the turbine, larger turbines that produce more megawatts are driving down the price of wind power around the world.

In wind power's early days, 750 kW was the industry's standard output for a single turbine. Now most new wind turbines crank out more than twice that amount of juice, around 2 MW—enough to power about 1,500 homes in the United States. In early 2005, Germany's REPower unveiled the world's largest turbine, a 5-MW monster for use in offshore wind farms. Each of its three blades, made of glass-carbon fiber and synthetic resins, is nearly 400 feet long. "It's like making a 747 wing three times," says Dr. Donald Aitken, senior consulting scientist for the Union of Concerned Scientists.

The economies of scale from the industry's growth have also driven costs down. Wind, along with solar, are the two fastest-growing energy sources in the world. Wind added more than 15,000 MW in 2005, to pass 74,000 MW of installed capacity worldwide. The rapidly increasing volumes, along with improved technology, have driven wind-energy costs down by an order of magnitude from more than 30 cents per kilowatt-hour in 1980 to as low as 4 cents per kilowatt-hour in some areas today.

BREAKTHROUGH OPPORTUNITY

Variable-Length Blades

Even the world's best wind-power sites, rated class 7 (on a scale of 1 to 7) in industry parlance, have wind-speed variability—that's just the nature of this energy resource. But what if you could vary the size of your wind-turbine blades, depending on the wind conditions, for optimum energy production? That's the premise of a potential breakthrough technology from 25-year wind-industry veteran Energy Unlimited in West Conshohocken, Pennsylvania, called the Variblade. Representing one of a number of innovation opportunities in turbine components, such as gearboxes and motors, the "blade within a blade" design contains a retractable blade extension. A controller in the base of the tower responds to changes in wind speed, extending the inside blade in lighter wind and retracting it in heavier breezes. Conventional turbines actually have to be shut off when the wind is too strong, to prevent damage. Energy Unlimited claims that the adjustability saves significant wear and tear on the turbine and gearbox and allows for increased use. But more important, it can boost electricity production by up to 25%, meaning more revenue to the wind-farm operator from the utility buying the power. "It's a pretty fixed-cost industry," says David Frost, vice president of strategy and development, "so a twenty-five percent increase in output gives you a thirty to forty percent increase in cash flow." Energy Unlimited has been operating Variblade prototypes since 2002 near Palm Springs, California.

The wind turbines of the twenty-first century are bigger, cheaper, and more reliable—industry average uptime is about 98.6%, which is better than for coal and natural-gas plants. Obviously the wind needs to be blowing steadily—neither too fast nor too slow—but that's why the industry chooses its wind farm sites carefully. These large turbines also address a wind-power issue that often causes local opposition to wind farms and pits clean-energy advocates against fellow green-minded citizens: bird and bat safety. Many believe the concern is overblown (pardon the pun), but the issue is very real for utilities and developers seeking site permits.

Since today's blades are so large, they actually spin much more slowly than their much smaller ancestors, making it easier for birds to see and avoid them. Most turbines also no longer use trellis-type support towers, which became inviting places for birds to perch or nest when the blades weren't spinning, with mortal consequences when the breezes began anew. But for bottom-line purposes, today's turbines generate much more energy per manufacturing, construction, and maintenance dollar than they did in the past, and that's shown up directly in the falling kilowatt-hour prices.

But larger turbines—and having so many more of them—are creating a demand crunch. As the solar industry contends with a shortage of silicon feedstock as outlined in the previous chapter, wind power is facing a comparable challenge: a shortage of, and higher prices for, wind turbines. Huge growth in worldwide demand in 2005 and 2006 has turbine manufacturers scrambling to keep up, while the rise in global steel prices sparked by rapid economic expansion in China and India is raising the cost of turbines' raw materials. A lot of steel, for example, goes into a 200-foot tower. That has put upward pressure on wind-turbine prices in some areas. Heavy and growing demand for other necessary parts, such as blades, gearboxes, and generators, makes component manufacturers such as blade-industry leader LM GlasFiber of Lunderskov, Denmark, very attractive growth opportunities in the near term. Turbine maker Suzlon thought so in March 2006 when it paid $565 million to acquire Belgian gearbox manufacturer Hansen Transmissions International, which also guaranteed a steady supply of gearboxes for Suzlon's own turbines.

But most industry principals see supply catching up with demand very shortly; GE, for one, sees its wind business continuing the growth rates that boosted its wind-power revenue from $2 billion in 2005 to some $3 billion in 2006. In both wind and solar, current price increases reflect an overheated industry coping with supply issues. They're not a result of technology being new and unproven, as in the early days of both industries.

The largest turbines do pose one unique, often deal-breaking challenge in remote areas and developing countries: They're simply too big to move to the designated site and erect there. Many wind-rich places such as Inner Mongolia, parts of India, and even the more remote prairies of the American Midwest lack roads, transport vehicles, and construction equipment that are capable of moving and installing multimegawatt behemoths.

That's led to a resurgence of growth in midsized turbines, like Vestas's V47 660-kW model. So even though the larger turbines are more cost-effective once they're up and running, there will be strong demand for midrange turbines, particularly with significant chunks of the wind industry's growth coming from developing nations.

BREAKTHROUGH OPPORTUNITY

Hybrid Wind-Hydroelectric

The intermittent nature of wind power makes it an ideal partner with a more easily controlled energy source such as hydropower. That's why several wind-hydroelectric hybrid pilot projects are under way in the United States and elsewhere, under the auspices of NREL, the International Energy Agency, and other bodies. The good news is that reliable wind and hydroelectric resources are often located in the same regions, such as the Pacific Northwest, the Missouri River Basin, Scandinavia, Switzerland, and Australia. Along the Columbia River in central Washington State, a team of engineers from Grant County Public Utility District, NREL, and Northern Arizona University is testing the integration of 16 MW of power from the nearby Nine Canyon wind farm with the hydroelectric output from the Wanapum and Priest Rapids dams. If successful and cost effective, projects like these could be a boon for wind developers and their investors, and for power integration engineering consultancies such as EnerNex in Knoxville, Tennessee, which is working on several NREL wind-hydroelectric test projects. For smaller, on-site generation to power farms or villages, there's also good potential in combining one or two wind turbines in a hybrid system with a small solar PV array or a generator running diesel or biodiesel. A U.S. Department of Agriculture test of a 150-kW wind–biodiesel plant near Amarillo, Texas, is scheduled for completion in March 2008.

THE FIXED-COST ADVANTAGE

The current demand-driven rise in wind-energy costs, however, does not change one fundamental advantage of wind power over electricity generated from fossil fuels: a fixed price. Wind-farm developers might command a higher price per kilowatt-hour from the purchasing utility than they did 2 years ago, owing to higher capital costs and the ability to charge what a market driven by high demand will bear. But that price is still locked in for the length of the contract, because wind is not subject to the vagaries of fuel costs.

But *Ah*, you might say, *what if the wind doesn't blow and the utility has to supplement the wind-farm output with other power sources?* It doesn't really change the pricing formula. Virtually all utility-scale wind farms are planned with highly sophisticated computer models predicting wind strength and consistency. It simply doesn't make financial sense to build them in places subject to frequent calm days, so most wind farms deliver pretty well on what their developers promise. And the vast majority of utility-scale wind farms deliver their output to the power grid, where their electrons mix with those coming from coal, natural gas, nuclear, geothermal, or hydroelectric plants. So in a sense, wind power is almost always supplemented by electricity from other sources; utility load planners figure in the intermittent nature of wind already.

In many areas of the United States and around the world, utilities are making wind a bigger part of their energy mix because of renewable portfolio standard (RPS) mandates. Nearly half the states now have such mandates, with voters making Washington State one of the newest RPS members via a successful ballot measure in the November 2006 election. The mandate requires Washington to get 15% of the state's power from clean sources by 2020. Many predict that the 110th Congress will move toward a national RPS for the United States. But whether national or state by state, since wind is usually the most cost-competitive clean power source, RPSs have been and will continue to be a major industry driver in states such as Texas, California, and Pennsylvania, and in much of the Midwest.

The incorporation of wind into a utility's overall electricity mix is also being driven by so-called green power. The term refers to residential or commercial electricity buyers' option to purchase a cleaner energy mix than their local utility's standard offering. Although green power can include electricity produced from landfill gas, geothermal sources, small hydroelectric, or solar, the vast majority of green power comes from wind farms. Austin Energy's GreenChoice and Xcel Energy's Windsource are two of the most successful green-power programs, but there are more than 600 others around the United States offered by both investor-owned and public, municipal utilities.

A variation on this is the option to purchase renewable energy certificates (RECs), or "green tags." These are essentially direct payments to third-party agents such as 3 Phases Energy Services in San Francisco; Sterling Planet in Norcross, Georgia; and NativeEnergy in Charlotte, Vermont, which specializes in wind power generated on Native American land. REC companies funnel the money to fund new wind farms and other clean-energy projects. For corporations, the purchase of RECs can be an important part of an overall sustainability strategy. Wells Fargo, for example, buys enough RECs from 3 Phases to offset 42% of its electricity use, making the banking giant the largest buyer of green power in the nation.

For businesses much of the financial payoff from RECs is an indirect one: positive public relations, goodwill, and improved attraction and retention of loyal customers and employees. But as GHG emissions mandates and carbon-trading markets become more of a fact of doing business in the United States and worldwide, RECs are becoming increasingly attractive.

That's why some of the nation's largest and best-known companies and organizations are turning to RECs as part of a green-power strategy. Combining RECs with direct purchases of wind energy and other forms of clean energy, pharmaceutical giant Johnson & Johnson bought 30% of its electricity in the United States from green-power sources in 2006. Staples purchased 20%, Starbucks 25%, and Sprint Nextel's operational headquarters 47%. Some may be surprised to learn that the nation's third-largest buyer of green power is the U.S. Air Force, purchasing more than 457,000 kilowatt-hours (kWh) of green electricity annually, or 2% of its total, in 2006.

Buying some utilities' green-power options, however, can yield direct, tangible business benefits. As we noted at the beginning of the chapter with the recent experience of customers in Colorado and Texas, green power can sometimes be cheaper than standard utility rates, but today that's a rare and often temporary phenomenon. The real financial advantage of green power is its fixed cost. A growing number of green-power customers are learning that the ability to lock in a consistent fuel charge for up to 10 years is a great business plum. It converts a variable budget line item into a fixed cost, or a volatile monthly household charge into something more consistent. Even if the initial green-power charge is a bit higher, many companies, government agencies, college campuses, and even military bases think it's worth it.

"Having to deal with the price volatility of natural gas-fired peaker plants is not a good way to do business," says J. Michael Horowitz, senior analyst of the clean technology and industrial growth research team at Pacific Growth Equities, an investment bank in San Francisco. "In my opinion, the higher highs and lower lows of natural gas prices are going to continue for some time. That is a business model killer."

QUICK PAYOFF

Semiconductor chip maker Advanced Micro Devices (AMD) is one of 400 businesses that buy Austin Energy's GreenChoice power for its Austin, Texas, factories and offices. Having signed up for 100% GreenChoice, AMD gets both the 10-year rate lock-in and direct cost savings, as the GreenChoice premium dipped below the natural gas fuel charge in January 2006, as described at the beginning of the chapter. "It helps AMD reduce overall energy costs," says Craig Garcia, the company's director of global corporate services. "As the price of energy derived from traditional fossil fuels continues to increase, green power is purchased at a fixed rate over the life of the contract." AMD expected to break even on its GreenChoice power in 3 years; instead, thanks to the rising cost of the natural gas–fired power that it *wasn't* buying, it reached the break-even point in just 1 year.

"We thought [GreenChoice for businesses] would move slowly, that it'd be just the hard-core greenies or those who believed conventional prices would soar," says Austin Energy GreenChoice sales rep Elizabeth Kasprowicz. "Now I can't keep them off me. It's becoming more and more chichi to be green, and price lock is the total clincher."

While Austin Energy remains the leader in locked-in pricing, it's not alone. As of mid-2006, two other utilities offered green power at long-term fixed rates: Oregon's Eugene Water & Electric Board and Washington State's Clallam County Public Utility District. Seven other utilities in Colorado, Iowa, Minnesota, Oklahoma, and Wisconsin exempt their green-power customers from fuel-surcharge increases. Fixed rates enable both commercial and residential customers to enter into stable, multiyear contracts for green power. And the average green-power price premium has dropped an average of 8% annually since 2000, according to NREL, with increasing numbers of consumers and businesses taking note. The number of residential buyers of green power more than tripled from 131,000 in 2000 to 430,000 in 2005, and number of nonresidential users (buying much more power per facility than homeowners) neared 9,000 in 2005. More than 600 investor-owned and municipal utilities across the United States offer a green-power option.

BREAKTHROUGH OPPORTUNITY

Building-Integrated Wind

There's an odd sight on the rooftop edge of the city of Austin's otherwise drab Wireless Communication Services Office building. Mounted side by side on the parapet are what appear to be eight oversized window fans. But these blades-in-frames aren't using electricity; they're generating it. They're a test project of a new technology in the wind business. Instead of turbine blades atop towers high in the sky, building-integrated wind power brings wind generation right into a building's architecture. The turbines in Austin, just 400 W each, are a test of the Architectural Wind System from AeroVironment in Monrovia, California, whose main business is control systems for pilotless aircraft and quick charging of batteries. Another pilot project, on the roof of the London Climate Change Agency in the United Kingdom, combines with building-integrated solar PV panels to produce 84 kW of power. A series of 1.5-kW turbines from Aerotecture International in Chicago will be deployed on the Ford Calumet Environmental Center in the Windy City, due to open in 2007. If these projects and others prove viable, that could unlock a huge market previously unreachable by tower-mounted, on-site wind power: dense urban areas. These so-called urban wind systems not only feature appropriate scale but are also designed to efficiently harness the variable, swirling winds of cities in ways that large turbines can't. Dutch company Ecofys has trademarked perhaps the catchiest name for products in this promising sector: Urban Turbines.

TAPPING THE OCEAN: WAVES AND TIDES

While thousands of wind turbines sprout to harness the currents of the atmosphere, clean-energy developers around the globe are working to perfect turbines powered by the movement of the sea. The basic technology concept is comparable: using natural currents to turn turbine blades to generate electricity. In one emerging tidal power technology, in fact, the turbines are driven not by the motion of water but instead by air currents forced through a tube by the push and pull of the tide.

Wave and tidal power remain nascent, pilot-phase technologies but hold great potential for a number of U.S. and European companies. Some observers have likened the field to the wind-power industry in the 1980s: still an offbeat curiosity to the mainstream but full of pioneering inventors with substantial promise for both significant power generation and the attraction of investment capital.

Unlike wind energy, the technology is not yet dominated by very large companies. There's still plenty of room for entrepreneurs and their backing investors to get in on the wave and tidal action. Not that all the big players are on the sidelines, however: GE and European energy giants E.ON of Germany and Norsk Hydro of Norway have all begun investing in their own wave and tidal projects or in smaller technology companies.

Some wave-power technologies, such as AquaEnergy's AquaBuOYs in Makah Bay off Washington State's Olympic Peninsula, rely on the heaving up-and-down motion of buoys to drive turbines. AquaEnergy, a unit of Finavera Renewables of Dublin, Ireland, says the project will deliver 1,500 MWH of juice to the local power grid annually, starting in 2007. Finavera's much larger project using the same technology off the coast of South Africa, scheduled to be completed by 2011, aims to deliver 360,000 MWH per year. Another company, Ocean Power Delivery of Edinburgh, Scotland, taps wave action with a floating 492-foot sectioned tube named Pelamis, after a genus of venomous sea snakes. Between each section is a hydraulic ram that, in reaction to the movements of waves, pushes fluid to drive a hydraulic motor that generates power. Ocean Power Delivery, whose investors include GE, Norsk Hydro, and Merrill Lynch, is building its first commercial Pelamis "power plant" off the coast of Portugal.

Tidal power, by contrast, is usually harnessed much closer to shore. Could New York City be the world's leader in clean energy produced in city limits? That's the grand vision of Verdant Power, which is testing tidal turbines in the East River, which is technically not a river but a tidal strait between Manhattan and Long Island. Verdant's turbines are like small underwater windmills, with tidal flows turning the blades. A $10 million, 18-month test of the first two turbines began in late 2006. Arlington, Virginia–based Verdant hopes to produce 10 MW in the project's first phase, with three other possible East River sites promising a potential total of 40 MW in the long term. On the Pacific coast, the city of San Francisco is studying the feasibility of placing underwater turbines near the Golden Gate Bridge and aiming to begin a 1 to 3 MW pilot project in 2009. One technology under consideration uses the power of the Golden Gate tides (among the world's strongest) to force high-speed air through a so-called Venturi tube to turn turbine blades—a sort of enclosed wind turbine underwater. The "Venturi effect" is similar to the wind-tunnel phenomenon that occurs between tall buildings.

WIND FORECAST: STEADY BREEZES

We're very bullish on wind power now. All the growth elements are in place: reliable technology, industry experience and maturity, and heavy investment from global manufacturing giants, large influential electric utilities, and many of the world's largest and most respected financiers. Add in wind power's cost competitiveness, an increasingly favorable government policy climate around the world, and huge potential growth in China and India, and the future looks breezy and bright.

Are there potential speed bumps (or wind breaks)? Absolutely. As the developers of the large proposed wind farm off the shores of Cape Cod, Massachusetts, can tell you, local opposition to wind projects, whether from the classic NIMBY ("not in my backyard") syndrome or legitimate concerns such as migratory bird kills, can be fierce. The current turbine shortage, from high demand and pressure on steel supplies, will drive up costs in the short term. And regulatory hurdles, such as delays in extending the all-important U.S. PTC, can certainly put the brakes on individual projects or even the whole industry.

But we believe that these potential blips will not significantly slow overall industry trends. The Democrat-controlled 110th U.S. Congress should be more predisposed to support clean energy in general and the extension of the PTC in particular. The Cape Wind project may never happen, but that will be the exception, not the rule among U.S. projects; work on other offshore wind farms, in fact, is proceeding off the coasts of Long Island and Texas. Turbine manufacturers around the world are ramping up production capacity to address the turbine shortage, an investment that should pay off quickly. Wind power, as the world's most cost-competitive clean-energy choice for large-scale generation, will be an increasing part of the electricity mix of large and small utilities worldwide.

With some notable exceptions that we've detailed throughout the chapter, wind is and will remain a large players' game. And it is without a doubt a global industry, with U.S., European, and Asian companies and their financial partners chasing markets around the world. For American job seekers, in fact, there's good potential within offshore suppliers seeking expanded presence in the United States, as Gamesa, Suzlon, Vestas, and other companies have shown in recent years. Although there are several breakthrough opportunities for entrepreneurial start-ups and small investors as different technology niches develop, the current landscape of utility-scale wind farms favors large, well-capitalized manufacturers and wind developers. Big players and big bucks—that's the sweet spot of the wind industry for some time to come.

THE CLEAN-TECH CONSUMER

Spend less green on green: Sure, hard-core greenies are willing to pay their utilities a small premium for electricity from clean-energy sources such as wind and solar. But in the next few years, that green-power niche (typically less than 5% of ratepayers in utility districts that offer green power) will likely become a mass market, luring not just enviros but bargain hunters as well. As wind energy continues to dip below the cost of natural gas in the next few years, more utilities across the United States will emulate the success of Austin Energy's cheaper green power. Particularly look for locked-in pricing, which will become more available as wind power offers more cost stability than natural gas and coal.

Own your own wind turbine: The big manufacturers and utility giants are generally focusing on ever-larger wind turbines, deployed in greater and greater numbers. But there's a significant growth niche in small-scale wind:

a single turbine providing on-site power for a residence, small business, or farm. An average wind speed of about 12 miles per hour (mph) is considered minimum for an installation to be cost effective. Fast-growing Southwest Windpower in Flagstaff, Arizona (www.windenergy.com), has captured more than 60% of the U.S. market. Its flagship turbine, the Skystream 3.7, snagged a 2006 Best of What's New award from *Popular Science* magazine. It cranks out about 400 kWh a month and costs between $8,000 and $10,000, including installation. Other notable suppliers include Abundant Renewable Energy in Newberg, Oregon (www.abundantre.com), and Bergey Windpower in Norman, Oklahoma (www.bergey.com), whose president Mike Bergey and his father Karl pioneered the small wind business in the 1970s. One key to the residential market is tax rebates and incentives, so check the current policies in your state: California, Pennsylvania, and Wisconsin are among those currently offering the best subsidies. Also check your local zoning ordinances; towers range from 35 to 110 feet tall, making these smaller turbines better suited for rural and open areas than for Main Street or the suburbs.

TEN TO WATCH

Acciona
Pamplona, Spain
www.acciona.com
Madrid Stock Exchange: ANA

The Spanish utility's Acciona Energía unit is one of the most aggressive, fast-growing, clean-energy players in one of the world's hottest markets. Acciona Energía is active in solar and biofuels too but is particularly worth watching in wind; its wind-power subsidiary EHN is one of the world's top five owners of wind farms. In 2006, it opened the largest wind-turbine factory in China, where it plans to build 400 to 600 MW of 1.5-MW turbines in Nantong. Acciona holds a 20% stake in Endesa, another Spanish company actively pursuing wind power.

Austin Energy
Austin, Texas
www.austinenergy.com

The unequivocal leader in green power, Austin Energy sells more than 400 million kWh a year of clean energy, mostly wind power. That accounts for 17% of all the green power sold in the United States. More important, Austin's clean energy sometimes sells for less than conventional electricity and is available at a fixed rate for up to 10 years. Austin Energy's wind ventures range from big wind farms to a pilot project of eight building-integrated wind turbines, from technology provider AeroVironment, on the rooftop of a local city government building.

FPL Group
Juno Beach, Florida
www.fpl.com
New York Stock Exchange: FPL

Formerly Florida Power & Light, this utility giant's FPL Energy subsidiary symbolizes the role of large utilities in moving wind power forward in the United States. FPL Energy is the nation's largest owner of wind farms—somewhat ironically, as there are no utility-scale wind farms in Florida or in any other wind resource–poor southeastern state. But hit California, Texas, Pennsylvania, or Minnesota, and you'll find FPL's name all over the state. As of late 2006, FPL had 47 wind farms in 15 states.

Gamesa
Madrid, Spain
www.gamesa.es
Madrid Stock Exchange: GAM

Vying with GE and Germany's Enercon for the number 2 spot among global wind-turbine manufacturers, Gamesa benefits from the fast-growing Spanish wind market and a strongly increased presence in the United States. The company has opened a turbine plant in Ebensburg, Pennsylvania, that employs 200 people, with another 100 at its U.S. headquarters in Philadelphia, and has inked a $700 million pact with Goldman Sachs–

owned Horizon Wind Energy for enough turbines to produce 600 MW on U.S. wind farms.

General Electric

Fairfield, Connecticut
www.ge.com
New York Stock Exchange: GE

Just about every aspect of the clean tech revolution feels the impact of GE. We include the company in this chapter's "Ten to Watch" section because of its powerful global influence on the wind-power industry. As a major manufacturer of wind turbines, GE both helps drive down costs in those industries and capitalizes on the resulting increased demand. Beyond its top position supplying the U.S. market, GE is winning big chunks of business against its traditional European rivals in emerging markets such as China. GE Power Systems (now GE Energy, based in Atlanta) astutely entered the business by acquisition, picking up Enron Wind from the wreckage of the imploding energy company in 2002. (GE joined the solar industry in similar fashion, buying then-bankrupt solar company AstroPower 2 years later.) Wind turbines, related equipment, and services accounted for about $3 billion of GE Energy's $20 billion business in 2006. GE's workhorse is its 1.5-MW turbine, with more than 5,000 installed worldwide.

Horizon Wind Energy

Houston, Texas
www.horizonwind.com

Horizon's fascinating saga began when Baghdad-born Selim Zilkha founded Zilkha Energy in the 1980s to buy and sell oil leases in the Gulf of Mexico. After selling that company, Zilkha saw a new business opportunity in building wind farms in Texas and elsewhere. In 2000, 73-year-old Zilkha (already listed as one of the *Forbes* 400 richest people in America) and his son Michael bought a small Houston wind company for $6 million and renamed it Zilkha Renewable Energy. Zilkha's rapid growth in wind caught the attention of Goldman Sachs, which acquired the company in 2005. Some observers call that move a turning point for clean tech—Wall Street's unconditional stamp of approval. Goldman Sachs renamed the company Horizon Wind Energy and in March 2007 announced plans to sell Horizon to Portuguese utility Energias de Portugal for about $2 billion.

Iberdrola

Bilbao, Spain
www.iberdrola.com
Madrid Stock Exchange: IBE

Operating wind farms in ten countries from Poland to Brazil, Spanish utility Iberdrola is bidding to be the world's largest producer of wind energy. Its $22.5 billion acquisition of ScottishPower, whose approval was pending as this book went to press, would create Europe's third largest utility and a wind energy powerhouse. Iberdrola bought three United States wind developers in 2006, and taking over ScottishPower would land it PPM Energy of Portland, Oregon, the ScottishPower unit aiming to operate 3,500 MW of wind in the United States by 2010. Iberdrola's total clean-energy capacity, most of it wind power, grew 16% in 2006.

Southwest Windpower

Flagstaff, Arizona
www.windenergy.com

The only small company on our "Ten to Watch" list in wind, Southwest Windpower has found entrepreneurial success in a niche that the big companies haven't pursued: small single turbines for the on-site, mainly residential market. In 2006, Southwest grew its U.S. small-wind market share to 65% with the 1.8-kW Skystream 3.7 turbine, whose $8,000 to $10,000 cost was roughly half the price of competitors' models. The market for small-scale wind in the United States grew 62% to $17 million in 2005, and 80% of Southwest's sales go to homeowners.

Suzlon Energy
Pune, India
www.suzlon.com
Mumbai Stock Exchange: SEL

Aggressive and consistently profitable, India's Suzlon is one of the world's fastest-growing wind-turbine manufacturers, now the largest pure-play wind company in market capitalization and number 5 in global sales. Suzlon is riding the growth curve of wind in India, now the globe's fourth-largest market, but is also winning business in China, Europe, and the United States. Per Hornung Pedersen, the head of its international headquarters (Suzlon Energy A/S) in Århus, Denmark, is the former CEO of Danish wind pioneer NEG Micon, which Vestas acquired in 2003. Suzlon is able to leverage low manufacturing costs in India but also opened blade factories in China and the United States (a 200-employee plant in Pipestone, Minnesota) in late 2006. To help ensure a steady supply of components, Suzlon acquired Belgian gearbox manufacturer Hansen Transmissions International in 2006 for €465 million.

Vestas Wind Systems
Randers, Denmark
www.vestas.com
Munich Stock Exchange: VWS

With 30,000 wind turbines installed in 50 countries and a 34% market share, Denmark's Vestas remains number 1 in global wind-turbine manufacturing, still ahead of its fast-growing Spanish, American, and Indian competitors. Vestas solidified its status by acquiring its largest Danish rival, NEG Micon, in 2004. It's a leader in driving down wind-power costs with bigger turbines, significantly increasing production of 100-meter, 3-MW models. Vestas is also very active in midsized turbines; its workhorse 660-kW V47 model is a popular choice in remote areas and parts of developing nations without adequate roads or equipment to transport and erect larger turbines.

3

BIOFUELS AND BIOMATERIALS

Developing Next-Generation Refineries and Feedstocks

Inside a nondescript warehouse in West Seattle's gritty industrial district, next to train tracks that carry goods across the West and adjacent to the Interstate 5 corridor that moves cars and trucks from the borders of Canada to Mexico, a new vision for America's transportation future is emerging. Using 7,000-gallon metal tanks salvaged from an old Rainier Brewery facility and a proprietary continuous-batch refining process, Imperium Renewables is hoping to brew up a revolution of its own as it turns virgin soybean, canola, and other oils into biodiesel fuel.

Imperium is one of a number of innovative companies involved in the rapidly expanding market for biofuels such as ethanol and biodiesel. The Seattle-based firm, one of the first VC-backed biodiesel producers in the United States, makes biodiesel for use in diesel trucks and cars, industrial motors, and home heating oil. "The industry is just starting to take off," says Martin Tobias, Imperium's charismatic CEO and a partner at VC firm Ignition Partners, based in Bellevue, Washington. "The growth potential, with the ability for consumers and industry to switch over to biofuels, is immense."

The business opportunities of biofuels and biomaterials are indeed vast. According to Clean Edge research, the total biofuels market alone will expand from $20.5 billion in 2006 (for both ethanol and biodiesel) to more than $80.9 billion by 2016. Biofuels, coupled with electric hybrids, high-efficiency diesels, and other fuel-sipping vehicles, offer the great promise of significantly reducing the need for imported oil supplies. In a resource-constrained world, biofuels are becoming the stuff of big business—with ADM, Cargill, ChevronTexaco, General Motors (GM), Ford, and others starting to aggressively advocate and advance the manufacturing and adoption of alternative fuels and vehicles. Cooperatives and smaller independent firms account for their fair share of the market too. The Renewable Fuels Association trade group's "Ethanol Industry Outlook 2005" report found that these smaller organizations account for nearly three quarters of the industry in the United States.

In 2006, ethanol represented a market of more than 12 billion gallons, valued at more than $18 billion in annual revenue, according to Clean Edge research. In the United States, ethanol is blended with gasoline in mixes ranging from 2% to 85% ethanol. In Brazil, which has already undergone a major infrastructure transformation to become the world's leading ethanol producer and user, ethanol mixes go all the way up to 100% for automobile use.

Biodiesel is currently a much smaller market than ethanol, but it's growing rapidly and can serve industrial fleets, trucks, automobiles, and machines that run on diesel—without the need for any retrofitting. Biodiesel is typically available in blends of 2%, 5%, 20% and even higher—all the way up to 99% biodiesel. The U.S. biodiesel market tripled from 25 million gallons in 2004 to 75 million gallons in 2005 and was on track to reach 150 million gallons in 2006, according to the National Biodiesel Board. The industry even has a celebrity face, music legend Willie Nelson, whose BioWillie brand has helped popularize biodiesel with long-haul truckers and consumers in the U.S. heartland. By 2008, well over 300 million gallons of biodiesel may be refined annually in the United States. Globally, biodiesel production now exceeds 750 million gallons yearly, for an annual market worth approximately $2 billion.

In this chapter, we'll look at the potential financial gains offered by the emerging biofuels and biomaterials sector, the political and environmental drivers behind them, what's required to put them on solid footing, and some of the potential hurdles to be overcome. We'll see how a new *carbohydrate*-based economy—one built on plant crops that can be harvested and wastes that can be recovered—will begin to displace the *hydrocarbon* economy and its reliance on the drilling and refining of carbon-intensive fossil fuels. And we'll uncover the opportunities and challenges that await today's biological pioneers in their battle to wean the United States and other nations off of fossil fuels—while turning a profit.

Many start-up companies such as Imperium are taking aim at the rising biofuels boom, and Tobias hopes to follow in the industry-reinventing tradition of his home region on Puget Sound. Seattle has been home to its fair share of emerging industries over the past century—minting millionaires and billionaires in the process. First came the aviation industry boom led by Boeing, then the personal computer software revolution via Bill Gates and Microsoft, followed by the coffee craze brewed up by Starbucks and the online shopping frenzy of Jeff Bezos's Amazon.com. Is there a more typical image of twenty-first-century life than sitting in the airport Starbucks, browsing on Amazon.com with Internet Explorer, before you board a Boeing 757 to fly home? Tobias and other industry players have a good shot to make that picture include a biofuels fill-up stop on the drive home from the airport.

Imperium's first processing facility, located not far from historic Boeing Field, can pump out about 5 million gallons of biodiesel a year. Its next facility, in Grays Harbor, Washington, was expected to produce 100 million gallons a year when it came online in mid-2007. Imperium's technology makes biodiesel manufacturing possible in the heart of urban areas, suburban outskirts, or just about anywhere, rather than only in centralized facilities deep in the Midwest. "Our model is a bit different from what's been done to date," explains Tobias. "Rather than processing in a centralized command and control model far from users, we can process biodiesel near the point of use, using local crops such as soybeans or canola."

With such significant growth potential, Imperium's fortunes, along with those of a host of other emerging and established companies, will hinge on many variables. How large will the market for biodiesel and ethanol be in the next 3, 5, 10 years? Will supply and demand grow in an orderly fashion? What type of impact could rising commodity prices for soybeans, corn, sugar cane, and other food crops have on the burgeoning sector? How quickly will cellulosic ethanol production ramp up, replacing the need to rely on food crops such as corn for energy? Will the large conglomerates such as ADM and Cargill dominate the sector, making it difficult for small start-ups such as Imperium to succeed?

These questions raise a number of important challenges and opportunities for entrepreneurs, corporate managers, policy makers, and others playing in the increasingly heated biofuels and biomaterials marketplace. Whoever the winners and losers (and there will be a significant number of both of them), the shift to plant-based fuels and materials has begun in earnest. These are some of the key developments and trends:

- In Brazil—the world's first country to transition from petroleum-based transportation to widespread use of biofuels—more than 70% of all new cars sold in 2005 were flex-fuel vehicles (FFVs) capable of using regular gasoline or ethanol fuel blends. The blends in Brazil range from about 25% all the way up to 100% ethanol. Just 2 years earlier, the proportion of new vehicles capable of running on ethanol in Brazil was less than 10%. A reported 40% of the country's total automobile fuels now comes from ethanol, with the price for 100% ethanol being less than half that of petrol gasoline.
- In 2006, ethanol (primarily produced from sugar cane in Brazil and corn in the United States) was a global industry of more than 12 billion gallons a year. Ethanol, in small blends of up to 10%, can be used in most internal-combustion vehicles on the road today, without any modification. Higher blends, such as E85 (85% ethanol) in the United States, require special FFVs. The global ethanol market has growth rates in the double digits each year.
- ADM, the major agricultural and food conglomerate, is forging a huge and growing business in the biofuels market. The company produced 1 billion gallons of corn-based ethanol in 2005, equaling more than 25% of total U.S. ethanol production and 11% of the world total. Ethanol now represents the fastest growing business unit for the company and equaled nearly a quarter of the company's 2005 operating profits. ADM also operates biodiesel refineries in Germany and is building a biodiesel refinery in North Dakota that will be second in size only to Imperium's 100-million-gallon facility. How seriously does ADM take the biofuels business? In 2006, the company named an energy executive, former ChevronTexaco vice president Patricia Woertz, as its new CEO. Woertz makes ADM the largest U.S. company headed by a woman, and she's its first CEO from outside the controlling-interest Andreas family since 1970.

- A range of innovative companies are looking to find better and cheaper ways to make ethanol from nonfood crops. These companies hope to make cellulosic ethanol from agricultural waste such as corn stover and rice straw and from "energy crops" grown solely to be processed into fuels, such as switchgrass and miscanthus. One of them, Iogen in Ottawa, Ontario, has received nearly $80 million (Canadian) in investments from heavy hitters such as Royal Dutch Shell, Petro-Canada, and Goldman Sachs. Iogen's goal is to replace corn with cellulosic crops and waste streams as the primary feedstock for ethanol.
- Bioplastics are catching on. DuPont, one of the top three chemical manufacturers in the world, is investing approximately 10% of its annual $1.3 billion research budget on developing technologies that take carbohydrates and turn them into plastics and other materials. CEO Charles O. Holliday Jr. told the *New York Times* that more than 10% of the company's products are already made from nonpetrochemical substances, and he expects that number to grow to an astounding 25% by 2010.
- Toyota, the auto manufacturing powerhouse that made HEVs a mass-market phenomenon, is on an ambitious mission to dominate the world's market for bioplastics. The company is aiming to supply no less than two thirds of the world's total output of bioplastics by 2020. According to the company's own estimates, this would represent 20 million tons of Toyota-manufactured bioplastics, worth about $38 billion in annual revenues.

GETTING TO PRICE PARITY

One of the key dynamics contributing to the growth of biofuels, like other clean technologies, relates to economies of scale in manufacturing. As production ramps up and technologies improve, costs come down. And in a volatile, high-cost, fossil-fuel world, they can reach price parity with their conventional counterparts.

In fact, during brief periods in several states in the United States in 2005, fuel blends containing ethanol and biodiesel achieved what the industry calls price inversion—they dipped below the costs of regular gasoline and diesel fuel at the pump. In the Midwest early that summer, some stations sold a gallon of 10% ethanol blend for 7 to 10 cents less than regular gas. In Brazil, the world's leading producer and user of ethanol, thanks to a large supply of inexpensive sugar cane as its feedstock, ethanol costs 15% to 40% less than gasoline. "Both ethanol and biodiesel are going through a building boom," says Eric Bowen, vice president of energy and director of biofuels at Sigma Capital in San Francisco, an investment bank focused on project finance. "If petroleum prices keep going up, there's no reason why these fuels shouldn't be cheaper."

Although expanded production capacity and increased supply are pushing down costs for ethanol and biodiesel, another factor has an even greater effect: commodity prices. In the United States, most ethanol is made from corn, and most biodiesel from soybean oil; in Europe, rapeseed oil is the standard biodiesel feedstock. Although prices have been historically low, commodity prices can be volatile—as evidenced by the recent increase in the cost of corn. Feedstock prices account for more than half the cost of biofuel, so there's only so much that production volumes and efficiency can do when corn or soybean prices spike.

But much like the thin-film and nanotechnology breakthroughs that may wean solar cells from silicon wafers and dramatically drive down solar energy costs, the biofuels industry has high hopes for so-called next-generation feedstocks. Although the project is still in the laboratory phase, biodiesel chemists see big potential in certain forms of algae that consist of 50% oil. GreenFuel Technologies in Cambridge, Massachusetts, for one, has raised more than $13 million in venture capital to develop its technology that harnesses algae to produce biofuels from power plant emissions.

As we discuss at length later in the chapter, ethanol refiners are working on producing cellulosic ethanol from agricultural waste products such as rice straw and vineyard prunings, a process that analysts say could bring ethanol prices down below $1 a gallon. Switchgrass is a fibrous, fast-growing perennial native to the Great Plains that could challenge corn for ethanol production. "Harvesting basically means you just mow it every year," says Bowen.

BACK TO THE FUTURE

With so much activity taking place in the biofuels sector, you'd think that the concept was relatively new. But not so. "The use of vegetable oils for engine fuels may seem insignificant today," said one innovator. "But such oils may become in the course of time as important as the petroleum and coal tar products of the present time." Sound like a clean-tech futurist of 2007? Actually, it was Rudolf Diesel, the father of the diesel engine, speaking back in 1912.

One of the transportation sector's other great legends, Henry Ford, also believed that the future of energy and materials would come not from petroleum but from plant-based materials. Both Diesel and Ford believed strongly in the connection between energy security and local, home-grown solutions. Now, nearly 100 years since the introduction of the Model T, their visions are starting to come true.

Diesel's first engine, demonstrated at the World Exhibition in Paris in 1900, was actually developed to run on peanut oil. Diesel believed the future belonged to a range of biofuels that could be locally harvested by farmers to fuel their machinery and tractors, not petroleum. Ford possessed a similar vision: He dreamed of manufacturing cars made of plant-based materials that ran on plant-based fuels. The Model T, the first mass-manufactured car, was introduced by Ford in 1908 to operate on both ethanol blends and gasoline.

"The fuel of the future is going to come from fruit like that sumac out by the road, or from apples, weeds, sawdust—almost anything," Ford said in a *New York Times* interview in 1925. "There is fuel in every bit of vegetable matter that can be fermented. There's enough alcohol in one year's yield of an acre of potatoes to drive the machinery necessary to cultivate the fields for a hundred years."

Ford's support and interest in bio-based fuels, along with others in the auto industry, culminated in the "chemurgy" movement of the 1930s. Conferences were held throughout the country in support of agriculture, industry, and science to promote the use of plant-based alcohol fuels and materials. In Europe as well, ethanol fuels were popular during the 1920s and 1930s. It was used as an octane booster at levels ranging from 10% to 30% in Denmark, France, the United Kingdom, and other European nations.

Two key developments, however, changed the course of history, putting biofuels onto the back burner. First, oil remained relatively inexpensive throughout most of the twentieth century, making it difficult for ethanol and biodiesel to compete. In most cases, ethanol and biodiesel cost more than the prevailing cost of gasoline and conventional diesel. Second, in the 1930s, there was a battle in the United States between using lead or ethanol as an additive in motor engines to reduce the knocking in engines. The federal government and industry put their influential weight behind lead-based additives for more than 50 years, rather than ethanol. It wasn't until after 1987, when lead additives were banned because of their high toxicity, that ethanol reemerged as a viable option.

But today's promise of a biofuels and bio-based plastics boom has much more solid footing—and provides some important points of differentiation from the past. The reasons are varied: the inexorable rise of the cost of oil; the national security costs involved in relying on volatile foreign sources of energy; technological breakthroughs in the efficient production of biofuels and biopolymers; and a growing worldwide agri-tech movement that aims to wean nations off depleting oil supplies. Most important, biofuels have reached the realm of the clean-tech holy grail: They're beginning to compete on a pure cost basis at the consumer level. Ethanol, as discussed earlier, is now cheaper than gasoline in the world's most dynamic ethanol market, Brazil, and biodiesel is cheaper than conventional diesel in the world's largest biodiesel market, Germany.

PRIMING THE PUMP

So where do investors and innovators go from here? The great challenge of the day is bringing down costs, increasing output without outstripping feedstock supply, and putting distribution and infrastructure in place.

The U.S. federal government is behind one recent activity that has really primed the pump: It is requiring that 7.5 billion gallons of the nation's fuel come from ethanol and biodiesel by 2012, up more than 90% from 4 billion gallons in 2005 and up nearly eightfold from the beginning of the century. Part of the Energy Policy Act of 2005, this nationwide renewable fuel standard (RFS) includes a tax credit of 51 cents per gallon of regular ethanol, as well as loans for developers and additional incentives for the development and expansion of cellulosic ethanol production. In President

Bush's 2007 State of the Union address, he called for increasing the mandate nearly fivefold to 35 billion gallons by 2017. Brazil, the current world leader in ethanol production, continues to ramp up refining, and China is now the third largest ethanol market in the world, with its eyes on continued expansion.

BREAKTHROUGH OPPORTUNITY

Next-Generation Biorefineries

One of the biggest issues raised by biofuel critics is the relative cost and energy efficiency of biofuels compared with oil-based products. They claim that once you include the cost of petroleum-based fertilizer, fossil fuel–based energy, and other inputs necessary for biofuel production, the math just doesn't play out. Although most of these assertions have been disproved, anything to reduce the cost of the refining process plays in biofuels' favor. So, what if a distiller could replace the need for using fossil-fuel inputs during the biofuel refining process? Panda Energy of Houston and E3 Biofuels of Mead, Nebraska, are both aiming to do just that. Some of their next-generation facilities use cow manure from nearby cattle feedlots to power all or part of their distilleries' fuel costs. The ethanol refining process also creates an important by-product: distiller's grain, which can be fed back to the same cows that provide power for the facility. We expect such closed-loop systems will become increasingly popular in the biofuels arena—and believe such developments offer engineers, farmers, ranchers, entrepreneurs, and project developers a range of unique and emerging opportunities.

The benefits of biofuels are becoming apparent to a wide range of stakeholders—and that's driving growth. One example can be found at a sprawling 130-acre aluminum rolling mill facility in Davenport, Iowa, operated by Alcoa, the world's leading producer of primary aluminum. At this plant, 100 forklift trucks, 40 pieces of heavy industrial equipment, and several emergency vehicles have run on biodiesel (B-20) since 2002. Alcoa senior staff mechanical engineer Dale Hupp likes biodiesel's recent price competitiveness but says its real pluses are operational: quieter engines, extended engine life, cleaner air inside the plant, and less maintenance, thanks to biodiesel's solvent properties, which are greater than those of petroleum diesel. "It's probably the best thing we ever did at our plant for our fleet and our employees," says Hupp, who first learned about biodiesel in an agricultural magazine at his parents' farm. "For us, the benefits have exceeded any cost considerations."

Fleets across the nation and world are also starting to operate on low blends of biodiesel—improving efficiency and reducing emissions in the process. From TriMet's public buses in Portland, Oregon, to U.S. naval, marine, and army locations around the world, vehicle fleets are becoming the largest user of biofuels in the nation.

Ethanol provides similar improvements. According to an Argonne National Laboratory study, ethanol blends of just 10% reduce global GHG emissions, such as carbon dioxide (CO_2), by 12% to 19%, compared with conventional gasoline. The Renewable Fuels Association says that ethanol reduces tailpipe carbon monoxide emissions by as much as 30% and tailpipe fine particulate matter emissions by 50%. For the United States, a nation that uses a quarter of the world's oil output but has only 3% of the world's remaining petroleum reserves, biofuels are gaining political steam.

25 BY '25

Just how big can a bio-based industry grow in the United States?

If a coalition of more than 100 farming, ranching, and agricultural groups, nonprofits, state and federal lawmakers, and companies has its way, the United States will greatly expand its energy supply from farm-based sources by 2025. The 25×'25 Work Group is a project of the Energy Future Coalition in Washington, D.C., an independent nonpartisan organization funded by private foundations. Its stated goal: "By 2025, America's working lands will provide 25 percent of the total energy consumed in the United States while continuing to produce abundant, safe and affordable food, feed, and fiber."

Deere & Company, the venerable equipment manufacturer that transformed American farms in an earlier era, sees a strong future in farm-based energy. An endorser of the 25×'25 Work Group initiative, the company supports ethanol and biodiesel industry targets and also operates John Deere Credit, a wind financing division to support farmers in deploying wind power on their lands, developing new revenue streams in the process.

The goal of the 25×'25 Work Group may sound audacious, but consider that Brazil, the fifth largest nation in the world, already gets approximately 30% of its transportation fuel from ethanol.

On the policy side, the 25×'25 Work Group has plenty of company in pushing for huge growth in biofuels use in the United States. In California, Governor Arnold Schwarzenegger signed Executive Order S-06-06 in early 2006 calling on an even more ambitious target. He ordered state agencies such as the California Energy Commission to develop plans to get 20% of the state's transportation fuel supply from ethanol and biodiesel by 2010 and *40%* by 2020. He'd like to see the majority of that fuel processed in the state. If California's past and present leadership in energy conservation and renewable electricity are any indication, the biofuels revolution is likely to have a bright future in the Golden State.

"It is critical that we do everything we can to reduce our dependence on petroleum-based fuels," said Schwarzenegger during the signing of the order. "Turning waste products [and plant crops] into energy is good for the state's economy, local job creation, and our environment."

Among states, California isn't alone. Minnesota has an RFS calling for 20% of its transportation fuels to come from ethanol by 2013; Iowa's goal is 25% by 2019. Montana and Hawaii both have standards targeting 10% ethanol in their fuel mix. Even the usually conservative U.S. Department of Energy projects that biofuels could displace up to 30% of the nation's current fuel use by 2030.

Whatever the exact targets, 25% by 2025, 40% by 2020, or something else, there's a land-rush mentality to move away from dependence on fossil fuels, in particular volatile, depleting supplies of foreign petroleum. Someone is going to figure out how to significantly ramp up biofuels processing, and farmers and rural communities are going to play a significant role in the transition.

FACING UP TO THE CORN CONUNDRUM

In 2005, the United States had more than enough excess corn crop to meet the needs of a fledgling ethanol industry. According to the American Coalition for Ethanol, approximately 1.6 billion bushels of corn went to ethanol production in 2005—about 12% of the nation's total corn crop. That provided enough fuel to power about 3% of the nation's light-duty vehicles. In 2006, however, the amount of U.S. corn processed into ethanol was projected to hit 2.15 billion bushels, a 36% jump. At this rate, we're likely to start reaching limits to growth in the not too distant future. "The problem with corn is that you can't grow enough of it to get a meaningful displacement of oil," says Thomas Koehler, vice president of Pacific Ethanol, a major West Coast producer and distributor of biofuels. "There's a limit to how much corn we can grow."

A 2005 report from the Energy Foundation, a clean-energy and energy-efficiency grant maker in San Francisco, concurs. The foundation's *The New Harvest* report finds that "when the U.S. reaches the 2012 RFS goal of 7.5 billion gallons, ethanol production will have almost reached feedstock limits and still remain only around six percent of light duty vehicle fuel consumption. For ethanol to significantly reduce oil imports and improve national oil security, *feedstocks must shift from grains to cellulose* [italics ours] such as corn stover, wheat straw, and rice husks. That will require improved technologies to economically break down the stubborn molecular bonds of cellulose so that it can be easily fermented into ethanol."

A rancorous debate regarding the competing interests of fuel versus food is already cropping up, raising serious issues about diverting food crops for energy in a food-constrained world. Some are talking about the issue of peak food, not peak oil. Because of these constraints, we believe that significant reliance on food crops, such as corn, is not smart energy policy.

So while corn ethanol can provide up to about 8 billion gallons a year of ethanol in the United States without significant impacts on the food stream, we'll soon need to pursue other crops and waste streams for ethanol feedstocks. The powerful U.S. corn lobby won't like to hear this, but rather than shifting our current eggs-in-one-basket energy supply from the Middle East to the Midwest, why not diversify? Why not exploit a cornucopia of regional nonfood crops to meet our growing energy needs?

MAKING THE SWITCH

Biotech breakthroughs, as well as the cultivation of new crops, will help to enable the shift to a mass biofuels market. Nonfood energy crops offer a number of advantages over their food-crop brethren. Depending on the plant, they can often provide far more gallons of fuel per crop-acre and require significantly less water, fertilizers, and energy to produce than corn, which noted food industry author and ethanol critic Michael Pollan calls "the SUV of plants."

"If the endgame was corn-based ethanol in the U.S., there would be no real interest by the environmental or technology lobbies," says Sigma Capital's Bowen. "But with the promise of cellulosic ethanol, that's really shifted. Investors and environmentalists see corn ethanol as a necessary evil to get to where they want to go."

Replacements for food crops such as corn, sugar, and soybean are now being pursued aggressively around the globe. A number of studies show that there is more than enough land for biofuel crops to substantially displace petroleum.

In the United States, native, perennial crops like switchgrass can be grown on suboptimal farmland with limited water irrigation and fertilizer requirements. A group of researchers from federal labs, universities, environmental organizations, and the U.S. Department of Energy, called the RBAEF (Role of Biomass in America's Energy Future), found in their report, *Growing Energy: How Biofuels Can Help End America's Oil Dependence*, that farmers "could produce the equivalent of nearly 7.9 million barrels of oil per day by 2050. That amount is equal to more than 50 percent of our current total oil use in the transportation sector and more than three times as much as we import from the Persian Gulf alone." They reached such results by analyzing the opportunity for the deployment of cellulosic biofuels production coupled with improvements in car fuel efficiency.

Another report released by Battelle Memorial Institute, *Near-Term U.S. Biomass Potential*, found that waste streams and dedicated energy crops could provide 50 billion gallons of ethanol per year (more than 10 times the current supply of ethanol in the United States) without having "large impacts on the agricultural system." Other studies show that cellulosic ethanol, when widely available, could reduce GHG emissions by an astounding 90% over petrol gasoline, provide more yield per acre than corn, and use considerably less energy in the production and refining process.

Iogen, which is currently using wheat, oat, and barley straw in the world's first cellulosic ethanol demonstration plant in Ottawa, Canada, is looking at a number of energy crops and waste streams as potential ethanol feedstocks. The company has been working to crack the cellulosic ethanol code for more than 25 years. But with a recent infusion of cash from Shell and Goldman Sachs and its proof-of-concept demonstration plant that's using yeasts and enzymes to break down cellulose into sugars and then ethanol, it may be able to deliver a commercial-scale solution by 2012.

BREAKTHROUGH OPPORTUNITY

Cracking the Cellulosic Code

One of the biggest aims of the ethanol industry is to move beyond virgin feedstock such as corn and begin to use things such as corn stover (the stalks that remain after corn has been harvested), forestry wastes and wood residues, and fast-growing nonfood crops such as switchgrass. As we've pointed out, corn should be considered only a bridge to a robust ethanol future, since corn crops will not be able to support extensive growth of the industry. Cellulosic ethanol is one of the key ingredients to a successful renewable fuels future. Companies such as Iogen, Broin, and Abengoa are at the forefront of creating refineries that can process biomass and turn it into ethanol, while companies such as Diversa, Novozymes, and Dyadic are focusing on producing the enzymes that could enable a cellulosic future. This shift from food crops to waste residue and native grasses for ethanol production offers unique opportunities for a range of players, from farmers to biotech firms to project developers to investors. Any player, large or small, that makes significant headway on cracking the cellulosic code will open up a huge market and reap the financial benefits.

China, for its part, is already looking to move away from its reliance on corn and wheat for ethanol production. The world's most populous nation is indeed worried about the competition between grain for fuel production and domestic food supplies. Government officials say the nation is considering new biofuel feedstock using cassava, sweet sorghum, sugar cane, and sweet potatoes. They are also looking into using agricultural and other wastes for use in cellulosic ethanol production.

In India, the jatropha tree, which produces an oil-rich nonedible fruit, is gaining admirers in the biodiesel world. The tree is drought resistant and considered an optimal source of oil for biodiesel because its fruit bears oil-rich seeds. The oil is so pure that it can be used for transportation fuel in diesel-powered vehicles and equipment without extensive refining. D1, a British biodiesel company that operates a global portfolio of planting and refining operations, has begun planting jatropha in India for the build-out of its biodiesel operations in that country. D1 is also setting up jatropha-centered operations in Africa, Asia, and other nations. India's government estimates that the country has nearly 100 million acres of land suitable for growing the tree.

As noted earlier in the chapter, algae has been identified as another potential source for biodiesel and ethanol by academics and researchers for some time. GreenFuel Technologies of Cambridge, Massachusetts, is one of the first companies to turn that theory into practice. Still in an early stage, the company captures CO_2, a global-warming pollutant created during electricity generation in power plants, feeds it into an algae bio-reactor, and then turns the algae into biofuels.

If successful, the company could tap pollutants for energy—a green entrepreneur's dream come true. Rather than planting farm crops, algae can be harvested from sewage, smokestacks, and other waste streams, as well as in ponds, offering a nearly perpetual supply of feedstocks. In the race to develop the fuel and material sources of the future, a score of other scientists, companies, and entrepreneurs are using and developing microbes, enzymes, and fungi to break down cellulosic materials. Dr. J. Craig Venter, the scientist best known for his earlier conquest of decoding the human genome, is now working to develop genes that can break down cellulosic material. His new company, Synthetic Genomics in Rockville, Maryland, is one of a number of companies, large and small, joining Iogen in the race to make cellulosic ethanol a reality. Other players include bio-tech companies Ceres, Diversa, Novozymes, and Genencor. "Investors should look at ethanol as a multibillion-dollar market that can grow thirty percent a year for the next ten years," says Vinod Khosla, the famed venture capitalist and cofounder of Sun Microsystems. "In that time, we can irreversibly forge a path that can get us independent of petroleum." Khosla himself aims to be at the forefront of this sector and has placed bets on a number of biofuel companies, including Cilion and Mascoma.

SPEED BUMPS AND POTHOLES

As in any emerging sector, not all is sanguine on the biofuels and biomaterials front. The rapidly expanding industry faces a host of challenges. A number of industry stalwarts, as noted earlier, are concerned about energy needs competing with food crops. If we are not careful, they say, we could face the issue of peak food rather than peak oil. Others claim that there are significant issues arising from environmental degradation in the farming and processing of biomaterials feedstocks. These and other issues are like potholes and speed bumps on a country road—if not addressed or understood, they could derail, or at least seriously impede, the growth of the industry.

Toby Janson-Smith, director of the Climate, Community & Biodiversity Alliance, an initiative of Conservation International, says that biofuel crop production is already a major contributor to deforestation and biodiversity loss in the developing world. In Malaysia and Indonesia, in particular Borneo, large areas of pristine rain forest are being cleared for the production of biofuel crops such as palm and castor oil. This certainly represents a significant unexpected consequence of the global biofuels trade. Most biofuel innovators are looking to solve environmental issues and make money at the same time—not exacerbate and increase environmental degradation. "The irony of green fuel production causing deforestation shouldn't be overlooked," says Janson-Smith, "and needs to be addressed by political and business leaders."

The use of genetically modified organisms (GMOs) to optimize plant crops for biofuels production looms as another significant issue that's already dividing environmentalists and nations in their enthusiasm for biofuels. Most of Europe and much of the developing world continue to have bans on GMOs, meaning that crops genetically altered and optimized for biofuels production could face serious opposition. That controversy could affect industry investors too. Will Europeans and other countries continue to demand that their biofuels be GMO-free? Separating the two issues becomes all the more difficult because many scientists believe that

GMO crops can spread, mutate, and impact nearby non-GMO crops. Today, the majority of U.S. corn and soybean feedstock is a GMO product, which means that ethanol and biodiesel manufactured in the United States is primarily a genetically manipulated product. One company, NatureWorks LLC, already offers certified bio-based products that contain no genetic materials.

And what about the potential use of rendered inedible animal remains (cattle, pigs, poultry, and the like) being used to produce biofuels? Will vegetarians buy biodiesel made from rendered pig parts? Would the biodiesel need to be labeled as a meat product?

Yet another challenge facing ethanol is that its energy content is less than that of gasoline, which means that mileage in conventional vehicles is less for a gallon of ethanol than for a gallon of gasoline. On average, E85 gets about 80% of the mileage performance of gasoline in today's vehicles. This lower energy content must be calculated into the cost of ethanol blends at the pump. In Brazil, high-ethanol blends cost about half as much as imported gasoline, making the economic decision to purchase ethanol an easy one. In the United States, where E85 still tracks the pricing of gasoline, the economics aren't as simple.

But technological breakthroughs could eventually help with the equation. Automaker Saab claims to have a prototype car that achieves better mileage with ethanol than with gasoline. In 2006, at the annual Shell European Eco-marathon, a race that has been held since 1985 to test alternative transportation concepts devised by European students, an ethanol car won the top spot for being the most fuel-efficient vehicle. The biofuels-powered, ultra-lightweight one-seater designed by French high school students achieved a fuel efficiency of 2,885 kilometers (1,792 miles) on a single liter of fuel (a liter is approximately a quarter of a gallon). The futuristic concept car also produced the lowest GHG emissions among the more than 200 prototypes entered in the race.

Other critics, such as longtime vocal ethanol opponent David Pimentel of Cornell University, have claimed that ethanol production uses more energy than it yields and doesn't offer significant advantages over gasoline. But there's a general consensus among academics, researchers, technologists, and industrialists that biofuels and bio-based materials are now net-energy positive—that is, the final product yields more energy than the energy required to produce it—and do make economic sense.

Dan Kammen and Alexander Farrell of the Energy and Resources Group at the University of California, Berkeley, released a report in early 2006 that evaluated the findings of six earlier ethanol studies, including Pimentel's, and found that "producing ethanol from corn uses much less petroleum than producing gasoline."

"It is better to use various inputs to grow corn and make ethanol and use that in your car than it is to use gasoline and fossil fuels directly," explains Kammen, who is also founding director of Cal-Berkeley's Renewable and Appropriate Energy Laboratory. "The people who are saying ethanol is bad are just plain wrong."

Kammen's assertion will be even more true as companies and nations figure out how to cost-effectively produce ethanol from cellulosic materials. A study by Argonne National Laboratory found that cellulosic ethanol made from switchgrass could deliver 1 unit of ethanol at the pump using only 0.10 units of fossil energy—a significant improvement over corn-based ethanol and revolutionary in its implications.

More and more famous names in business and popular culture are moving into biofuels as investors and users—and they are set on solving many of the issues that could slow the growth of biofuels. Among them is Sir Richard Branson of the United Kingdom, the avid trend spotter and founder and head of the Virgin Group of music, airline, and cell phone service fame. In late 2006, as part of the Clinton Global Initiative, Branson said he would spend up to $3 billion to develop renewable fuels. He's formed a new unit entitled Virgin Fuels to achieve this goal—and taken a $60 million stake in California-based ethanol start-up Cilion as the unit's first investment. He's in good company. His fellow mogul and the world's richest man, Bill Gates, has also taken an interest in biofuels and invested $84 million in West Coast ethanol distributor and processor Pacific Ethanol.

So while there are potholes and road bumps that must be navigated, we believe the road to a biofuels future is quite bright. None other than the Indy Racing League, sanctioning body of the popular IndyCar Series, was to switch to an all-ethanol formula in 2007, which should remove any doubts about ethanol as a high-performance fuel.

Like all technology developments, it will take many factors for nature-harvested biofuels and biomaterials to truly boom and sustain long-term growth. Considerable investment by governments, corporations, and venture capitalists; a realignment of policy initiatives; technological breakthroughs; and a growth in consumer demand will all need to play a role. But this time, the future seems to be on biofuels' and bioplastics' side.

CLOSER TO HOME

We believe that given the high cost of energy to transport materials, it may not always make economic or environmental sense to continue to ship bio-feedstocks or biofuels over long distances. A number of innovative players agree and are working to change this scenario.

Pacific Ethanol, Imperium Renewables, D1, and other companies are looking at ways to process biofuels closer to their source of use to overcome this issue, increasingly with locally harvested crops. In 2006, Imperium and ChevronTexaco both unveiled plans to invest in regional biodiesel processing facilities, one in Washington State and the other in Texas. Each facility is projected to be pumping out 100 million gallons in annual capacity by 2008 to serve local biodiesel markets.

BREAKTHROUGH OPPORTUNITY

Go Local

A number of biofuel pioneers are taking a contrarian approach to the way we process fossil fuels. Rather than ship raw feedstock thousands of miles to refineries, and then ship processed fuels hundreds or thousands of miles to end users, why not make the entire process more local? In this new energy model, you grow your crops regionally and process and refine the oil or feedstock near the point of use. Companies such as Imperium Renewables, Pacific Ethanol, and SeQuential Biofuels are working to make this a reality. While we aren't recommending that readers of this book go out and try to build a regional processing facility, we do believe there are opportunities for farmers, local agriculture groups, universities, lawyers, policy makers, and of course entrepreneurs to play a role in helping to establish regional production of biofuels. It's happening in places as diverse as Seattle and Pune, India—and will become a growing movement in years to come.

The concept of regional processing of biofuels has become a very attractive element to farming interests. Corn in the Midwest, canola oil in the Northwest, sugar cane in Brazil, rice straw in Asia—each region has its own star feedstocks. And politicians have taken note—many of today's RFSs have requirements that a portion of fuels come from locally harvested crops and are produced in regional refineries.

"We'll be able to stop shipping money to the Middle East and Venezuela for oil," explains Rhys Roth, codirector of the nonprofit Climate Solutions in Olympia, Washington, "and instead spend it in local communities to create both biofuels and jobs. We're talking about the regionalization of ethanol—where you can use local supplies and processing facilities to make ethanol from forest thinnings, wheat straw, new energy crops, just about any regionally available feedstock."

Right now corn farmers in Iowa and other states in the Midwest dominate ethanol production in the United States, and sugar cane dominates in Brazil. But this is just the beginning of the expansion of ethanol, biodiesel, and other biofuels markets, and the local-versus-central, corn-versus-cellulosic issues are going to take time to distill. Therein lies the opportunity for companies and organizations that can tap into this rapidly expanding market and uncover new methods of production and distribution. The United States, China, and India, for example, all plan to at least double their biofuels production between now and 2012.

Another issue that could be either a boon or a barrier to the producers of biofuels is by-products. The refining of both ethanol and biodiesel results in prodigious amounts of nonfuel by-products in the production process. In the case of biodiesel, the manufacturing process results in glycerin, which can be converted into soaps, cosmetics, and other products. The main by-product of ethanol is distiller's grain, which is used as nutritional feed for dairy cows and cattle. To fully capture the value of the refining process, refiners and processors must find useful applications for these by-products and build out markets. For instance, 1 bushel of corn yields about 18 pounds of distiller's grain and 2.7 gallons of ethanol.

VeraSun Energy, a publicly traded biofuel refiner in Brookings, South Dakota, may have found one solution. In late 2006 the company said it would open a new refinery that would make biodiesel from distiller's grain. In other words, the company hopes to produce both ethanol and biodiesel from one feedstock, such as corn. This breakthrough could change the face of the biofuel-refining business.

A number of other refiners are working to build new high-value "coproducts" that can create additional revenue streams, offset or replace energy costs, and enable new bio-based materials.

ONE WORD OF ADVICE

As we noted earlier, the future carbohydrate economy will be not just about biofuels but also about biomaterials. In the 1967 film *The Graduate*, a wealthy family friend at a cocktail party offers that famous word of unsolicited career advice to Dustin Hoffman's young Benjamin Braddock character: *plastics*. If the film were made today, he'd more likely mention bioplastics, which promise to be not only cheaper to manufacture but also easier to dispose of and environmentally superior. Unlike conventional plastics, which are difficult to recycle, bio-based plastics can be formulated to be both biodegradable and easily recycled. Most important, they're not made from high-cost petroleum.

DuPont, as noted earlier, is taking the concept seriously. In 2007 it was scheduled to introduce Sorona, a new product made up of corn and other biodegradable materials. It can be used in everything from carpeting to clothing. The company believes that by 2010, 25% of its plastics business will be based on materials other than petroleum. "For DuPont, the question was, 'What can biology do that chemistry can't?'" explains John Ranieri, the company's vice president of bio-based materials. "By definition, you have something that's environmentally sustainable."

Toyota, the global auto behemoth that pioneered the HEV market, is now setting its sights on bioplastics as one of its next big growth sectors. In what would sound like an audacious goal by just about any other company, Toyota says it plans to manufacture 20 million tons of bioplastics per year by 2020—capturing what it predicts would be two-thirds of the global market for bio-based plastics at the time and generating annual revenue for the company of $38 billion.

Honda and Mazda are working on biopolymer developments of their own, but not with such ambitious stated goals as Toyota's. Honda recently announced that it has developed plant-based interior fabrics for use in car seats and other interior surfaces. Mazda has also developed a plant-based material, working with Hiroshima University, which it says can withstand the heat that builds up in cars on hot summer days.

ADM, in partnership with biotechnology firm Metabolix, has unveiled plans to pursue bioplastics development to complement its ethanol and biodiesel efforts. The company was building a plant in Iowa that was scheduled to open in 2008 to make plastics from corn and other biodegradable materials. While oil prices are likely to rise in coming years and increase the cost of petroleum-based plastics, the company believes that plant-based plastics could be cheaper, as well as more environmentally sustainable. "As the world's demand for petroleum continues to increase, ADM believes that this facility is a positive step towards producing renewable plastics that offer the global marketplace an alternative to traditional petroleum-derived plastics," said G. Allen Andreas, then the company's CEO, in early 2006.

And will there be a market for all of these new bioplastics? The answer seems to be yes.

In late 2005 the world's largest retailer, Wal-Mart, began a transition to use PLA (polylactic acid derived from corn) in its packaging. The company has cited the stable prices for PLA, in marked contrast to volatile pricing of petroleum-based plastics, as one compelling reason for the switch. Using PLA from NatureWorks LLC, a stand-alone entity in Minneapolis owned by food and agricultural giant Cargill, Wal-Mart plans to replace existing packaging with PLA products in a series of phases through its supply chain. These include PLA in containers for vegetable packaging and gift cards, bread bags, and doughnut boxes—all told, more than *100 million* packages per year. "With this change to packaging made from corn, we will save the equivalent of 800,000 gallons of gasoline and reduce more than 11 million pounds of greenhouse gas emissions from polluting our environment," says Matt Kistler, vice president for product development and private brands in the Sam's Club division of Wal-Mart.

SHIFTING INTO GEAR

For markets to really take off, however, biofuels must overcome the classic chicken-and-egg dilemma. For a robust market to develop, not only must the fuels be refined but also the vehicles that can run on them must be readily available to consumers (at least in the case of ethanol) and the distribution channels and gas station pumps must be in place to deliver the fuel. The same is true for bio-based plastics and other bio-based materials. A market won't materialize without supply and distribution in place and easy consumer access. And no matter how much consumers say they care about the environment, price nearly always trumps nature. In other words, biofuels and bioplastics need to reach cost parity with conventional fuels and materials to compete successfully.

As we've uncovered in this chapter, the shift is well under way, but the biofuels and biopolymers industry will need a significant push to take it from the realm of promise to ubiquity. We'll need thousands of E85 fueling stations, not hundreds, if the United States is to move beyond low biofuel blends and toward major E85 distribution. We'll need bio-based packaging used in every Wal-Mart, not just a handful of test stores. And bioplastics will need to be featured prominently in every Toyota car, not just as floor mats in a select number of Japan-only models.

To a large extent, much as it has for the last century, politics will dictate how the biomaterials revolution plays out. Just as lead-based additives won out over ethanol during the early to mid-twentieth century because of government support, the current political environment and activities will have a huge influence on the success level of ethanol, biodiesel, and bioplastics. But most indications point to an alignment in clean tech's favor. Biofuels and biomaterials please such diverse constituents as farmers, Wall Street investors, corporations, and environmentalists. "I was at a hearing on biofuels in Washington, D.C.," explains DuPont's Ranieri. "On one side of me were the red-state corn growers, and on the other side were the blue-state, edgy, Ivy League–educated NGO types. And they were all in support. This is the only truly bipartisan issue that I've seen in years."

The phenomenal growth of biofuels in the United States indeed owes a great deal to government policies and supports. The first significant driver in recent history was the transition from the banned additive MTBE (methyl tertiary-butyl ether) in California to ethanol. At first, politicians didn't think farmers and industry could meet supply needs, but ethanol producers were able to respond rapidly and proved such fears wrong. Now, more than 25 additional states have followed California's lead in banning MTBE, and there's a rush to transition to ethanol throughout much of the country. The other significant driver of the U.S. biofuels market is the 52-cent tax credit and the nation's RFS. At the regional level, a number of states have instituted their own RFS calling for increased percentages of biofuels.

"The thing that makes the biofuels movement so exciting and powerful is that it bridges so many divides: economic and political, urban and rural, liberal and conservative," explains Climate Solutions' Roth.

Former Central Intelligence Agency chief R. James Woolsey feels that way. Along with former secretary of state George Shultz, he has been on a crusade to advance plug-in hybrids and E85, urging the rapid transition to a biofuels-based economy. He sees a future in which cars could get the equivalent of 200 to 500 miles per gallon of petrol-based gasoline. As amazing as that may sound, the math pans out. Imagine a plug-in hybrid that gets the equivalent of 80 miles per gallon—very doable with today's emerging battery and engine technologies. Now imagine that same car has a flex-fuel tank that runs on 85% ethanol and 15% gasoline. Such a state-of-the-art vehicle could travel approximately 800 miles on approximately 2 gallons of petrol gasoline and 11 gallons of ethanol (this calculation accounts for ethanol's lower energy density)—for the equivalent of 400 miles per every gallon of petroleum. And if the car were optimized to run on ethanol, like Saab seems to have done with its pilot technology, the overall mileage for such vehicles could be even higher.

Detroit automakers GM and Ford, who both missed out on the early development of the hybrid markets, aren't letting ethanol issues hold them back. In 2006, the two companies were set to manufacture more than half a million FFVs, adding to the more than 4 million FFVs already on the road. It costs the automakers less than $200 to make an automobile E85 capable. GM launched a big "Live Green, Go Yellow" (the color of corn) campaign during the 2006 Super Bowl—which was followed by a major media push in magazines, on TV, and other media outlets. The company will send yellow gas caps, free of charge, to any of the nearly 2 million owners of a GM FFV. In November 2006, the CEOs of GM, Ford, and DaimlerChrysler announced their intention to have 50% of their annual production by 2012 be vehicles designed for E85 flex-fuel or biodiesel.

Not surprisingly, Toyota, Honda, and other overseas competitors aren't standing still. Toyota announced plans to introduce, as early as 2008, an ethanol FFV for the Brazilian market, as well as potentially for the U.S. market. Honda planned to introduce clean-burning, low-emission diesel cars into the U.S. market in 2009 that meet California's strict air-quality standards. Diesel cars are more efficient, going about 30% farther than a gasoline engine on a gallon of fuel, and they can run on biodiesel.

With only 1,000 E85 fueling stations in the United States, and a similarly small number of biodiesel outlets, however, most consumers can't currently fuel up with high-biofuel blends. Thousands of fueling stations will be needed to meet the needs of consumers driving the 5 million-plus FFVs that were scheduled to be on the roads by 2007, and the millions of diesel trucks and cars already on America's roads.

BREAKTHROUGH OPPORTUNITY

Branded Biofuels Distribution

Not many consumers can find easy access to high-blend biofuels like E85 and B50—but that could change dramatically in the near future. One company, SeQuential Biofuels, is aiming to open multiple biofuel stations across the Northwest; its first station opened in Eugene, Oregon, in 2006. Willie Nelson's BioWillie brand has biodiesel retail outlets in more than eight southern and western states. Wal-Mart has said it hopes to begin selling biofuels at up to 400 gas stations it operates at Wal-Mart and Sam's Club stores. We believe there will be a good mix of start-ups and Wal-Marts that will need to push the big guys into action. And some of the new brands should find success, offering opportunity for regional entrepreneurs to get into the distribution game, whether it be for automobile fueling or home heating.

Senator Barack Obama of Illinois proposed a unique solution to the chicken-and-egg dilemma. He introduced legislation in 2006 that would require oil companies that earned more than $1 billion in the first quarter of 2006 to invest no less than 1% of their profits into installing E85 or other alternative-fuel pumps at gas stations across the United States. It is estimated that the bill would create more than 7,000 new E85 pumps in the country. But until such broader access is in place, most American drivers will need to be content fueling up with smaller blends of ethanol that can be used in most internal-combustion engines. More than a third of the gas sold in the country today uses ethanol in blends up to 10%.

DuPont and BP may also crack the code with something other than ethanol. The two companies are developing a form of biobutanol (a bio-based fuel similar to ethanol) that can be used in regular internal-combustion engines with no retrofitting and that has an energy density greater than that of ethanol. The companies planned to introduce biobutanol made from sugar beets in the United Kingdom in 2007 as an additive to regular gasoline, and to unveil a next-generation product more broadly in 2010.

And bioplastics, some made from the by-products of biofuel production, face similar development and distribution challenges. If DuPont, Toyota, and others are to reach their ambitious goals, consumers will have to have ready access to their products in supermarkets and department stores.

While many of the issues, challenges, and conflicts facing the biofuels and biopolymers industry are not insignificant, we believe that they will prove to be more like bumps on the road than significant barriers. Our research leads us to believe that biofuels combined with hybrids, plug-in hybrids, and other high-efficiency vehicles provide a far better solution to our transportation fuel crisis in the near term—and offer much better growth and investment opportunities in that time frame—than the much-hyped hydrogen future. Biofuels can be deployed with very little change in infrastructure or cost, but a hydrogen transportation future will take at least 20 years to materialize and hundreds of billions of dollars in development, deployment, and infrastructure investment. Similarly, bioplastics are being embraced by large multinationals and emerging companies alike because they reduce the need for expensive petroleum-based feedstocks.

In a world in desperate need of a rapid shift away from depleting, high-cost, polluting fossil fuels, biofuels and biomaterials could be the ultimate goal. At last, the United States could wean itself off of foreign supplies of oil and stop the cycle of war and violence engendered by our reliance on a volatile, unreliable, predominantly foreign resource. It will take a concerted effort by policy makers, investors, and innovators, but the tide is turning. Out of today's current petrochemical crisis, we believe, will come immense opportunity for a new army of biofuel and biopolymer visionaries, entrepreneurs, and investors.

THE CLEAN-TECH CONSUMER

Fill 'er up with E85: For the majority of Americans, the initial use of ethanol will be as a minor blend in their conventional gasoline. Ethanol, in small blends, is already in more than a third of the gasoline sold nationally, though most consumers don't realize this. Those who want to fill up with E85 (85% ethanol and 15% gasoline) will need access to the special blend at their local gas station. Approximately 1,000 fueling stations, mostly in Minnesota, currently offer E85—but that number is expanding. According to some projections, the United States was to have had 2,000 E85 fueling stations by 2007, out of 170,000 fueling stations in the nation. You'll also need an FFV to run the stuff, but FFVs are growing in popularity too. There are already more than 4 million FFVs on the road. And both Ford and GM planned to ship more than half a million FFVs in 2006 and to continue to expand that number to half their annual vehicle production by 2012. If the momentum toward FFVs and E85 fueling stations continues, which we believe it will, your next car could very well fuel up with 85% ethanol made predominantly from locally harvested plants, rather than gasoline made from oil shipped in from the Middle East.

Wall to wall: DuPont is working on producing a new carpet that the company says will hold dyes better and stand up to more wear and tear. What's it made out of? Corn. Sorona, which the company said would be available by mid-2007, will appear in a range of products including carpets. Interface Engineering, a pioneer in bio-based carpets, has been shipping its own biodegradable and renewable product to consumers since 2000. And it's not just carpeting; food packaging, plastic utensils, comforters, pillows, and many other consumer products are now being made out of polylactic acid (PLA), a biopolymer derived from corn. With NatureWorks, DuPont, Interface, and even Toyota jockeying for position in the emerging bioplastics space, be on the lookout for more products and applications.

TEN TO WATCH

Archer Daniels Midland
Decatur, Illinois
www.admworld.com
New York Stock Exchange: ADM

ADM is in the midst of reinventing itself, going from an agribusiness leader and the self-proclaimed "supermarket to the world" to an "agri-energy" giant. In 2006 it appointed former ChevronTexaco executive Patricia Woertz as its CEO, and the company is now garnering about 20% of its operating profits from its biofuels business. ADM will need to move beyond its reliance on corn for its ethanol production—and follow in the footsteps of next-generation biorefinery innovators—but we believe it has the war chest, technology access, and vision to succeed.

Cilion
Menlo Park, California
www.cilion.com

Just what do the investors at Khosla Ventures (headed by famed VC investor Vinod Khosla) know about this upstart in California? In 2006 the venture firm partnered with Western Milling, California's largest grain-milling company, and put an initial $40 million into the start-up. The company raised an additional $200 million, making it the largest clean-energy venture deal of the year. The company says it's working on deploying modular, standardized 55-million-gallon-per-year ethanol plants that promise to be "cheaper and greener" than standard corn-to-ethanol plants. With the investors' past track records, and a big war chest, this is definitely a company to watch.

Diversa
San Diego, California
www.diversa.com
NASDAQ: DVSA

To break down virgin plant materials and agricultural and animal wastes into fuels and plastics, you need enzymes. One company working on this puzzle is Diversa, a biotech company that also develops enzymes for industrial, health, and nutrition applications. Since 1998 the company has been developing enzymes that convert plant material, such as corn and agricultural waste, into ethanol for fuel. The company is well positioned to continue to develop enzymes for next-generation biorefinery processes and cellulosic ethanol applications.

DuPont
Wilmington, Delaware
www.dupont.com
New York Stock Exchange: DD

The chemical industry can be a dirty and polluting business—and the majors, such as DuPont, Dow, and 3M, all face challenges and criticism. But a revolution is occurring within the chemistry business with a shift toward cleaner and greener approaches. We believe DuPont is at the forefront of this shift. Not only does the company say it's committed to producing up to 25% of its chemicals with nonpetroleum resources by 2010, but it also believes it's imperative to wean itself off petroleum-based feedstocks to remain relevant and competitive. Working with BP, it's also developing biobutanol, an alternative to ethanol that can be used in just about any standard internal-combustion engine vehicle. It won't be easy, but we believe DuPont could be one of the best-positioned multinationals for this type of transformation.

Imperium Renewables

Seattle, Washington
www.imperiumrenewables.com

The first American biodiesel company to raise VC, Imperium Renewables is on a mission to spread its wings and expand around the country and possibly the world. The company's proprietary "continuous flow" process might just enable it to lower costs and build out capacity. In early 2007, the company raised an additional $214 million in private and debt equity to help deliver on its plans. There will be a host of companies working to break into biofuels—but this company's early start, Seattle genesis, and early backing make it well positioned for the rapidly expanding biodiesel sector.

Iogen

Ottawa, Ontario, Canada
www.iogen.ca

Iogen is the largest company making cellulosic ethanol, the biofuel from next-generation feedstocks of wheat straw and other agricultural residues. A biotech company that's supplied enzymes to the paper, textile, and animal-feed industries for more than 30 years, Iogen is poised to capitalize on the growing demand for lower-cost ethanol worldwide. With backers including Shell, Petro-Canada, and Goldman Sachs, and a head start against the competition, Iogen could deliver on its cellulosic biofuels promise.

NatureWorks LLC

Minneapolis, Minnesota
www.natureworksllc.com

A wholly owned subsidiary of Cargill, NatureWorks has been a pioneer in developing PLA polymers since its founding in 1997. The company's polymers can be found in everything from pillows and comforters to shrink-wrap and carpeting. While the company got off to a bit of a rocky start (it was originally a joint venture of both Cargill and Dow Chemicals before Dow pulled out in 2005), the privately held company has a manufacturing capacity of 300 million pounds of PLA a year. With gasoline at more than $50 a barrel, the company says its products are now cost competitive with petroleum-based resins. As a result, the company reports that sales have been growing by more than 40% annually in recent years.

Novozymes

Bagsværd, Denmark
www.novozymes.com
Copenhagen Stock Exchange: NYZM B

Novozymes is the world leader in enzymes and microorganisms, with the largest product portfolio in the world. The company currently produces more than 100 types of enzymes and microorganisms used in more than 700 different products. Within clean technology, the company's enzymes are used for everything from wastewater treatment to renewable fuels. The company is working in the United States, Europe, Asia, and elsewhere to grow its ethanol portfolio and developing strategic partnerships to keep it on track. In June 2006, the company announced a joint partnership with China Resources Alcohol Corporation to conduct research on converting rice straw to ethanol, and in October 2006 it entered into an agreement with Broin in Sioux Falls, South Dakota, to develop ethanol from corn stover.

Toyota

Toyota City, Japan
www.toyota.com
New York Stock Exchange: TM

What qualifies one of the world's largest auto manufacturers for the biofuels and biomaterials "Ten to Watch"? Not only is Toyota looking to launch FFVs into Brazil and potentially other markets but it is also eyeing the biomaterials sector as one of its core new industries—hoping to develop a business unit worth more than $30 billion. We question whether the company can reach such lofty biopolymer goals, but we'd never discount a company that basically created an entire sector—the HEV—and then managed to dominate the space. Worth 10 times the market cap of GM, Toyota will continue to be a rising star.

VeraSun Energy Corporation
Brookings, South Dakota
www.verasun.com
New York Stock Exchange: VSE

In 2006, VeraSun was one of a number of ethanol companies to go public. Since its public unveiling, the stock has experienced some turbulence—coming off its IPO highs. Because of intense competition and a growing number of rivals, we expect to see companies try to differentiate and bring down biofuel prices to compete with petroleum-based gasoline and diesel. One thing we find particularly interesting about VeraSun is its claim that it can now turn distiller's grain, the major coproduct of ethanol, into biodiesel. Two biofuels from one feedstock could revolutionize the ethanol and biodiesel industry. They'll certainly have competition, but this makes the United States' second largest ethanol producer one to watch.

4

GREEN BUILDINGS

Leveraging Advanced Materials and the Power of "Negawatts"

On 42nd Street in midtown Manhattan, the Big Apple hubbub rushes past a large, fenced-off construction site that looks the same as the dozens of others around town. But the 54-story, crystalline-shell Bank of America Tower going up at One Bryant Park won't be just another high-rise when it opens in 2008. The Durst Organization, its developer, is aiming for it to be the world's greenest, most energy-efficient skyscraper. It's aiming to earn the highest level of green-building accreditation, the platinum level of the Leadership in Energy and Environmental Design (LEED) Green Building Rating System. The long list of twenty-first-century clean technologies being built in to make that happen include a subfloor displacement air ventilation system, floor-by-floor HVAC (heating, ventilating, and air-conditioning) control, maximum daylighting, ultra-efficient LED light fixtures, and a thermal storage system in the basement that produces ice overnight (when power demand is lowest) to help cool the building the next day.

Both commercial and residential buildings have entered a new world of operational and energy efficiency, one that bears little resemblance to the conservation efforts of the 1970s that focused on cutting back and "going without." Remember President Jimmy Carter by the fireside in his cardigan sweater in 1978, urging Americans to turn down their thermostats? Wipe that image from your memory banks. Efficiency enabled by today's clean tech is about doing everything we already do, but doing it cleaner, smarter, and better. And that's opening growth opportunities for job seekers, investors, and entrepreneurs in green building design and construction, on-site energy-management technology, and a host of other building and operation-wide efficiency arenas.

This chapter will explore that new world of efficiency, twenty-first-century style. We'll look at the growth opportunities being created by energy-saving innovations in buildings and industry that are transforming the business and economic landscape, creating new winners and losers. Energy-saving homes and office buildings have come a long way from the days of turn down the heat, turn off the lights, and don a heavy sweater. Today's commercial and residential green buildings generally use 30% less energy than their comparably sized nongreen counterparts (some save much more), and they're generally brighter, healthier, and more aesthetically pleasing. They're often built with little or no additional up-front cost, and they pay back not only in energy savings but also in better employee retention, attendance, and productivity.

THE SEXY SIDE OF EFFICIENCY

On the surface, technologies for energy and materials efficiency may not sound as sexy as those that deliver energy from clean resources such as wind, solar, or biofuels. But the field is attracting its share of entrepreneurs, corporate investors, and savvy business executives. They're finding market opportunities in technologies that drive energy-efficient improvements for industries, buildings, and water systems. Efficiency technologies that *save* energy, driven by the same confluence of forces that's fueling the growth of the sexier technologies that generate clean power, are now getting onto the radar screens of more and more companies and investors. Companies both large and small offer the opportunity for businesspeople and investors to play in the energy-efficiency world. Established, traditional giants of industrial and building controls such as GE, Honeywell, and Johnson Controls are stepping up their efforts in efficiency, making the field ripe for job seekers and corporate intrapreneurs. But there's plenty of activity in the start-up arena as well, as small growing companies, many of which we'll discuss in this chapter, eye those corporate giants as customers, technology licensees, or potential acquirers.

"By 2007, efficiency will be where the solar photovoltaic industry is today as an attractive investment opportunity," says Jonathan Livingston, senior program manager for emerging technologies at electric and gas utility PG&E in San Francisco. "You'll see one or two grand-slam plays, and in someone's garage today there's a breakthrough invention that'll get sold to a GE."

THE POLICY DRIVER

"Conservation may be a sign of personal virtue," Vice President Dick Cheney memorably told PBS's Jim Lehrer in 2001, "but it's not a sufficient basis for a sound, comprehensive energy policy." Cheney's assertion ignored a basic fact about efficiency: The cheapest (not to mention cleanest) kilowatt of electricity you'll ever buy is the one you *don't* use—and the one that the utility never has to produce at all. And governments from New York to California and Japan to Europe are proving that efficiency is not only sound energy policy, it's essential to economic competitiveness in this decade and beyond. Policy is a key driver of the efficiency sector, and entrepreneurs and investors would do well to target cities, regions, and countries that have implemented GHG reduction mandates such as the European Union, California, and the nine states in the U.S. northeast that have signed on to the Regional Greenhouse Gas Initiative. In areas like those, corporate operations, residential developers, and other big energy users are seeking out the latest, most cost-effective efficiency techniques and technologies to reduce power consumption—driving the business growth of those technologies. "You'll see a lot more 'net-zero energy' homes, for example, in areas with greenhouse gas caps," says Susan Munves, energy and green building program administrator for the city of Santa Monica, California. "When buildings actually have to measure their carbon emissions, that will be a big driver of growth."

With the long-term pricing trends of conventional fuels such as oil, coal, and natural gas on the rise, the payoff for investments in efficiency is greater than ever. Efficiency is a cornerstone of clean tech, and it should be a cornerstone of energy policy as well. "Green cars, homes, offices, appliances, designs, and renewable energies will be the biggest growth industry of the 21st century," wrote influential *New York Times* op-ed columnist Thomas L. Friedman in early 2006. "If we don't dominate that industry, China, India, Japan or Europe surely will."

The list of current energy-efficiency advances and breakthroughs goes on and on. Manufacturers using wireless sensors to optimize manufacturing equipment, heating and cooling, and other industrial processes are making their factories more energy efficient—and making products more cheaply than their competitors. "Tankless" home water heaters save power, water, and floor space, delivering hot showers on demand instead of heating water around the clock. In short, efficient products and processes today are harnessing leading-edge, profitable innovations in design and engineering around the world. Sure, turning down the thermostat never hurts. But today's technology often obviates the need for yesterday's heavy wool sweater.

Even the world's largest (and often most reviled) private employer, Wal-Mart Stores, has embraced energy-efficiency improvements in a big way. In an ambitious plan unveiled by chairman Lee Scott in late 2005, the giant retailer said it would double its truck fleet's fuel efficiency and cut store energy use by 30% over the next 10 years. "The whole thing hinges on mind-set," says Andy Ruben, Wal-Mart's vice president of corporate strategy/sustainability. "In order to succeed, any business needs to evolve, and saving energy by being smarter is needed in the world right now. When you think about everyday low cost, if you're not thinking about reducing the amount of waste in your Dumpster, or the amount of energy you're using, or how to lengthen product life cycles, then that's not truly lowest cost."

IF YOU BUILD IT . . .

Conventional wisdom has it that energy consumption in the United States breaks down fairly evenly into three categories. Give or take a few percentage points, it takes one-third of the energy pie to power transportation, one-third to drive industry, and one-third for the heating, cooling, and lighting of residential and commercial buildings.

But in recent years, a revisionist view emerged among green-minded architects. *Hey, wait a minute,* they said, *how much of that industry slice actually relates to the built environment?* Factories need lighting and heating too; it's not just the power to run the machines. And what about the power needed for construction—and the energy that goes into making and transporting building materials? With this new perspective, architects recalculated conventional energy use data from the Energy Information Administration of the U.S. Department of Energy. The built environment, they reckoned, is responsible for nearly half (48%) of all U.S. energy usage and (76%) of electricity demand.

"It's the architecture, stupid!" wrote veteran green architect Ed Mazria, principal at Mazria Odems Dzurec in Santa Fe, New Mexico, in an influential 2003 article in *Solar Today* magazine calling on architects to take the lead in energy-efficient design. It took some time, but mainstream professionals are taking up the cause. In late 2005, the 78,000-member American Institute of Architects officially called for building construction and operations to use 50% less energy from fossil fuels by 2010. That's creating big growth opportunities in energy efficiency, as it's often more cost effective for buildings and factories to invest in technologies that save power—the proverbial "negawatt"—than to produce more energy with solar PV panels or other sources of clean power.

BREAKTHROUGH OPPORTUNITY

Green Design

As the *economic* benefits of green and energy-efficient buildings become apparent to more developers and builders, the demand for advice and consulting on technologies and processes is skyrocketing among builders large and small. That's a great business opportunity for entrepreneurs and job seekers with expertise in green architecture, design, and engineering. The financial payoff from green building will be multifaceted, comprising direct savings from reduced energy use, higher value in the real estate market (including resale value), increased employee retention and productivity, and potential carbon credits from reduced CO_2 emissions. So a wide variety of skill sets can be brought to bear. There'll be demand for firms and individuals with expertise in very specific areas, such as the latest window glazing or HVAC improvements, as well as those skilled in green-building project management and accountability. Examples of current successful players include Enermodal Engineering in Kitchener, Ontario, and Interface Engineering in Portland, Oregon, whose booklet *Green Building Breakthrough: Engineering a Sustainable World* is a highly regarded reference in the field.

LEEDING THE WAY

Administered since 2000 by the U.S. Green Building Council (USGBC) in Washington, D.C., the LEED rating system contains several dozen criteria for buildings to meet in different areas, including energy efficiency and emissions, water usage, construction techniques, choice of building materials, and how far those materials have to be transported—a major energy use. The rating system is like a report card, with completed buildings earning grades ranging from LEED Certified up to LEED Silver, Gold, and Platinum.

LEED is not an ideal rating system, and it's under constant scrutiny and revision to be a more accurate representation of environmental benefits. Critics point out that a building's bike storage room gets as many LEED points as a major improvement in heating and air conditioning. But the USGBC has revamped the standard to place more emphasis on energy use, and on average, LEED buildings use 30% less energy than non-LEED counterparts with comparable square footage. "We are dedicated to continuous improvement," says Tom Hicks, vice president for LEED at the building council. "Energy use is an area that we're going to be a lot more focused on, going forward." Since 2000, the USGBC continues to add new categories in addition to new building construction for builders to seek LEED certification. These include commercial interiors, existing buildings (usually energy-saving overhauls), core-and-shell construction, homes, and residential neighborhoods.

"It's not a perfect evaluation method," says George Beeler, a green architect at AIM Associates in Petaluma, California. "But it's a good start and it's very well-accepted." LEED got a further boost in the fall of 2006 when the U.S. General Services Administration called it the most credible among five systems that rate the "green-ness" of buildings.

Some LEED-certified buildings are where you'd expect them—the offices of the Natural Resources Defense Council (NRDC) in Santa Monica, California, say, or the Institute of EcoTourism in Sedona, Arizona. Others, however, do not fit the green stereotype. The Detroit Lions' football headquarters and training facility in Allen Park, Michigan; a Shaw's superstore in Worcester, Massachusetts; the Washington State Penitentiary's replacement warehouse in Walla Walla; the Barksdale Air Force Base's physical fitness center in Shreveport, Louisiana; and the world's first

LEED-certified airport terminal—Delta's at Logan International Airport in Boston—show how mainstream LEED buildings have become. All told, more than 730 commercial projects have been certified as LEED buildings and 5,700 more under construction have applied to get LEED certification. In 2005, construction starts intending to be LEED-certified totaled $10 billion, or about 5% of all building projects worldwide. There are more than 35,000 LEED-accredited architects and other building professionals, with about 25 more passing the accreditation exam every day.

The energy footprint of a building, in LEED criteria or other rating systems, is not just the energy consumed in its operation. It also includes the energy demands in the manufacture and transport of building materials. That's causing green-construction professionals to source materials closer to home, while spurring growth in a range of building materials technologies. Often the goal is innovative use of waste products from other industries, such as fly ash. Essentially waste residue from coal-fired power plants, fly ash is a partial replacement for one of the most energy-intensive, high CO_2–emitting of all materials to make: cement. Other examples include roof shingles, made from scraps from the polyvinyl chloride pipe industry, and straw particleboard, created from agricultural waste, that replaces traditional drywall. Australian company Ortech and its U.S. unit, Durra Building Materials of Whitewright, Texas, have used ceiling and wall material made from wheat and rice straw in airports, hotels, and IMAX theaters.

THE EFFICIENCY DIVIDEND

With electricity and heating oil costs on the rise, the choice of energy-efficient building design would seem to be a no-brainer. But as in all areas of efficiency, real-world fiscal realities can contradict that. Often it's a matter of long-range versus short-range thinking. "Most buildings are built by developers, and their number one thing is lowest first cost," says Beeler. "But if you're going to own a building for any length of time, it's not at all true that building green costs more."

Enermodal Engineering, resource efficiency consultants to seven LEED buildings including Canada's first, is among the firms that track the payback period on electric utility costs for LEED projects. With the "LEED premium" of up-front construction costs ranging from 1% to 15%, Enermodal estimates energy payback periods as ranging from 3 to 10 years. "Energy consumption reductions will be realized over the entire life of a building," says R.K. Stewart, a principal at global architecture firm Gensler and president of the American Institute of Architects in 2007. "We need to look beyond the first impacts associated with constructing a facility and really consider what happens over the many decades that the facility will be used."

Those who design, work, and live in green buildings also need to consider advantages beyond lower utility bills. LEED-designed buildings boast a range of other business benefits, some "soft," but most with direct bottom-line payoffs. Improved indoor air quality and day-lit environments mean happier, healthier employees. That's not just touchy-feely betterment; it's a real payoff in improved retention and recruitment, with reduced absenteeism and attrition—a top priority in intellectual-capital industries. Worker productivity usually rises too. Energy savings may be the main goal, but many ancillary benefits follow.

What's more, an increasing number of green-building designers say you don't even have to wait for multiyear payback periods. Many efficient and environmentally sound structures cost no more, *or are cheaper*, than their conventional neighbors. On the banks of the Willamette River in Portland, the 16-story Center for Health & Healing at Oregon Health & Science University, which opened in late 2006, is another large project aiming for LEED's highest level of platinum. Water-chilled beams replace fans and other air-conditioning gear in some areas—the first U.S. application in a large building of that scheme, developed in Scandinavia. Captured rainwater (Portland has plenty of that) is used for toilets. Stone slabs on the ground floor store heat. Solar panels on the south façade of the 100,000-square-foot building generate power on-site and provide shade. Stairwells are ventilated with controlled outside breezes instead of energy-consuming fans and blowers.

And the bottom-line kicker? The electrical, mechanical, and plumbing systems are projected to cost 10% less than they do in a comparably sized office tower, a savings of $3 million. "We're delivering champagne on a beer budget," says lead project engineer Andy Frichtl, principal at Interface Engineering, the Portland consultancy that designed the systems. Then will come operating savings: an estimated $400,000 a year in electric power, 56% less potable water use, and reduced sewer bills, thanks to the center's nearly 100% on-site sewage and wastewater treatment.

A BIG PLAYERS' GAME TOO

Although small, regional design firms such as Interface are doing pioneering work in energy-saving green buildings, the industry's biggest players are in the game too. Turner Construction in New York, the largest and one of the oldest commercial construction firms in the United States, has completed more than 100 green projects, some before the LEED rating system came into being. Turner's green work includes the corporate headquarters of Alcoa, Duracell, Genzyme, and Reebok, and the 1.5-million-square-foot David L. Lawrence Convention Center in Pittsburgh, one of the world's largest LEED structures. Turner took home the 2006 corporate environmental leadership award from Global Green USA.

Turner's annual "market barometer" survey of corporate executives tracks business attitudes toward the economics of green building. In the 2005 study, 91% of execs who've had experience with green buildings say their initially higher construction costs will be recouped in energy and operations savings, with 8.1 years as the average payback period. Two thirds (68%) say green projects have a better return on investment than conventional buildings. Other benefits of green versus nongreen got even more votes: occupants' better health and well-being, 88%; greater value of the building, 84%; and improved worker productivity, 78%.

To a large extent, the efficient use of energy and water in buildings comes from working with nature rather than against it. The products and solutions use cutting-edge technology, but their goal is often the greater use of natural resources—sunlight instead of lightbulbs, outside breeze instead of conditioned air, rainwater instead of the city's water supply. "I'm an engineer, so I'm part of the problem we're trying to fix," says the USGBC's Hicks. "In the distant past, we used to design our buildings with nature in mind. But our technologies, especially heating and cooling, have allowed us to overcome nature. The cost of that, we now see, is paying for energy."

HOME GREEN HOME

For many years across the United States and around the world, millions of homeowners have cut their energy and water use—and their utility bills—with double-pane windows, front-loading washing machines, and hundreds of other products. What's new in the clean tech revolution is the emergence of production-scale, superefficient homes comprising entire new housing developments.

Tucked a few miles inland from the shores of Monterey Bay in the fertile Pajaro Valley, the city of Watsonville, California, is known as the strawberry capital of the world. It's also home to one of the nation's largest superefficient housing developments, Clarum Homes' Vista Montana. It's a community of 177 single-family homes, 80 townhouses, and 132 apartments, all meeting Clarum's Enviro-Homes standards of energy and water efficiency, improved indoor air quality, and ecofriendly materials like recycled wood for decks.

Enviro-Homes uses tankless hot water heaters, a technology common in Europe that's starting to catch on in the United States. Instead of a 40-gallon tank in the basement, the tankless system uses a compact, wall-mounted, gas-fired heat exchanger right in the water system that heats the water only when it's needed. Manufactured by companies noted for energy-efficient appliances such as Bosch in Germany and Rinnai and Noritz in Japan, tankless systems use up to 50% less energy than traditional gas-heated hot water and 70% less than electric hot water systems.

"In most homes we keep water hot 24-by-7, even though we're not using it most of the time," says Aaron Nitzkin, an advisor to Clarum on energy technologies. "The tankless system is essentially hot water on demand—but only then. And the hot water doesn't run out." It's one more example of how today's efficiency tech contrasts with the shorter showers (and Jimmy Carter's cardigans) of the scale-it-back, go-without conservation days of the past. In fact, there's a possible efficiency downside to this abundance. Unlimited hot water's a nice temptation for *longer* showers, which could send energy use and monthly bills back up. Even with tech innovation, personal behavior still matters.

Other efficiency products used by Clarum include the solar radiant barrier, an aluminum sheath below the roof that blocks summer heat to save 8% to 12% on air-conditioning, and the T-MASS wall, a Dow Chemical product that sandwiches a Styrofoam layer between concrete to double or triple the wall's insulation value, depending on climate.

Clarum built Vista Montana in conjunction with an NREL program called Zero Energy Homes. That means homes that produce as much or more power, usually with solar PV panels, as they actually use. The name is more of a goal than a reality in most cases, except for single-unit projects, but some full-scale residential developments come very close. Solar energy provides up to half the electricity for the residents of Vista Montana, and with efficiency measures cutting demand from 40% to 70% of a conventional home, zero energy use is not too far off.

Indeed, that's where the big savings in fossil fuel energy come—in the *combination* of efficient design with clean-energy generation. In hot, sunny climates, something as simple as a white instead of dark-hued roof can save as much energy needed for cooling as would be generated by a multithousand-dollar rooftop solar array.

The National Association of Home Builders has called green building its industry's most significant new development in decades, and it's that kind of large-scale clout that's transforming efficiency in U.S. homes. In the United States and other countries, energy efficiency is starting to near the top of lists of factors that home buyers are seeking, along with good schools, friendly neighbors, resale value potential, and other traditional criteria. One 2006 survey in Toronto and Ottawa found that 90% of buyers were seeking energy efficiency in their new homes.

SYSTEMIC CHANGE

Such trends mean that Clarum has plenty of company. Wisconsin's largest home builder, Veridian Homes in Madison, saves enough energy in every 10 homes it builds to power an eleventh one. Shea Homes in San Diego, the nation's largest family-owned home builder, has built more than 400 zero-energy residences. "If this is going to be a systemic change for the masses, it can't just be custom superefficient homes here and there," says Nitzkin. "It has to be production homes, a couple hundred at a time. Then you'll get people thinking about the total operating cost of their home over the years, not just the listing price. That hasn't really happened before, but it's starting to." So if you're looking to enter the burgeoning zero-energy home business, keep an eye out for large builders like these with the production muscle to scale up quickly as demand grows.

As with vehicle fuel efficiency, Japan and Europe are also leading developers and users of energy-efficient homes. PanaHome, a unit of Panasonic's parent company Matsushita, is one of Japan's leading prefab home manufacturers and aims to make 15% of its output zero-energy homes in

2006. British architect Bill Dunster is pushing the concept of zero-energy development, or ZED; his BedZED is an 84-residence project in South London that uses triple-glazed windows, wind-driven ventilation, solar PV, and other technologies to drastically cut power needs. In Austria, efficient housing advocates predict that one quarter of new homes by 2010 will be so-called passive houses, which use up to 75% less energy than conventional homes do for heating and power.

BREAKTHROUGH OPPORTUNITY

Next-Generation Insulation

Like many clean technologies, aerogel isn't new. It was first invented in 1931 but wasn't commercialized until more recently. Aerogel is the lightest solid known to scientists, weighing little more than air. It offers unique insulating qualities that make it two to eight times more effective than traditional insulating materials. Aspen Aerogels, based in Northborough, Massachusetts, is one start-up company that's developed insulation products based on nanotechnology. While still too expensive to include in most building applications today, Aspen's insulation technology is being used for industrial, military, and commercial applications for everything from deep-sea oil drilling pipelines to foot-warming shoe inserts. It's a longer-term, potentially lucrative opportunity for entrepreneurs and investors. One day, aerogel could supply high-performance, price-competitive insulation for the building market, as Aspen or another company is able to ramp up production and significantly lower costs. Aspen, the global leader in the sector, received $50 million in Series D financing from the likes of Lehman Brothers, Reservoir Capital Group, and RockPort Capital Partners in 2005 to ramp up its commercialization with a new manufacturing facility. Other start-ups to watch include Aerogel Composite in Bloomfield, Connecticut, and Airglass in Staffanstorp, Sweden, which makes a transparent, aerogel-based material that insulates much better than glass.

STINGY LIGHTBULBS

LED technology sounds pretty geeky. It's a semiconductor-based, solid-state technology that illuminates most of the world's cell phones and clock radios. In recent years, several large and small companies have begun making LED lighting products that replace incandescent and fluorescent bulbs in commercial buildings and municipal applications such as traffic lights and highway exit signs. So how's an LED products company getting meetings with former Secretary of State George Shultz and Irmelin DiCaprio (matinee idol Leo's mom) during the same week in early 2006?

It's because lighting burns up about 22% of the electricity produced worldwide, so any technology that creates light more efficiently gets the attention of people who care about a cleaner energy future. In the strange-bedfellows world of clean tech, those people include Shultz, who's joined with former Central Intelligence Agency director R. James Woolsey and other political hawks in pushing clean energy as a national security issue, and DiCaprio, who works with her son's Leonardo DiCaprio Foundation to support climate change mitigation and environmental efforts around the world. Thus their respective confabs with Cree, a $400 million publicly held maker of LED lighting devices in Durham, North Carolina. To Cree's vice president of marketing and business development, Chris James, who worked in Silicon Valley for 20 years before moving east, it was quite a ride.

"This is what a technology executive dreams of doing," he says. "You want to change the world, but how do you get it started? You find influential people. We're on the tip of a business tidal wave like I've never seen in Silicon Valley. I was there during the [dot-com] bubble, where you'd try to spin a need for your technology. Well, here's a need you don't have to spin—cutting energy use—and the technologies are showing up."

The meeting with Irmelin DiCaprio led to Cree showcasing its wares at the 2006 Global Green USA pre-Oscar party in Hollywood, where movie stars such as Kate Bosworth and Daryl Hannah arrived in hybrid and biodiesel cars to greet the paparazzi on the "green carpet." (Two nights later, for the fourth straight year, Global Green coordinated the hybrid-car arrivals of even bigger stars, such as George Clooney, Charlize Theron, and Morgan Freeman, at the much more famous red carpet.) Far from the Tinseltown glitz back in Durham, Cree battles global LED competitors, such as Japan's Toyoda Gosei and Nichia, Germany's OSRAM, and the Netherlands' Philips, which took over full ownership of LED pioneer Lumileds from joint venture partner Agilent in 2005.

LED lights are up to 10 times more efficient than standard incandescent lights (which waste up to 90% of their energy as heat) and use 10% to 30% less electricity than compact fluorescent bulbs. Although LED prices are dropping, the bulbs remain more expensive in up-front costs, but they last 10 to 15 *years* in normal use. "Our goal," says James, "is to obsolete the lightbulb." Carmanah Technologies in Victoria, British Columbia, takes the technology a step further with solar-powered LEDs that light airport runways, ships, rail crossings, and bus shelters worldwide.

BREAKTHROUGH OPPORTUNITY

LED Lighting

The incandescent lightbulb's technology hasn't changed dramatically in more than a century, and that shows in its inefficient use of electricity. The compact fluorescent lightbulb, fast becoming popular, offers a sizable efficiency advantage, but it's really a bridge technology toward the most energy-efficient light source to date: the light-emitting diode (LED). LEDs offer the most promising long-term opportunity for both midsized players such as Cree and global lighting giants such as GE, Philips, and OSRAM. The high-brightness LED market will reach $6.8 billion in 2009, double its 2004 size, according to research firm Strategies Unlimited in Mountain View, California. Not bad, but that's mainly in traditional LED applications such as mobile devices. Over the longer term, Cree and others have their sights on much bigger fish: the current $55 billion global market for lightbulbs and light fixtures. The technology's still too expensive for most homeowners today, but we're very bullish on its potential for mass markets 5 to 10 years out.

NEGAWATTS: EFFICIENCY AS AN ENERGY RESOURCE

Tapping the energy of mighty rivers like the Columbia and the Snake, the Pacific Northwest has always been the leading U.S. region in hydroelectric power. It's also the home of one of North America's largest wind farms, PPM Energy's Stateline project along the Columbia. But in recent years, the utilities of Washington, Oregon, Idaho, and Montana have been pioneers in the use of the cleanest power source of all: efficiency.

Amory Lovins, founder of the Rocky Mountain Institute in Snowmass, Colorado, and one of the world's most respected efficiency technology gurus, first coined the term *negawatt* in 1989. It's a unit of conserved electricity—a megawatt that a power plant never has to generate because the demand for it has been eliminated by improved building design, energy-saving lightbulbs, more miserly appliances, more efficient use of the electrical grid, or hundreds of other efficiency measures. Utilities have refined the term to the official metric of an average megawatt—a megawatt delivered (or more accurately, not delivered) continuously for 1 year. In the Northwest, 1 average MW is equivalent to the power needed to light 585 homes for a year.

In 2005, the region's top 15 municipal and investor-owned utilities saved 108 average MW, or 63,000 homes' worth of juice. The region's largest power supplier, the federal government's Bonneville Power Administration, aimed to save 230 average MW in fiscal year 2006. Those efforts make efficiency the Northwest's second-largest "source" of electricity today, behind hydroelectric power. Money spent to promote efficiency is usually a better investment than building new power plants or buying more electrons on the wholesale market. Most of the utilities' efforts focus on reducing the load from residential and commercial buildings.

But before utilities could view efficiency as a power resource, utility regulators had to reform the system and create financial incentives for utilities to promote efficiency. It doesn't work if utilities' financial performance is tied only to how much energy they sell. The Northwest Power Act of 1980 allowed power generators to share a portion of their customers' savings from using less electricity, giving them a financial stake in the efficiency game.

Among utilities' large-scale efforts in efficiency is market transformation, a program in which utilities and regulators promote the manufacture and purchase of energy-saving products (appliances, building materials, and the like) with rebates, industrial training, consumer education, and marketing assistance. One metric of success: The four Pacific Northwest states represent just 4% of the U.S. population but buy 16% of the energy-saving compact fluorescent lightbulbs sold nationwide. "There's so much we can do when we get the incentives right," says Ralph Cavanagh, energy program director at the environmental advocacy group NRDC.

But in most areas in the United States aside from the Northwest, California, New York, and a few others, regulatory efforts to drive efficiency have a long way to go. The so-called decoupling of utility sales and profits has not yet happened in most regions, so utilities are lacking the biggest regulatory incentive to help homeowners and businesses be more efficient. For most utilities, profits grow when their customers use more energy, not less. Given that U.S. utility policies are a patchwork of regulation and deregulation, covering shareholder-owned utilities, municipals, rural electric cooperatives, and other ownership structures, most states face a challenging path to decoupling and other key efficiency incentives. For now, investors and entrepreneurs should keep a close eye on regional utility decoupling trends as a factor in potential business growth opportunities in efficiency products and services.

BREAKTHROUGH OPPORTUNITY

Energy-Management Systems

Long considered a plodding, slow-growth niche, technologies that help enterprises manage and conserve energy resources in their buildings and operations have become hot. Venture capital funding is starting to pick up, and it's a ripe opportunity for start-ups and entrepreneurs because the applications are so varied. MACH Energy in Walnut Creek, California, for example, uses pattern recognition software to help commercial real estate managers for customers such as ING and eBay identify potential electricity savings and shave demand accordingly, saving an average of 10 cents per square foot on energy costs. ConsumerPowerline in New York, a Deloitte "Fast 50" technology company in 2006, earns its revenue from sharing customers' energy savings after analyzing their operations and demand patterns. Seattle-based Verdiem specifically targets the energy pull of its customers' computer networks, via a software utility called Surveyor that cuts computer power usage by 5% to 15% annually. No matter what the approach, the value proposition to customers is simple and compelling: providing bottom-line savings. That will always be a good business to be in, and ever more so as energy costs increase worldwide.

California, a leader in state-directed efficiency initiatives since the 1970s, kicked its efforts into high gear after the deregulation fiasco that caused rolling blackouts and skyrocketing rate increases in the summer of 2001. If you're an entrepreneur or corporate executive looking to sell efficiency products and services today, California is a prime market. From 2006 to 2008, the California Public Utilities Commission will spend $2 billion on efficiency measures in by far the largest conservation campaign ever seen in the U.S. utility industry. The commission says that the money will save more than $5 billion in energy costs for homes and businesses in what would be the world's sixth largest economy if California were its own country. Those negawatts will eliminate demand that would have necessitated building three new large power plants in the state. "Before our utilities spend a dollar to buy power in the market or build a new-generation plant, they will first invest in ways to help us use energy more efficiently," says commissioner Susan Kennedy. The money covers rebates of $10 to $600 for efficient appliances, energy audits for buildings, efficient-design assistance, and an effort by the $30 million California Clean Energy Fund to back efficiency-related start-up companies. The fund includes $1 million to start a center of global leadership on efficiency technologies at the University of California, Davis, and the removal of barriers to the rapid commercialization of technologies developed there. (For a more detailed look at current and future technologies used by utilities themselves to operate more efficiently, see chapter 6, "Smart Grid").

CHINA AND INDIA: THE EFFICIENCY IMPERATIVE

In China alone, 400 million people are expected to move from the countryside to cities by 2020—one of the largest and fastest population migrations in human history. In India the trend is slower, but still considerable. The number of cities of more than 1 million people grew from 21 in 1991 to 35 a decade later, and India now has 9 megacities with populations exceeding 3 million, including Mumbai, one of the world's most populous cities at 13 million. The rural-to-urban migration is part of another massive transformation—the creation of unprecedented middle classes. Some projections place China's middle class at 200 million people in 2010—roughly the population of the United Kingdom, France, and Germany *combined* and larger than the adult population in the United States. And a great deal of them will want to be cooled by air conditioners at work and home, wash their clothes by machine, and generally live a much more energy-consumptive life. The same pattern is playing out in India, Brazil, Mexico, and across the globe. The year 2005 marked the first time that more humans lived in cities than in rural areas. That transformation will only accelerate, and it will be one of the defining trends of the twenty-first century.

Although environmentalist do-gooders and social-policy utopians might try, no one will be able to tell the members of these newly minted middle classes that they ought not to have access to personal transportation, be able to heat and cool their homes, and enjoy leisure activities and travel. Not if the twin engines of market forces and human nature have anything to say about it. The key, then, is making sure that heating and cooling systems, refrigerators, washing machines, and the buildings that house them use energy and water as cleanly and efficiently as possible—in other words, to avoid fueling the global middle classes of the twenty-first century with wasteful, inefficient twentieth-century technologies.

A modest glimpse of this clean-tech future can be found on the ninth floor of a nondescript Shanghai office block surrounded by a dozen of the city's endless parade of residential high-rises. Here the Shanghai Energy Conservation Supervision Center, run by China's first nonprofit energy-efficiency advocate, opened during the city's annual Energy Conservation Week in June 2006. It showcases the latest in energy-efficient technologies available for the swelling ranks of Chinese urban professionals, dubbed Chuppies by the buzzword purveyors of American marketing. Most of the featured products are manufactured in China, but most of the brands are foreign: Philips compact fluorescent lights, Owens Corning double-pane windows, Daikin compact air conditioners, Sakura stoves and ovens, Whirlpool washer-dryers and microwaves.

The center also features a scale model of a zero-energy, two-story office building in the Shanghai suburb of Xinzhuang. Powered by solar PV panels and a micro wind turbine, the project sports a green roof and a water recycling system from Spirax Sarco, a British manufacturer of steam- and water-capture products. Every visitor receives a "How to Save Energy in Daily Life" brochure. "Without energy, we cannot develop economically," says center vice-director Zhang Zhong Cheng. "And with their cars and homes, the middle class likes to show that they're rich! But I think the public is becoming much more aware of conservation and energy efficiency."

TWO NEW MANHATTANS A YEAR

Green building is also a relatively new concept in the developing world, but its early growth constitutes a huge potential market for foreign clean-tech manufacturers, designers, and consultants. "When you have a country [China] building the equivalent of two new Manhattans a year, the sheer amount of construction means big opportunities," says Barbara Finamore, director of NRDC's China Clean Energy Program. Or put another way, here's the advice to visitors to Beijing from Eric Martinot, visiting professor at the city's Tsinghua University, research fellow of the Worldwatch Institute, and lead author of the annual Ren21 report on global clean-energy development: "Never rely on any map that's more than three months old."

In 2006, China christened its first LEED-certified building, the 139,000-sqare-foot Ministry of Science and Technology headquarters in Beijing. An international coalition of companies called Accord21 (the American-Chinese Coalition Organized for Responsible Development in the 21st Century) collaborated on the project, which achieved the LEED Gold rating. Its efficiency features showcase the China opportunity for American companies and other foreign technology providers. The building includes energy-saving HVAC systems from Trane and Carrier, optimized building controls from Honeywell, and even waterless urinals from Falcon Waterfree Technologies, a Grand Rapids, Michigan company whose customer sites include India's Taj Mahal. "More and more, building green is becoming a marketing tool," says Finamore. "But who has the technologies to make it happen? They don't. The U.S., Europe, and Japan do."

The ministry building is not just a solitary, token effort. Under a national government directive to improve energy efficiency by 20%, 54 government buildings and 300 commercial structures in Beijing are undergoing retrofits, and some 1,700 other buildings are scheduled to do the same before Beijing hosts the 2008 Summer Olympics. Plus, *4 million* streetlamps are slated for efficiency upgrades.

Energy efficiency as a business service, a longtime growth opportunity for engineering consultants in the United States, is now starting to catch on in China. Beijing PowerU Technology is the first private energy-management contractor in China, providing clients such as hospitals with energy-savings advice and helping finance the purchase of more energy-efficient equipment. One of PowerU's investors is the China Environment Fund, China's first and largest VC fund devoted exclusively to clean-tech and environmental remediation investments.

LOW-HANGING FRUIT?

Finamore calls efficiency the low-hanging fruit of clean-tech opportunities in China, with the potential to save the equivalent energy of 17 new coal plants in Jiangsu Province alone, where NRDC is working with the provincial government. The key, she says, is achieving the mind-set change that took place (after years of effort) in California and the Pacific Northwest: getting utility and policy decision makers to view energy efficiency as a resource. In China's burgeoning manufacturing sector—the economic underpinning of the middle class—there are huge potential efficiency gains in the replacement or overhaul of industrial motors, fans, pumps, and chillers, many of which date back to the 1970s.

Then there's the growing market, for large global construction companies and the subcontractors who supply them, to bring energy efficiency to the new factories popping up all the time in China and India. San Francisco–based Bechtel worked with small consultancy Environmental Market Solutions in Takoma Park, Maryland, to design China's first LEED Gold factory for American telephone headset maker Plantronics in the eastern city of Suzhou. The $23 million manufacturing complex uses rainwater collection ponds, reverse-osmosis water purification, and daylighting to cut power use. Intel is also weighing green-building options for its new chip plants in the Shanghai area.

India and Mexico are founding members of the World Green Building

Council (WGBC), joining Australia, Canada, Japan, Spain, and the United States to help promote LEED-type building certification and LEED professional accreditation to construction markets worldwide. India is home to the first LEED Platinum building outside the United States, the Confederation of Indian Industry–Sohrabji Godrej Green Business Centre in Hyderabad. The U.S. LEED criteria often need to be tweaked to reflect local conditions in the specific countries. Water scarcity in India, for example, results in heavier weightings for use of clean technologies such as waterless urinals, storm water collection, and recycled gray water. Parasu Raman, the energetic chairman of the Indian Green Building Council and vice chairman of the WGBC, views green building as an important economic boost to India's construction industry and has called on the national government to require energy efficiency and other minimum green measures for all new buildings larger than 20,000 square feet.

THE NEW EFFICIENCY MIND-SET

In the clean tech revolution, the battle to cut the energy use of a computer network or use fly ash instead of cement in a concrete slab may not sound sexy. But a closer look reveals otherwise. From Wal-Mart's business strategy sessions in Arkansas to engineers studying HVAC systems in Oregon, from appliance-heating specialists in Japan to architects in London, the efficiency goal is inspiring and emboldening radical new designs, new ways of thinking, and a new realization that energy savings translate directly into dollar savings and improved overall value.

A new mind-set is emerging in which *saving energy* constitutes an *energy resource*—the cheapest and cleanest resource of all. This mind-set now affects decisions by governments, corporations, and investors worldwide. And when you combine efficiency with clean energy—a power-saving building design, say, with solar PV cells generating electricity on the roof—you've created a new type of entity that at certain times actually produces more power than it uses.

Energy efficiency in buildings and commercial operations often flies under the radar as VC investors, corporate developers, and the media focus on more visible or tangible clean-tech opportunities such as wind farms and biofuels refineries. But the efficiency-as-a-resource mind-set is gaining new converts at a rapid pace worldwide, bringing with it dramatic growth opportunities for a wide range of entrepreneurs, consultants, investors, and job seekers. It may be as simple as changing a lightbulb (to an LED) or as complex as designing a skyscraper, but efficiency is a critical growth opportunity in the clean tech revolution and should not be overlooked.

THE CLEAN-TECH CONSUMER

Go tankless: Why keep your water hot all the time when you need it only a couple of times a day? Common in Europe and Japan and starting to catch on in the United States, "tankless" water heaters replace a 40-gallon tank with a compact, wall-mounted, gas-fired heat exchanger right in the water system. They can cut your water-heating energy bill in half if you currently heat with natural gas, and by 70% if you use electricity to heat water. Added benefit: increased storage space in the basement where the water tank used to be. Leading manufacturers include Bosch, Noritz, and Rinnai.

Blue jeans in the wall: A fast-growing niche in the repurposed-materials sector is building insulation made from recycled denim insulation, such as the UltraTouch brand from Bonded Logic in Chandler, Arizona. It's made from scraps from blue-jeans manufacturers, as well as used jeans donated by consumers—even from celebrities Lindsay Lohan and Gwen Stefani, who gave theirs to a Habitat for Humanity green building project in the Bronx, New York.

TEN TO WATCH

Aspen Aerogels

Northborough, Massachusetts
www.aerogel.com

Aspen is one company poised to capitalize on the demand for next-generation technology to insulate buildings. Aerogel, invented in 1931 but commercialized only recently, is a highly insulating material that's the lightest material known to science. Aspen, with big VC backing in its coffers, is working on nanotechnology breakthroughs to make aerogel more cost competitive with traditional insulators. Lux Research, a leading nanotech researcher, named Aspen one of 2006's most attractive nanotech start-ups for large companies seeking innovative partners.

Clarum Homes
Palo Alto, California
www.clarum.com

Clarum began building homes with solar electric power in 1999 and remains a leader in energy-efficient design among production-scale residential builders. Its Enviro-Home, dating back to 2002, gets high ratings for efficiency, green building materials, and progress toward the goal of net-zero energy usage. Every new residence Clarum builds is an Enviro-Home. With most of its business in California, Clarum is well positioned to profit from the state's mandated financial incentives in its Million Solar Roofs program and landmark GHG reduction legislation. And as the real estate market softens, Clarum has a creative clean-tech take on the latest trend of home builders and realtors giving away cars and plasma TVs to lure buyers. In one Clarum development, buying an Enviro-Home gets you a free Toyota Prius hybrid.

Cree
Durham, North Carolina
www.cree.com
NASDAQ: CREE

Cree is a midsized public company going toe-to-toe with global giants such as GE, OSRAM, and Philips in the market for lighting using LED technology, the most energy-efficient lighting method. But that advanced technology comes at a price; LEDs are still considerably more expensive (at least in up-front costs) than compact fluorescent or traditional incandescent bulbs. That could change by around 2012. Cree is well positioned with several key patents and products, but this sector remains a longer-term play.

The Durst Organization
New York
www.durst.org

A true green-building pioneer, this influential Big Apple developer opened the world's first environmentally designed skyscraper, the Condé Nast building at Four Times Square, even before the LEED rating system debuted in 2000. Durst had the first green skyscraper and is now codeveloping the biggest, the 54-story Bank of America Tower at One Bryant Park. Principals Douglas and Jody Durst, grandsons of Joseph Durst, who started the company in 1915, are leading advocates for green buildings as a smart, leading-edge investment. Their activities are widely followed by large commercial developers in New York and other key cities worldwide.

Interface Engineering
Portland, Oregon
www.interfaceengineering.com

Although its engineering design consultancy dates back to the 1960s, Interface's current practice exemplifies the new breed of firms providing expertise on green design and energy efficiency worldwide. Most of its projects are in the eco-conscious Pacific Northwest, but its influence is spreading, thanks to pioneering work on the "green premium" cost factors of green buildings—namely, that it can be minimal. Its budget-conscious work on Oregon Health & Science University's Center for Health & Healing, expected to earn LEED's highest rating of Platinum, is considered a model for others to deliver highly efficient buildings without big added costs.

Ortech
Braeside, Victoria, Australia
www.ortech.com.au

Ortech pioneered the manufacture of ceiling and wall panels from wheat or rice straw, replacing traditional drywall. It's a fast-growing exemplar of the diverse business sector of converting waste products to clean, energy-efficient building materials. Its Durra brand products are used in sports arenas, Hilton hotels, IMAX theaters, and three Australian airports. Ortech's U.S. arm is Durra Building Materials (www.durra.com) in Whitewright, Texas.

PanaHome
Osaka, Japan
www.panahome.jp/english
Tokyo Stock Exchange: 6752

Publicly traded with two Matsushita companies as major shareholders, PanaHome is Japan's leading residential builder specializing in healthy, energy-efficient homes. The $2.3 billion company was the first home builder in Japan, the world's second-largest solar-energy market behind Germany, to offer prefabricated homes with solar cell arrays. Its Eco-Life Homes now represent about 35% of its portfolio.

Rinnai
Nagoya, Japan
www.rinnai.co.jp
Tokyo Stock Exchange: 5947

The world's largest manufacturer of gas appliances, Rinnai is a leader in energy-saving products, especially game-changing devices such as the tankless water heater. Instead of keeping large amounts of water heated around the clock "just in case," the tankless device from Rinnai (and other global players such as Bosch, Noritz, and Rheem) heats water on demand, cutting energy use by anywhere from 10% to 70%. The big pitch to consumers is that "the hot water never runs out." It's a big seller in Japan and Europe that's catching on in the United States, where Rinnai is stepping up marketing efforts to capitalize on the current growth in energy-efficient home design.

Turner Construction
New York
www.turnerconstruction.com/greenbuildings

More than a century old, Turner Construction, a unit of Turner Corporation of Dallas, Texas, first identified green building as a growth opportunity in 1995. More large construction firms are entering the sector now, but Turner remains a leader, with more than 100 green and/or LEED-certified buildings around the world. Its stable of green buildings includes the David L. Lawrence Convention Center in Pittsburgh, the world's largest LEED project at 1.5 million square feet, and several headquarters buildings for Fortune 500 companies.

Wal-Mart Stores
Bentonville, Arkansas
www.walmartstores.com
New York Stock Exchange: WMT

Wal-Mart certainly raised some eyebrows with its massive energy-efficiency initiative launched in late 2005 and expanded and formalized as "Sustainability 360" in February 2007. What was America's most visible symbol of low-price, big-box unsustainability and controversial labor relations really up to, talking about saving energy and reducing GHGs? Wal-Mart CEO Lee Scott says the company will invest $500 million a year in efficiency, waste elimination, and GHG-reduction efforts in store and warehouse design, operations, and transportation. The world's largest retailer is also using its market pull to give preference (like prime shelf space) to those among its 60,000 suppliers who set their own efficiency goals. The company's first experimental energy-efficient stores in McKinney, Texas, and Aurora, Colorado, use on-site solar and wind power, LED lights in grocery cases, captured rainwater, daylighting, and other technologies to cut resource use by (so far) 10% or more. Whether Wal-Mart will really make good on its goals remains to be seen, but even small efficiency improvements will have a huge multiplier effect because of the company's size and market influence.

5

PERSONAL TRANSPORTATION

Designing Ultra-Efficient, Low-Emissions, High-Performance Vehicles

It's a beautiful day for a drive just north of San Francisco in Marin County, California. Rays of the late-afternoon January sun, beaming between purple-gray clouds like stage lighting, frame stunning vistas of majestic Mount Tamalpais. But behind the wheel of the Toyota Prius that he's converted to a plug-in hybrid, Ron Gremban isn't paying attention to any of it. "Look at that!" he says, pointing to the mid-dashboard graphic display showing how much kinetic energy from the car's brakes is going to recharge its batteries. "Thirty-five amps of regenerative braking. That's all energy that's not being wasted." Elsewhere on the screen is the most important number: on the current tank of gas, the car's getting 79.5 mpg.

Back in 1968 as an engineering student at California Institute of Technology, Gremban helped design and drive an electric battery-powered Volkswagen bus, the "Voltswagen," from Los Angeles to Boston to win the Great Electric Car Race against a team from MIT. Today he's leader of technology development for the California Cars Initiative (CalCars), a nonprofit group of engineers and marketers working with auto and component manufacturers to promote the plug-in hybrid—a standard gas–electric hybrid like the Prius, equipped with extra batteries and a plug-in module enabling the use of household electricity to charge them.

Unlike regular hybrids that use a gasoline engine in combination with an electric motor most of the time, plug-ins can run on purely electric power—delivered in an overnight battery charge from a standard home wall socket—for the first 25 to 30 miles of local driving speeds. That means virtually no gasoline burned for driving around town, which constitutes the vast majority of vehicle use around the world. "GAS OPT," reads Gremban's license plate. The technology delivers dramatic cuts in hybrid vehicle fuel consumption—50% to 70% better than a standard Prius, which is already pretty stingy. And if the extra battery charge runs out or you forgot to plug it in, the car operates like a regular hybrid, with the gas engine charging the battery and kicking in for power when needed. So there's no limited-range problem, a deal-killer for the all-electric vehicles (EVs) on the market in the 1990s that never grew beyond a small niche. A number of technology innovators and political leaders have even talked about pairing a plug-in hybrid with flex-fuel technologies (a fuel tank that can run on a mix of up to 85% ethanol and 15% petrol gasoline). In this type of vehicle, you might drive up to *500 miles* before burning up a gallon of petrol-based gasoline. That makes it, if you will, a true "hybrid" hybrid—and one that we see as one of the greatest potential breakthroughs, and business opportunities, in vehicle efficiency.

Welcome to today's world of clean-tech transportation, a world full of vast business and investment opportunities and fraught with high risk. Designing ultra-efficient, low-emissions vehicles to serve the mobility needs of the carbon-constrained, high-oil price years and decades ahead is truly one of industry's biggest challenges. These trends have already shaken up the global automobile industry, which cranks out 65 million new vehicles a year, in a major way, rewarding sellers of efficient vehicles and even opening the door for start-up clean-car companies in one of the world's highest entry-barrier businesses.

Motorized transportation is a broad and diverse industry, comprising aviation, boats and ships of all sizes, passenger and freight locomotives, light rail, buses, long-haul trucks, and many other forms of conveyance. But we believe that the most compelling opportunities for clean tech—and many of the biggest challenges—come in the world of personal transportation. That's the focus of this chapter.

THE NAME OF THE GAME: FUEL EFFICIENCY

There are nearly 800 million cars and light trucks on the road today worldwide, and the new consumers of China, India, and other growing nations are joining the ranks of the world's car owners at a breakneck pace. Current market growth rates will place 1 billion cars on the roads of the world by 2020, and if China ever reaches American ownership rates of three vehicles for every four people, it alone will have 1.1 billion cars by 2031. In the United States, according to J.D. Power and Associates, only 1% of cars are purchased by first-time buyers; in China, it's *84%*. The U.S. Department of Energy's Energy Information Administration projects that 43% of the world's increase in oil demand between 2003 and 2030 will come from China, India, and the other developing nations of Asia. At that rate, neither affordable petroleum resources nor livable CO_2 levels can be sustained without significant changes in vehicle technology. That presents the opportunity for a wide range of large and small players, from the world's largest auto companies to start-up suppliers of efficient batteries and carbon-composite materials to reduce vehicle weight.

Improvements in vehicle fuel efficiency present a huge opportunity for auto manufacturers and their suppliers, particularly in the United States. Enviro-zealots love to single out SUVs, but average gas mileage standards across the *entire* U.S. vehicle fleet are the lowest among all of the world's industrial countries or regions. The current average gas mileage for the U.S. auto and light truck fleet is 20.8 mpg (in 2004, the last full year for which data is available), whereas the European Union and Japan currently average about *double* that, at 40 mpg and 46 mpg, respectively, according to the Pew Center on Global Climate Change. Even China has stricter fuel-efficiency standards than the United States, with requirements averaging 35 mpg. In the United States, the corporate average fuel economy measure of miles per gallon has actually *dropped* since 1987, when it was 22.0 mpg, going in the opposite direction of almost every other country. In the United States, only California has plans to try to catch up with other nations. Even so, at current projections, it won't even match China's 2008 targets until 2016.

BREAKTHROUGH OPPORTUNITY

Carbon-Composite Materials

The new Boeing 787 Dreamliner, dubbed "Boeing's Plastic Dream Machine" by *Business Week* because of its extensive use of carbon fiber composites, has been one of the fastest-selling jets in commercial aviation history. Could composites—the stuff of tennis rackets, high-performance skis, and bicycles—have a similar impact on next-generation car and light-truck design? Carbon fiber weighs just one fifth as much as the steel it replaces, but it's so strong that today's Formula 1 race cars *require* it in the auto body. Fuel efficiency mavens such as the Rocky Mountain Institute's Amory Lovins have been pushing composites for years—a 10% drop in auto weight improves fuel economy by 7%—and many industry R&D efforts are under way. A Ford–GM–DaimlerChrysler consortium is working with the Polymer Matrix Composites Group at the U.S. Department of Energy's Oak Ridge National Laboratory to break the biggest barrier to widespread carbon-fiber use in mainstream vehicle design: cost. Prices today are $8 to $10 per pound; they'd have to drop to $3 to $5 per pound to compete with steel. Solving the cost issue presents a lucrative tech opportunity for companies ranging from GM to Atmospheric Glow Technologies, a University of Tennessee spinoff whose plasma-processing technology could dramatically cut carbon-fiber production costs.

There are many factors behind the financial woes of Ford and GM, but their lack of leadership (until very recently) on fuel efficiency has clearly bitten them as gas prices have shot up. "I think it's now clear to virtually everyone in Detroit that if our government had had the courage ten years ago to raise mileage standards, they might not be in quite the level of complete economic meltdown they're in today," says Christopher Flavin, president of the Worldwatch Institute, an environmental research nonprofit in Washington, D.C.

Ford, DaimlerChrysler, and especially GM are now putting much more R&D and marketing muscle behind vehicles that run on something besides gasoline—primarily ethanol or electric power. Whether it's real high-volume commitment or too-little-too-late lip service remains to be seen, and many in the clean-tech and environmental communities, burned by years of false hopes and broken promises from the Big Three, are understandably skeptical. But the companies seem to recognize that current and future shareholder value (and possibly, in Ford's case, survival) depends at least partially on producing much cleaner, more fuel-efficient vehicles, and they're pursuing a range of potentially breakthrough technologies to make it happen. "GM will be one hundred years old in 2008, and for the entire time our products have been ninety-nine to one hundred percent petroleum-based," says Tony Posawatz, vehicle line director in charge of electric-powered cars and trucks at GM's Warren Technology Center in Warren, Michigan. "That's not a good business strategy going forward."

In 2006, Ford turned to an auto industry outsider, former Boeing executive vice president Alan Mulally, to reverse its dwindling fortunes. Mulally brought not only an industry outsider's fresh perspective to Ford's CEO job but also a keen sense that focusing on fuel efficiency can play a key role in reversing an American industrial icon's decline against foreign competition. At the end of Mulally's tenure at Boeing, for the first time in 6 years, the aircraft manufacturer had more planes ordered in a 6-month period (the first half of 2006) than its longtime European nemesis Airbus, mainly on the strength of its new 787 commercial jet. Known as the Dreamliner, the 300-seat 787 championed by Mulally is the most fuel-efficient long-distance commercial plane ever built. Its revolutionary wing and fuselage design contains 50% plastic composites, which include resins and fibers of carbon, boron, graphite, and glass; they're used today in high-end bicycle frames and top-of-the-line sports cars. The most advanced commercial aircraft in the sky today use no more than 25% composites. Lighter, stronger, longer-lasting, and easier to maintain than traditional aluminum alloy, the composites (and other design advances) will help Boeing's twin-engine 787 use 20% less fuel and cost 10% less to maintain than comparably sized planes. Airlines plan for it to begin flying commercially in mid-2008.

Airbus found itself plagued by management turmoil and manufacturing delays in 2006, but aviation analysts say that the European aircraft maker's woes were at least partially strategic. Airbus lost its lead when it did not put the same emphasis on fuel efficiency in its new designs as Boeing did, focusing instead on the hulking, double-deck, 555-seat A380 and the A350, more comparable to the 787 in size but without as much use of composites and other energy-saving technologies.

"What do you do when fuel is the price of champagne?" Boeing asked in a three-page ad in *Aviation Week* in 2006. Oil may not be there yet, but as its price neared $80 a barrel in the summer of 2006, Boeing's efficiency strategy was clearly paying off with its customers—the increasingly fuel cost–conscious airlines around the world. As Ford's new CEO, Mulally calls enhancing fuel efficiency one of the company's biggest short-term challenges. "With the business environment we have," he told *Business Week* in September 2006, "higher oil prices will be with us for a while."

Another huge segment of the personal transportation sector, often overlooked in the United States, is the worldwide market for single-passenger vehicles: motorbikes, mopeds, scooters, motorcycles, and tuk-tuks—the popular Southeast Asian conveyance that's essentially a motorized rickshaw. These vehicles may be relatively fuel-efficient compared with large cars and SUVs, but emissions are another story. Tuk-tuks, older-model Vespa scooters, and other motorbikes often use two-stroke engines—one of the world's dirtiest internal-combustion technologies. In the two-stroke process, the engine's lubricant is burned along with the fuel, so normal operation produces the same belching, bluish smoke as an old junker car that's "burning oil"—as anyone who's spent time choking in a Bangkok traffic jam can tell you. The CO_2 emissions are high too—even higher than for SUVs, some have claimed, although there haven't been solid scientific studies. Whatever the actual comparative pollution level, we see a huge business opportunity in cleaner technologies for the nearly $40 billion worldwide motorcycle–motorbike–scooter market, and several companies in the United States and overseas are moving aggressively to meet that need.

HYBRID ELECTRIC VEHICLES, PLUG-IN HYBRID ELECTRIC VEHICLES, AND ALL-ELECTRIC VEHICLES

The auto industry's biggest challenge is the transition away from petroleum (traditional gasoline and diesel) as vehicles' primary power source to two different forms of energy: electricity and biofuels. In chapter 3 ("Biofuels and Biomaterials: Developing Next-Generation Refineries and Feedstocks"), we covered the business challenges and opportunities in producing ethanol, biodiesel, and other biofuels to power millions of vehicles. This chapter will focus primarily on the opportunities from the use of electric power to augment, and in some cases completely replace, the gasoline engine. "Hybrid electric vehicles usually outperform their conventional counterparts, which a lot of people find hard to believe," says Bill Rankin, president and CEO of UQM Technologies, a vehicle electric motor supplier in Frederick, Colorado. "In terms of energy delivered to the vehicle, gasoline engines are only twenty-seven percent efficient, and diesels, thirty-three percent, because most energy is wasted as heat. By contrast, electric motors deliver ninety-four percent efficiency to the vehicle."

Electric power is not the only path to a cleaner, more efficient vehicle, but we believe that it encompasses most of the key growth and investment opportunities for clean vehicles in the near- to mid-term. Electric vehicles also include the long-hyped and much-debunked hydrogen fuel-cell vehicle (FCV), because a fuel cell essentially produces electric power from its fuel source. Briefly, these are the four categories of vehicles we'll examine in more depth below:

- **HEVs.** On the market for several years now and rapidly gaining mainstream acceptance, hybrid electric vehicles (HEVs) have helped Toyota and (more recently) Honda boost market share and market capitalization value. They're one of the great clean-tech business success stories to date and an immediate market opportunity for current players who are ramping up production and rolling out new models. "Hybrid models will eventually become the new automotive standard," wrote global investment giant Alliance Bernstein in a June 2006 report entitled *The Emergence of Hybrid Vehicles: A Game-Changing Technology with Big Implications*. But we view them, to an extent, as a precursor to even more efficient, lower-emissions vehicles in the other two electric-vehicle categories.
- **PHEVs.** Plug-in hybrid electric vehicles (PHEVs) are on the verge of a transition from the domain of "Prius hackers" reengineering hybrids into plug-in models in their garages to the production lines of global automakers. That opens up compelling growth opportunities for entrepreneurs (and their investors) to work with the big companies on battery technologies and other key components. GM surprised many industry observers by being the first automaker to announce PHEV

production plans, unveiling a plug-in version of the Saturn VUE hybrid SUV at the Los Angeles Auto Show in November 2006. "There finally seems to be momentum among the big car companies for the plug-in concept," says veteran clean-vehicle observer Jim Motavalli, editor of *E, the Environmental Magazine* and author of *Forward Drive: The Race to Build "Clean" Cars for the Future* (Sierra Club Books, 2001).

- **EVs.** "Who killed the electric car?" asked the title of an acclaimed 2006 documentary film about U.S. automakers' pulling the plug on their electric vehicles (EVs) in the early 2000s. Now the car's response might be a line from another movie, of the Monty Python variety: "I'm not dead yet!" New entrepreneurial developments at both the high and low end of the market, from Silicon Valley to Norway to India (and even in Detroit), suggest exciting new potential for the EV.
- **FCVs.** The saga of the much-hyped "hydrogen economy," based on cars powered by hydrogen fuel cells, could fill an entire book—and has, more than once. Our assessment of the near-term growth and investment opportunities in fuel-cell vehicles (FCVs) is fairly skeptical, but we recognize it's a "wild card" sector where big breakthroughs are certainly possible. Honda's sleek new hydrogen-fueled FCX Concept, rolled out at the 2006 Los Angeles Auto Show, brings the long-promised technology closer to wide-scale commercial reality. But reaching affordable price points and building a widely accessible hydrogen-fueling infrastructure remain huge challenges.

EVs and PHEVs that draw power from a charging station or standard wall socket have raised the question: Is that really clean energy? Sure, emissions and fossil-fuel consumption are dramatically reduced on the road, say skeptics, but what if the electrons charging your battery overnight are coming from a dirty coal plant? Is that really cleaner than burning the equivalent gasoline? In a word, yes. Studies by a number of agencies, including the Electric Power Research Institute (EPRI), Argonne National Laboratory, and the California Air Resources Board have all concluded that running cars on electricity from today's U.S. power grid (that is, about 50% coal-fired), instead of gas or diesel, reduces overall GHG emissions anywhere from 22% to 61%. A big reason why: most battery-charging takes place overnight, when power demand drops dramatically and utilities have excess generating capacity, an effect known as "valley filling." A December 2006 study by the U.S. Department of Energy's Pacific Northwest National Laboratory (PNNL) concluded that such off-peak utility generation and transmission could power 84% of the 220 million vehicles in the United States if they were PHEVs.

If you live in a region where more wind or hydroelectric generates the juice—or it's coming from your own rooftop solar panels—your electric-car advantage is even better. With the market share of clean energy rising around the world, the advantages of grid power versus petroleum will continue to improve. "PHEVs and EVs are the only cars that get cleaner as they get older," says CalCars founder Felix Kramer, "because the grid gets cleaner every decade." And you can't beat the cost savings. At an average utility rate of 10 cents per kilowatt-hour, you're paying the equivalent of about 60 cents a gallon to run on electricity.

HYBRID ELECTRIC VEHICLES: SQUARELY IN THE MAINSTREAM

Today's gas–electric hybrid cars have been called the most significant innovation in the auto industry since the automatic transmission—some even say since the gasoline engine replaced the Stanley Steamer. J.D. Power and Associates predicted that hybrid sales in the United States would top 400,000 in 2007, nearly a sixfold increase from 70,000 just 3 years earlier. Families driving a 45-miles-per-gallon Toyota Prius today get legroom and cargo space comparable to that of a Camry sedan, Toyota's worldwide best seller (which has a hybrid version of its own, launched in 2006—the first Toyota hybrid built in the United States, in Georgetown, Kentucky). Or they can choose a hybrid full-size sedan (the Camry or a Honda Accord), small SUV (Ford Escape or GM Saturn VUE), large SUV (Toyota Highlander, Mercury Mariner), full-size luxury SUV (Lexus RX 400h), or pickup truck (Chevy Silverado).

That's just a sampling, and there'll be many more hybrid models in the next few years. Nissan, after lagging fellow Japanese competitors Toyota and Honda, finally released a hybrid Altima in 2007 with technology licensed from Toyota and will develop its own HEV technology for vehicles aimed at the 2010 model year. But bear in mind that not all hybrids are created equal. Many, notably the Lexus models, use the electric motor more for its power boost to the gasoline engine than to run as often as possible in emissions-free electric mode. That can mean very little improvement in gas mileage or emissions compared with the nonhybrid counterpart model; you're paying the hybrid premium for extra power (and perhaps pride of HEV ownership). Hybrid-electric is a flexible technology adaptable to many different market segments, but not all HEVs are as clean as others. Regardless, it's a huge potential market. AllianceBernstein, one of the world's largest publicly traded asset management firms with some $660 billion in assets, is particularly bullish on the sector. The firm predicts that hybrids (including plug-ins) will comprise 50% of global new car sales by 2015 and a stunning 85% by 2030.

Sometimes the financial advantage of a HEV goes beyond savings on fuel expense. Hybrid buyers in the United States get a federal tax credit of between $250 and $3,150, depending on the HEV model. And people working at a growing number of high-tech firms and other companies, including Google, HP, Timberland, and Yahoo!, receive up to $5,000 from their employer toward the purchase of the highest-mileage hybrids.

The appeal of hybrids, and their breakneck sales growth, has extended far beyond the green-minded and has proven there needn't be a trade-off between fuel efficiency and performance. *Motor Trend* magazine, Detroit's bible of speed and style since 1949, bestowed its coveted Car of the Year honor on Toyota's Prius in 2003, Honda's lineup of Civics (including the hybrid) 2 years later, and the Toyota Camry, including its hybrid version, in 2007. These honors didn't come just because the hybrids save gas. "The Prius is a capable, comfortable, fun-to-drive car that just happens to get spectacular fuel economy," wrote then editor-in-chief Kevin Smith. "It also provides a promising look at a future where extreme fuel-efficiency, ultra-low emissions, and exceptional performance will happily coexist." No trade-off at all—it's just a better car. It's helped put Toyota on pace to surpass GM as the world's largest automaker; the company expects to sell 1 million hybrids annually worldwide by 2010.

"When we launched the Prius in the U.S. in July 2000, the star of the Detroit Auto Show earlier that year was the Hummer H2," says Celeste Migliore, national marketing manager of advanced technology vehicles for Toyota USA in Torrance, California. "Hybrids were an unknown quantity. Now the Prius has become our 'halo' for the Toyota brand, and we're branding our Hybrid Synergy Drive technology across all models." Toyota, which initially eschewed traditional advertising for the Prius, clearly caught a wave of market forces that place it an enviable position moving forward as HEVs, PHEVs, and EVs evolve. "Our feeling is that we don't create demand, we facilitate it," says Migliore. "It's really hard to *make* a product cool. You can't do it—your customers have to do it."

Hybrid car production is also booming in China (along with overall auto manufacturing there), with Toyota, Hyundai, and Volkswagen all producing hybrids in partnership with local Chinese carmakers. They have plenty of competition from China's own manufacturers. At least five—Dongfeng, Chery, Geely, Chang'an, and China FAW—planned to start manufacturing and selling hybrids in China by early 2007.

BREAKTHROUGH OPPORTUNITY

Next-Generation Batteries

Short of the daunting task of starting your own car company (we'll get to that later in the chapter), where's the opportunity for clean-tech entrepreneurs and their investors to capitalize on the growth of hybrid and electric vehicles sold by the world's automotive giants? Those giants are all looking for breakthroughs in the batteries that store and deliver the electric power needed to run the car. With some notable exceptions, PHEVs and EVs in particular are generally evolving from the nickel–metal hydride (NiMH) batteries of today's Prius to lighter-weight, greater-power-density lithium-ion batteries—the same technology powering most laptop computers, cell phones, and iPods. Lithium-ion batteries seem to hold the most promise because they store about twice the energy as the equivalent weight of NiMH batteries currently used in the Prius. Their traditional problem is they heat up too much (the engineers call it "thermal runaway"), but some pioneering battery manufacturers are using new materials such as phosphates and nanotechnologies to address the heat problem and reduce weight as well. The challenge and opportunity is scaling up lithium-ion technology to store and deliver enough power to run a car, while controlling thermal runaway. It's a growing sector attracting large and small companies, including A123 Systems in Watertown, Massachusetts; Valence Technology in Austin, Texas; Altairnano in Reno, Nevada; Electrovaya in Mississauga, Ontario, Canada; VARTA in Hannover, Germany; and Saft in Paris, France. (The latter two are part of a joint venture with Johnson Controls to supply batteries for DaimlerChrysler's PHEV Sprinter van). Electro Energy in Danbury, Connecticut, is aiming for both the EV and electric scooter market with its next-generation "bipolar" NiMH battery design, while Firefly Energy in Peoria, Illinois, a spinoff from Caterpillar, hopes to serve the EV market with a transformed lead–acid battery design that replaces the lead with graphite foam. Then there's EEStor in Cedar Park, Texas, known as one of Kleiner Perkins's most secretive investments. EEStor is looking to replace batteries altogether with a ceramic, aluminum oxide, and glass energy-storage device that could power high-performance electric sports cars. It's a big-risk, big-reward bet, but Kleiner Perkins is known for those.

PLUG-IN HYBRID ELECTRIC VEHICLE: THE NEXT BIG THING?

Many believe that PHEVs represent one of the best transportation growth opportunities in the near- to mid-term. Calling plug-in technology "truly game-changing," AllianceBernstein predicts that lithium-ion batteries will gain the necessary power capability and fall in price before 2012, paving the way for widespread PHEV commercialization. "Plug-in hybrids represent a real near-term solution to America's overreliance on foreign oil imports and energy prices that escalate the cost of everything and threaten the very economic life of our nation," said Austin, Texas, mayor Will Wynn at the January 2006 launch of Plug-In Partners, a coalition of businesses, utilities, and more than 40 U.S. cities formed to demonstrate a ready market for PHEVs. Austin offered $1 million worth of rebates in 2006 to help its citizens and businesses buy plug-in hybrids when they're commercially available; advocates are pushing to make that happen in the next several years.

GM, Ford, and Toyota all disclosed in the first half of 2006 that they're working on plug-in hybrid development. Then GM stole a march on its rivals by rolling out its Saturn VUE plug-in plans, albeit without any production targets or timetable, at the 2006 Los Angeles Auto Show in November. "GM and Toyota are both saying they want to be first in plug-ins," says CalCars' Kramer. "It's good to have a horse race."

GM took another interesting tack in that race at the Detroit Auto Show in January 2007. After pouring some $1 billion into R&D for hydrogen FCVs still years from wide commercialization, GM signaled a new direction toward an electric future with the E-flex platform, a plug-in hybrid with a twist. Instead of the common HEV configuration of a gasoline engine and electric motor both powering the car's wheels at different times or in combination, the E-flex chassis uses 100% electric power from its batteries for propulsion. A small 1-liter, three-cylinder gas engine is used only to power the onboard generator. In other words, the serial (rather than parallel) hybrid design operates as an electric car all the time, not just at low speeds. GM committed to the E-flex for production (though without a timetable), but the first model on the platform, the four-door Chevy Volt sport coupe, is only a concept car. The platform is "flex" because GM says it can accommodate a flexible ethanol mix in the gas engine, a hydrogen fuel cell to power the batteries, or other variations.

"Instead of a singular architecture with fuel cells, we'll have a platform that can share a lot of stuff," says Posawatz, a GM vehicle line veteran whose previous rollouts included not-so-clean gas hogs such as the Chevrolet Avalanche and Cadillac EXT. "That's much more of an intriguing business proposition." GM's also opening the door to innovators in the battery sector, looking to form a team or partnership with companies that can crack the price, power-delivery, and heat-control barriers in lithium-ion technology. It could be an ambitious bet with a big payoff for GM, but its track record in clean tech leaves many skeptical. "We're very pleased that they've put a stake in the ground here," says CalCars' Kramer, "but they could go for a decade saying it's not ready."

Meanwhile, PHEVs from DaimlerChrysler are already on the road in customer tests of the Sprinter passenger van. Testers include the South Coast Air Quality Management District in Southern California, the Kansas City Power Authority, and the New York Times Company. It's a true test—the 40 vans include some with gasoline engines, some with diesel, some using lithium-ion batteries, and others using NiMH. DaimlerChrysler has no current plans for volume production, says Loren Beard, the company's senior manager of environment and energy planning.

To be sure, plug-in hybrids face technical challenges, especially the development of next-generation batteries to improve storage of the electricity that powers the car in its initial all-electric mode—and make it more affordable. But PHEV advocates say we're not too far away, and as noted above, a lot of R&D efforts and VC dollars are pursuing the opportunity. "I don't think we need new show-stopper technology; we just need to improve what we have," says Kramer. "It's a question of chemistry, not physics." In the meantime, while waiting for PHEVs from the auto companies, some entrepreneurs have found a niche in selling plug-in conversion kits to current HEV owners. Companies offering such kits include EnergyCS (under the brand EDrive) in Monrovia, California; Hybrids Plus in Boulder, Colorado; and Hymotion in Concord, Ontario, Canada. But it isn't cheap—a typical conversion runs $10,000 to $12,000.

BREAKTHROUGH OPPORTUNITY

Flex-Fuel Plug-Ins

Which is a better and cleaner growth opportunity, a flex-fuel vehicle (FFV) that can run on up to 85% ethanol (100% in Brazil), or a plug-in hybrid humming along on electricity for drives around town? Why not combine both? This is the ultimate in fuel efficiency for the internal-combustion engine; it's been estimated that a PHEV with flex-fuel capability, running on E85, can get 400 to 500 miles per gallon of the 15% petroleum gasoline in the tank. This is the vision outlined by two U.S. national security experts who are now clean-tech mavens, R. James Woolsey (ex-head of the Central Intelligence Agency) and Robert "Bud" McFarlane (national security advisor to President Ronald Reagan), who rightly note that both the ethanol and the electricity are produced domestically. Silicon Valley Business Leaders for Alternative Energy, a who's who of the high-tech CEO digerati, has joined the chorus as well. They're calling for a crash government program to encourage development of FFV PHEVs, but their interest suggests a funding and market opportunity for those who can commercialize the technology. Ford tantalized some in early 2006 with its intention to develop a flex-fuel version of its Escape hybrid SUV, but it's only a concept vehicle—and not a plug-in. This opportunity is wide open.

ELECTRIC VEHICLES: NO LONGER A TRADE-OFF

Electric cars of the past usually involved asking people to make a trade-off. With some notable exceptions such as GM's EV-1 car and Toyota's RAV-4 small electric SUV, most commercial electric cars developed in the 1990s had limited range of 150 miles or less on a battery charge, acceleration that most drivers would call wimpy, small size, and styling (or lack thereof) that appealed only to the extreme alternative-lifestyle demographic. For many reasons—some alleged by environmental activists to be conspiratorial—most automakers stopped making commercial electric cars by the early 2000s. Some EVs are still on the road and the technology has a very loyal following, but it has been little more than a tiny blip in the global vehicle market. Until now.

Tesla Motors, Silicon Valley's first auto company, is out to prove that the all-electric car can be high-performance, sexy, and profitable. The $92,000 Tesla Roadster sports car, powered by more than 6,300 tiny lithium-ion batteries charged from a home socket, does 0 to 60 in 4 seconds. It's caught major buzz among California's well-heeled high-tech crowd, selling out its first production run of 250 cars in a few months, with the company now ramping up to build a few thousand. The cars were scheduled to hit the road in late 2007. *Forbes* called it "the new car that best lived up to the hype" in 2006.

Tesla CEO and cofounder Martin Eberhard, a successful high-tech entrepreneur, is out to chart a dramatic new future for EVs that's light-years away from what he calls the "ugly pathetic little cars" of the 1990s. "Electric vehicles in the past were designed by people who viewed driving as a necessary evil," he says. "We wanted to build a car that doesn't force you to make a choice between performance and efficiency." Tesla is starting at the high end of the market with the Roadster, then plans to get broader and cheaper with a five-passenger, all-electric sedan selling for $50,000 to $65,000 in 2009. It's aiming to build and sell 10,000 to 30,000 of those annually. "As an entrepreneur I've learned that the right time to enter a market is when your product is just barely possible," says Eberhard. "If it's really easy, then you're too late."

We agree with the business potential of Eberhard's vision. But we're even more intrigued by the opportunity, exemplified by Tesla, of EV technology (and its variations) enabling a whole new type of car company.

Rather than trying to beat the world's auto giants at their own game, as last century's visionaries, such as Preston Tucker and John DeLorean, tried to do and ultimately failed, Tesla and other EV manufacturers are carving out a whole new business opportunity and model inspired by Silicon Valley. Tesla will eschew a dealer network, for example, and own its service centers, but is partnering with a range of technology providers (such as British race car legend Lotus for the Roadster chassis) in designing its car. And it's working on deals with solar PV installers, such as Solar City in Foster City, California, to jointly sell both the Roadster and the clean-energy source—rooftop solar panels—that can power it at your home.

Taking the new-model, high-tech car company concept a step further, several efforts are under way around the world to design new, clean, ultra-efficient vehicles in a collaborative, open-source process. Initiatives such as the Germany-based OScar (www.theoscarproject.com) and the Open Source Green Vehicle (www.osgv.org) are tapping the expertise of hundreds of engineers worldwide to create a fuel-efficient, next-generation vehicle. The Rocky Mountain Institute has followed this model for some time, placing its Hypercar hydrogen FCV design in the public domain for improvement and tweaking by outside collaborators. We're not sure what these business models or investment opportunities will look like yet. But bringing the open source process from high tech to the auto industry is an exciting development partially mirrored by the open-source efforts, which we'll explore in the next chapter, to modernize the electrical grid.

Much of the current growth in EV sales is occurring outside the United States. One of the most promising EV manufacturers is REVA Electric Car in Bangalore, India, which has more than 1,000 small electric sedans on the road in India and another 600 in the United Kingdom under the brand GoinGreen. REVA received $20 million in funding in December 2006 from two prominent U.S. investors, the private equity Global Environment Fund and noted VC firm Draper Fisher Jurvetson. Some of the funds will go to expand capacity of REVA's Bangalore production plant from 6,000 cars a year toward its eventual goal of 30,000.

What REVA calls its ElectriCity car is a niche play for urban motorists and commuters, with a top speed of just 40 mph and a range of only 48 miles on a charge. But with London, Rome, Athens, and other cities offering exemptions from their inner-city driving restrictions and "congestion charges"—and free parking—to clean-power vehicles and EVs, start-ups like REVA see a big opportunity. The REVA car uses eight 6-volt lead-acid batteries, but its range could expand as lithium-ion and other battery technologies advance.

FUEL-CELL VEHICLES: "20 YEARS AWAY" DRAWS CLOSER

Recent developments give hope that the wild-card promise of the so-called hydrogen economy for transportation, seemingly 20 years away every year, may be drawing a bit closer. We still believe it's a long-term opportunity—mainly because of the huge costs and logistical challenges of building out an infrastructure for hydrogen fuel distribution and because for now, vehicles powered by grid electricity offer a much better business and investment bet. As GM's Posawatz says, "There is infrastructure for electricity throughout the world that exists today."

Honda says it will make a limited-production hydrogen FCV in 2008, likely based in some measure on its snazzy FCX Concept model shown in late 2006. The company has an earlier-generation FCX in a customer test with a Southern California family. Ford has small numbers (fewer than 50) of fuel cell–powered Focus and Explorer concept vehicles out in tests in the United States, and GM plans to roll out 100 Equinox SUVs with fuel cells in 2007.

But Honda may have the biggest potential breakthrough development in the next generation of its Home Energy Station. The device currently taps into a residential natural gas supply so that owners of Honda's Civic GX, powered by compressed natural gas (CNG) and available in California and New York for about $25,000, can refuel at home. Most hydrogen produced worldwide for industrial and agricultural uses is extracted from natural gas, so Honda is working to duplicate that process in its home device to fuel hydrogen cars. The concept of hydrogen home fueling could help the industry leapfrog the need for a massive overhaul of nationwide filling-station infrastructure. "One can truly start envisioning a future hydrogen economy when you take a look at the Home Energy Station III," writes Tyler Hamilton in his popular clean-tech blog *Clean Break*.

UNSUNG OPPORTUNITY: ELECTRIC MOTORBIKES AND SCOOTERS

Often overlooked in the buzz about EVs, particularly in the United States, is the two- and three-wheel variety—the tens of thousands of battery-powered scooters, mopeds, motorbikes, and bicycles buzzing along the world's roads and streets, mainly in or near cities. These light electric vehicles (LEVs) have been around for years, but current advances in materials, battery, and engine technologies have made electric scooters a hot item for urban commuters, notably in Europe and China.

Today's high-end electric motorbikes can be as snazzy as the Vespa scooter without the price tag and gasoline, are easily recharged at home overnight, can hit increasingly high speeds, and are much quicker than taking the bus. Making a Tesla Motors–like bid to carve out some of the high-end market is start-up Vectrix in Newport, Rhode Island. With Carlo DiBiagio, the former CEO of Italy's legendary Ducati Motor Holding, on board as chief operating officer, Vectrix is billing its vehicle as "the world's first high-performance, all-electric maxi-scooter." It claims a top speed of 62 mph and a range of 68 miles per charge. With an undisclosed equity investment from vehicle systems manufacturer Parker Hannifin, Vectrix plans to launch its scooter first in Italy in 2007. North America, Taiwan, and Southeast Asia will follow. For a product not yet on the market, Vectrix has some pretty good buzz: It earned Frost & Sullivan's Technology Innovation and Leadership Award for 2006.

Mini electric scooters, by comparison, top out at 20 to 25 mph and have a range of 30 miles or less. Some leading players in the United States include Evader in Bellevue, Washington, and EVT America in Miami. But the field is wide open, with lots of room for new innovators and entrepreneurs who can increase speeds and charging times, expand driving range, or cut costs.

Some 75% of the world's LEVs—more than 8 million—are sold annually in China. But there's one problem that potential sellers need to know about. For several controversial reasons, some cities, including China's fifth-largest, Guangzhou, have begun banning LEVs. City officials cite safety concerns and potential pollution from improper disposal of the scooters' lead-acid batteries, but LEV advocates charge that there's been undue influence from automakers, who, they're quick to point out, also use lead-acid batteries in their products. But the LEV industry got very good news when Beijing's city government voted to repeal the capital's ban before it took effect in January 2006, rightly citing LEVs' contribution to relieving vehicle congestion. And Shanghai has no ban, so China's two largest cities remain an open market.

As in electric cars, there's an opportunity for innovators in the battery sector to team up with U.S. and foreign vehicle manufacturers. New York–based Advanced Battery Technologies, for example, is supplying polymer lithium-ion batteries for electric scooters from Taiwan's Ayingsi for the Chinese market. The batteries, using electrode nanomaterials from Altairnano, took only 15 minutes to recharge in a 2006 test, compared with 2 hours or more for most scooter batteries on the market today.

SIGN OF THE TIMES: THE X PRIZE FOR VEHICLES

In 2004, the X PRIZE Foundation awarded $10 million to SpaceShipOne, the winning design for a two-person spacecraft that's opened the door to space travel as a pastime for consumers, albeit very wealthy ones. In 2006, the foundation turned its sights toward clean vehicles, deciding that one of its next multimillion-dollar prizes will go to the best new design of a super-fuel-efficient vehicle. Mark Goodstein of high-tech incubator Idealab became the X PRIZE Foundation's new executive director to lead this effort. "The X PRIZE is about changing paradigms," says Goodstein. "The current paradigm is that it's perfectly acceptable to drive a car that only gets 20 or 30 miles per gallon."

The new paradigm may be hybrid, plug-in hybrid, all-electric, fuel-cell, some combination thereof, or something entirely new. There will be winners and losers in all these sectors, with new entrants already shaking up the personal transportation industry, a trend that's likely to continue. If innovators can figure out how to launch billionaires into space, the idea goes, what about a new, safe, fun, and dramatically better way to drive millions of families to their jobs, schools, and soccer games across the globe in ultra-efficient, low-emissions, high-performance vehicles? Now *that* sounds like a business opportunity.

THE CLEAN-TECH CONSUMER

Car-share. We're not talking about the carpool days of old, but the increasingly popular concept of "car sharing." Talk about a distributed model! Instead of you or your family owning one, two, or three cars (like most Americans), what about having access to a car just when you need it? This is a particularly intriguing and useful concept for folks who live in dense urban areas (where parking can cost as much as a monthly car payment); for families who occasionally need access to an additional car; and for fleet managers for cities and companies. Here's how it works: for a small monthly fee and an hourly/day rate, you can lease a car when you need it. The cars are usually parked within walking blocks of your home or business. There are a number of leading car-share programs, such as Flexcar and Zipcar, sprouting up in cities across the United States.

Scoot around town, cleanly. If you want to motor around your city or town in style, with no engine emissions at all, how about an all-electric motorbike or scooter that you recharge overnight in a standard wall socket? Today's options, increasingly popular in the cities of Europe and Asia, are getting more varied every year. Low-end models (small, low-speed, 30-mile range) from makers such as Evader and EVT America start at just a couple thousand bucks. At the high end, Vectrix's sexy electric maxi-scooter can reach 62 mph (keep that helmet on) and has a range of nearly 70 miles on a battery charge, but you'll face an estimated $7,000 sticker price. Vectrix planned to debut in Italy in 2007, with rollouts in North America and other European countries to follow.

TEN TO WATCH

CalCars
Palo Alto, California
www.calcars.org

Founded in 2002 as the nonprofit California Cars Initiative to promote the development of PHEVs, CalCars is now looking to launch a for-profit venture in the PHEV field. Business possibilities include delivering plug-in conversion kits for HEVs already on the road, licensing PHEV designs to big auto manufacturers, or a number of other variations. But regardless of its future business plans, or whether those plans eventually make money, CalCars will continue to be a key PHEV player to watch for its advocacy, technology leadership, and grass-roots influence in an industry that often needs a good kick from the outside.

Chery

Wuhu, China
www.cheryglobal.com

Although Chery's talks with legendary U.S. auto entrepreneur Malcolm Bricklin to sell the first Chinese car in the United States collapsed in late 2006, Chery's launch of the first Chinese-made hybrid in its home market makes the company a clean-tech notable. The assembled-in-China Toyota Prius is the only HEV available in China today, and thanks to high taxes on Japanese auto parts, its price equates to about $40,000 in U.S. dollars. That's crimping sales in a big way, but Chery hopes that its four-door A5 ISG hybrid sedan, selling for about half that price when it hits the market in 2007, will win over China's fast-growing class of new car buyers. Chery's first-mover advantage will be put to the test quickly, as domestic competitors Chang'an, China FAW, Dongfeng, and Geely all had plans to launch hybrids in China in 2007 or 2008.

EEStor

Cedar Park, Texas

Talk about "stealth mode." As this book went to press, not only did advanced battery developer EEStor decline to talk to the media but it didn't even have a Web site. Yet the company outside Austin is generating quite a buzz around Silicon Valley and elsewhere for its patented ultracapacitor technology that could far surpass lithium-ion batteries in both power and affordability. The resulting potential for clean-vehicle breakthroughs is vast, and that's attracted the likes of VC investor Kleiner Perkins for funding and former Dell vice chairman Morton Topfer to an EEStor board seat.

General Motors
Detroit
www.gm.com
New York Stock Exchange: GM

GM's environmental misdeeds, from commercializing the gas-guzzling Hummer to killing off the innovative EV-1 electric car, are legendary. More recently, the company, founded in 1908, has been accused of sacrificing the hybrid and electric near term for the far-off pipe dream of hydrogen FCVs. But change is coming, likely spurred by billions of dollars in red ink. With the first commercially announced PHEV (the Saturn VUE Green Line) and especially the E-flex platform that delivers 100% electric power to the axles, GM finally signaled a new direction in late 2006 and early 2007. If GM can leverage its massive size for market momentum rather than market inertia, it will definitely be one to watch in clean transportation.

Honda
Tokyo, Japan
www.honda.com
New York Stock Exchange: HMC

Honda brought the first hybrid car to America, the two-seat, funky-looking Insight—still the highest-rated mileage car in the United States Toyota's much more practical Prius grabbed the top hybrid spot in the early 2000s and hasn't looked back, but Honda has jumped back into close contention with the redesigned Civic hybrid and a hybrid version (albeit not with a great mileage improvement) of the top-selling Accord. But Honda's real impact may be longer-term, as it looks to leverage its leadership in cars powered by CNG into the world of hydrogen. Honda is looking to convert its backyard CNG filling station, the Home Energy Station III, to pump hydrogen as well as natural gas. Although it's some years off, that could help solve the chicken-and-egg dilemma of nowhere to refuel hydrogen FCVs as their production expands (and their costs decline) beyond 2010.

REVA Electric Car
Bangalore, India
www.revaindia.com

REVA Electric Car is actually the world's number one producer of EVs. Its small, battery-powered ElectriCity sedans sell mainly in India, with sales growing in the United Kingdom under the brand GoinGreen. REVA has been under the radar in the United States until recently, when a $20 million infusion from VC leader Draper Fisher Jurvetson and the Global Environment Fund private equity manager caught many observers' attention. With a low-priced product and manufacturing ready to ramp up, REVA is well positioned to deliver clean vehicles in fast-growing Asian markets as well as in the increasingly vehicle-restricting cities of Europe and, perhaps beyond 2012, the United States.

Tesla Motors
San Carlos, California
www.teslamotors.com

Like its namesake, twentieth-century electricity pioneer Nikola Tesla, Silicon Valley's first car company is aiming for big breakthroughs in both technology and perception. It's building and selling the world's first commercial all-electric sports car, the $92,000 Tesla Roadster. With high-profile investors including Google founders Sergey Brin and Larry Page, Tesla is bringing high performance, sleek design, and ultrachic cachet to a vehicle category long regarded as tree-hugging and dorky. Tesla has longer-term plans to broaden its market into the tens of thousands with a more moderately priced (though still costly) electric sedan for $50,000 to $65,000 in 2009. And it has opened a new revenue stream, looking to sell its battery-pack technology to other EV companies; potential buyers include Norway's Th!nk Global. Many are watching to see if Tesla can deliver under the spotlight that it has actively courted to date.

Toyota
Toyota City, Japan
www.toyota.com
New York Stock Exchange: TM

Toyota's Prius not only brought HEVs into the automotive mainstream in the United States and around the world, but it also raised the awareness of clean tech and the business success that it can deliver. By pioneering hybrid vehicle systems, Toyota has garnered millions in revenue both from Prius sales and from licensing aspects of its Hybrid Synergy Drive technology to competitors Ford, Nissan, and others. Hybrids and overall leadership on vehicle fuel efficiency helped put Toyota on pace to surpass GM in 2007 as the world's number-one seller of cars and trucks. So now what? In the short term, keep an eye on sales of the hybrid version of the Camry, the perennial top-selling car in the U.S. market; the hybrid Camry is Toyota's first HEV built in the United States. Toyota has been coy to date about its plans for offering a plug-in hybrid option, and GM actually became the first automaker to announce a PHEV model, a plug-in version of the Saturn VUE Green Line hybrid SUV. But we still expect to see a Toyota plug-in on the market first.

Valence Technology
Austin, Texas
www.valence.com
NASDAQ: VLNC

"The battle for batteries" is a critical piece of clean transportation now, with billions of dollars of business at stake. Valence is one of many small companies positioning themselves to deliver the technologies that can make EVs, including hybrids and PHEVs, safe, reliable and affordable. Concept PHEVs have used Valence's phosphate-based, Saphion lithium-ion batteries, which are lighter and store more energy that nickel metal hydride. A smaller form-factor version of the Saphion powers mobile electronics devices, another market with significant business potential for clean alternatives.

Vectrix
Newport, Rhode Island
www.vectrix.com

Tesla Motors may have a kindred spirit in the two-wheeled vehicle world in the form of Vectrix, a flashy start-up bringing snazzy design and all-electric power to so-called maxi-scooters—high-end motorbikes. Vectrix was slated for commercial launch in 2007 in Italy, home of its chief operating officer, former Ducati Motor Holding CEO Carlo DiBiagio. It's aiming for the hip Vespa crowd with a 125-volt, nickel metal hydride battery-powered cycle with a top speed of 62 mph. U.S. launch was expected by the end of 2007. If Vectrix succeeds with its motto of "Cool people drive electric" motto, it (along with Tesla) will help boost the clean transportation market by redefining EV power as cool, hip, and trendy. To add credibility, not to mention capital, Vectrix's investors include the $7 billion global vehicle components manufacturer Parker Hannifin.

6

SMART GRID

Creating an Intelligent, Distributed, Twenty-First-Century Grid

Texas is synonymous with *big*. Not only is it the largest state in the continental United States but also its people rank among the top 10 most obese; the state is home to 3 of the 10 largest cities in the nation; and the state's unofficial motto is "Everything's big in Texas." So it's intriguing to find the appropriately named Richard E. Smalley Institute for Nanoscale Science and Technology located in the heart of Houston at the acclaimed Rice University. Founded in 1993 as the brainchild of the late Nobel Prize winner Richard (Rick) Smalley, who is considered one of the early fathers of nanotechnology, the institute is a global leader in advanced energy and nanotech research.

Before his death from cancer in 2005 at age 62, Smalley and his team came up with a list of the 10 greatest challenges facing humanity. At the top of the list were energy and water, followed by food, environment, poverty, terrorism and war, disease, education, democracy, and population growth. The scientists understood that energy and water stood at the base of many of the other challenges. Without access to clean, reliable, and abundant supplies of each, you would only exacerbate the issues of food, environment, war, disease and so on. The institute, under Smalley's guidance, decided to focus a good deal of its efforts on the intersection of energy and nanotechnology, conducting research, writing papers, and convening meetings.

Smalley, a brilliant, inspired, and tireless researcher and educator, offered an innovative solution to the energy crisis. He painted a vision of a future in which electrical energy would be transported and stored by a vast network of highly efficient and energy-dense nanowires, or what researchers call "armchair quantum wires," which would move electrons over far greater distances than they can travel today. "The problem is that our current wire—copper and aluminum cable—isn't sufficient for sending hundreds of gigawatts from place to place or over thousands of miles," says Dr. Wade Adams, the Smalley Institute's current director. "The average reach of today's grid is closer to two hundred miles, maybe double that. So you aren't currently able to ship energy from sun-rich Arizona to New York City."

Instead of having to transport heavy, polluting, and carbon-based mass (coal, oil, gas), as is done today for the majority of our energy sources, Smalley envisioned an energy future in which both centralized and distributed renewable energy sources could feed into a grid that could carry electrons thousands of miles, say from a wind farm in the Great Plains to the urban masses on the east and west coasts. Electricity would be stored on-site in nano-based batteries and other backup systems at millions of locations connected to the grid. Smalley called this the "distributed storage generation grid."

Can Smalley's vision of a distributed storage generation grid become a reality? In this chapter, we'll look more closely at the potential growth and investment opportunities presented by a nano-enabled electricity grid, along with less ambitious but equally compelling concepts that are dramatically reshaping the utility landscape in the form of a smart grid. We'll uncover a number of companies developing smart meters that can help users and utilities more efficiently track and manage their use of energy and water; companies applying a new generation of demand-side management products and services that replace the need for new fossil fuel–based energy-generation plants; and organizations that are reenvisioning the grid to be more like the Internet, with built-in redundancy and reliability. In all of these developments, and beyond, we will look at the very real opportunity to create jobs, wealth, and economic competitiveness for companies, investors, nations, and regions that lead the way.

FROM THE BOTTOM UP

The industrial shift that's taking place in the delivery of electricity offers a growing range of opportunities for investors, job seekers, companies, utility managers, and others. In particular, we see room for innovation in reworking the grid (the massive infrastructure that enables the transmission and distribution of electrons) to look more like the Internet—a massive two-way network that is flexible, secure, and imminently redundant.

Most of the world's energy today comes from large, centralized, generation facilities, including massive power plants and oil refineries of a size once unimaginable. Utilities and fuel processors have historically worked on a large scale to take advantage of centralized production and to leverage existing distribution networks to deliver their products and services: namely, electrons and liquid and gaseous fuels.

To a large extent, the clean tech revolution will not follow this centralized, top-down approach.

Instead, it will look increasingly like the computer and Internet revolutions that preceded it, embracing the distributed business models made so popular, powerful, and profitable in the 1990s. This new way of sourcing, processing, generating, transmitting, distributing, and storing energy will be driven by a new breed of entrepreneurs, electronics and semiconductor manufacturers, information technology managers, and other trailblazing clean-tech pioneers who look nothing like the oil and utility barons of old. These innovators are pushing the envelope on what many have called end-to-end smart-grid solutions in which intelligence is embedded across the electric utility system: from generation to transmission and distribution to smart appliances and wireless devices.

"Cheap silicon in the field will rewrite the way we manage the electric grid," wrote researchers Roger Anderson and Albert Boulanger in the March 2004 issue of *Mechanical Engineering* magazine. "Widespread wireless computing on every critical node of the Smart Grid will deliver business intelligence. It will incorporate self-healing, self-organizing, Web services, and peer-to-peer computing among networks of connected assets. Each field computer will have enough memory so that it can capture its own best practices and be its own data historian."

Imagine rooftop-based solar modules powering not tens of thousands but tens of *millions* of homes and businesses during the day and storing backup energy for use during electricity shortages and unexpected power outages. Consider advanced fuel-cell systems that provide electricity, hot water, and heat to a home or business and can feed extra electrons into the grid during times of peak demand or meet other demand-side management needs. Envision name-brand refrigerators, washing machines, and other appliances that are smart enough to power up and down to help utility-grid managers deal with the vagaries of volatile supply and demand and to enable consumers to reduce their energy bills. A true bottom-up revolution!

Nancy Floyd, cofounder and managing director of Nth Power, a leading energy technology VC firm in San Francisco, sees big opportunities in this distributed revolution. "Think about renewable and distributed energy once it's at price parity with conventional energy," she explains. "We'll see the Googles of clean energy, the Ciscos of smart intelligence."

BREAKTHROUGH OPPORTUNITY

Smart Appliances

To have a smart grid, you need not only an advanced transmission and delivery infrastructure but also millions of "smart appliances" and devices that are able to communicate with the grid and power up and down on command. Although such systems are still in the development stage, researchers such as Pacific Northwest National Labs (PNNL), Bonneville Power Administration, and Electric Power Research Institute (EPRI) are working to test such systems to enable grid operators to manage the flow of electrons to thousands of devices in the field. The likely winners in this arena will be two groups: the utilities that adopt smart-appliance standards and capabilities and the companies that provide the wireless sensors, software, and intelligence to operate such devices. Invensys Controls (which has developed a technology to enable smart-appliance deployment), IBM, and Whirlpool are just some of the early players that have been working to develop, deploy, and test smart appliances and the communications, computer, and control technologies that enable them. Keep an eye on PNNL's GridWise Alliance, and other test-bed projects (mostly on the U.S. West Coast), to see how these developments unfold and where new opportunities might open up.

GET SMART

One of the biggest potential business opportunities arising from the confluence of clean tech and high tech is the electric utility grid. Not only does the smart grid have the potential for an entrepreneurial business boom along the lines of high tech but it also *incorporates* many of the leading-edge innovations of high tech in the production and delivery of energy and water. The modernization of antiquated energy generation and distribution systems is heeding lessons from the development of the computer, the Internet, and wireless industries, often using these systems for data delivery, processing, and feedback. After years of disregard, utilities are finally beginning to embrace the Information Age. To improve reliability and efficiency, *information* about the generation and usage of electricity and water is becoming as important as the commodities themselves. But the adoption of many of these new technologies has been slow to date; utilities and governing bodies will need to push for smart-grid adoption if we are to see any significant change.

The current North American grid is largely based on technology created and developed more than a century ago. Thomas Edison, Nikola Tesla, and George Westinghouse, the forefathers of the electric industry, would all feel relatively at home with much of today's technology. During the same time period that the Wright brothers' Flyer gave way to supersonic jets and Guglielmo Marconi's first transatlantic radio transmission beget Web streaming and YouTube, the electric grid hasn't changed that much. Of equal concern, the majority of North American grid infrastructure (valued at more than $100 billion) is composed of transmission lines, transformers, and circuit breakers that are 25 to 40 years old and in desperate need of replacement.

As we've learned all too well with recent large-scale blackouts, the current grid is no longer suited to the needs of an information-driven and security-conscious society that requires always-on energy with a high level of reliability. The grid has proven woefully ill prepared to deal with the impacts of hurricanes, heat waves, and other foreseen and unforeseen natural disasters, accidents, and security threats.

The cost of this outdated system regarding human lives and the economy has been considerable. The East Coast power outage of August 2003 plunged more than 50 million people into darkness, claimed eight lives, and racked up an estimated $6 billion in economic losses. Two years later, Hurricanes Katrina, Rita, and Wilma left millions of people without electricity for weeks and took a huge toll on regional economies. EPRI, the electric utility industry's leading think tank in Palo Alto, California, estimates that the total cost for such grid failures across the United States is a staggering $50 billion to $100 billion a year.

In addition to outages, the North American grid wastes, or loses, up to 20% of the energy transmitted and distributed through its arteries. Antiquated transmission and distribution systems not only leak energy but also no longer provide the quality of electricity demanded by our information-intensive digital society. The current grid is akin to a massive one-way freeway with thousands of off-ramps onto all one-way streets. Unlike the Internet, which is built on a network of millions of connected yet independent nodes, each able to send and receive information, the massive electric system network has little two-way capability or redundancy built in. If one tributary or the main line goes down on the grid, it impacts everything downstream.

When a Cleveland, Ohio, transmission line overheated, sagged into a tree branch, and shut down on August 14, 2003, the effect cascaded through a power grid already strained by 90-degree heat throughout the Northeast and Midwest. The largest blackout in North American history eventually affected tens of millions, stretching from Cleveland to New York City and from Pennsylvania to Ontario. And when power goes out in a neighborhood, how do most electric utilities learn about it? From angry customers calling them on the phone!

In other words, today's grid isn't very intelligent.

BREAKTHROUGH OPPORTUNITY

Grid Monitoring

As we've seen so far in this chapter, putting computing power and digital information to use will be the name of the game in the future grid. Companies such as CURRENT Communications of Germantown, Maryland, and BPL Global of Pittsburgh are developing broadband over power line (BPL) tools that enable grid operators to track electrons by monitoring their flow and use over the same electric lines that provide power to homes and businesses. Overlaid on the existing electric distribution network, CURRENT's BPL network solution, according to the company, incorporates advanced digital communication and computing capabilities that provide real-time monitoring. One recent stamp of approval came from TXU Electric Delivery, which provides power to more than 3 million delivery points in Texas, making it the nation's sixth largest electric transmission and distribution company. TXU and CURRENT signed an agreement in late 2005 to transform TXU Electric Delivery's power distribution network into the nation's first broadband-enabled smart grid. Not only will the utility be able to use the system to enable smart-grid applications, acting as a backbone for utility applications, but it will be able to offer broadband services such as high-speed Internet to its customers via the same technology. BPL is still in its infancy, but we believe it offers considerable promise.

The Energy Future Coalition, a broad-based, nonpartisan alliance of business, labor, and environmental groups, sums up the dilemma well: "Running today's digital society through yesterday's grid is like running the Internet through an old switchboard." Picture Lily Tomlin as Ernestine, in her *Rowan & Martin's Laugh-In* routine from the 1970s, trying to emulate a high-speed Cisco router.

So clearly, the opportunity for modernizing the grid is immense. In North America alone there are more than 3,000 electric utilities serving nearly 140 million residential, commercial, and industrial customers. According to a report by the Center for Smart Energy, a research and advisory firm in Seattle, the North American electric utility industry represents about $275 billion in annual sales. That makes it 30% larger than the auto industry and roughly twice as large as the telecommunications business.

A smart grid will look very different from today's system—enabling utilities to more efficiently deploy both centralized and distributed energy, and for customers to more efficiently and economically monitor and manage their energy usage, adjust their consumption behavior, and more easily feed electrons from solar PV, fuel cells, and other distributed clean-energy sources into the grid.

The U.S. Department of Energy's National Energy Technology Laboratory, in recent working groups, has described some of the major characteristics for a modern smart grid, including:

- **Self-healing:** A grid that can rapidly detect, analyze, and respond to problems, and restore service quickly.
- **Empowering the consumer:** A grid able to incorporate consumer equipment and behavior in its design and operation.
- **Tolerant of attack:** A grid that stands resilient to physical and cyber security attack.
- **Twenty-first-century power quality:** A grid that provides a quality of power consistent with Digital Age consumer and industry needs.
- **Generation options:** A grid that accommodates a wide variety of local and regional generation technologies, including clean-energy sources such as solar, wind, biomass, geothermal, and small-scale hydroelectric.

In simple terms, the smart grid takes advantage of the latest developments in digital information technology to better manage and deliver a range of centralized and distributed-energy sources. The network is able to monitor and control the flow of electrons and ensure a two-way flow of electricity and information between a power-generation facility and the end user.

Microsoft chairman and cofounder Bill Gates sees the electric grid moving into its own silicon age, not dissimilar from the computer revolution. He recently told *Toronto Star* journalist and clean-tech blogger Tyler Hamilton that the electric industry's problems are very similar to those faced by the computer industry. "They need systems that are extremely reliable, redundant, that can switch over and do things in different ways very, very rapidly," said Gates.

ELECTRIC GOLD

How much money will be made in the transition to a new, more robust, smart grid? EPRI estimates that the building of the smart grid—what it likes to call the IntelliGrid—will cost $160 billion in the United States alone by 2025. This level of utility investment, if it occurs, represents a significant opportunity for providers of intelligent-grid products and services, including wireless meters, new advanced transformers, and monitoring equipment. EPRI believes that these costs would be easily offset by dramatically reducing annual losses from outages and wasted electricity and providing customers with new value-added, information-rich services. North American utilities are already spending nearly $10 billion annually, analysts estimate, on smart technologies, including automated meters that are transforming the grid into a digital, self-monitoring, and adaptive system.

But utilities, for reasons both intrinsic and external, are notorious for being slow to adopt new technologies. According to some estimates, the utility industry, on average, invests less than 1% of its revenue in R&D—lagging far behind the percentage of investment made by most other industrial sectors. To put it mildly, when utilities embrace change, they often do it slowly and carefully. Indeed, if a utility were a lover, it would be better known for its dependability than its passion.

Not all the blame, however, can be placed on the utilities' intransigence. The electric industry has enabled an age of wonder, powering much of the great innovation of the past century by literally turning on the lights in people's homes, powering the industrial growth engine, and enabling the computer and Internet revolutions. Like the railroads that also facilitated industrialization, the current grid was cobbled together piece by piece and region by region, rather than purposefully and holistically designed like the Internet.

The grid, for all its faults, has served us pretty well and was the first major and successful experiment in interconnection. Grid operators and electricity generators have been wary of messing with a system that has been ranked one of the greatest engineering achievements of the last century. The current system is 99.9% reliable, but it has been unable to keep up with growing demand. While electricity demand has expanded rapidly, investments in new transmission lines, energy efficiency, and on-site generation have lagged.

PUTTING A VALUE ON INTELLIGENCE

Unfortunately, incumbent regulations have been a significant obstacle to the need for massive investments in new transmission and distribution systems. Policies at both the regional and national level have focused mainly on adding more generating capacity, thereby supporting the development of new coal and natural gas-fired power plants much more than energy efficiency and grid management.

Many industry experts have called for the decoupling of profits from generation to overcome the current perverse incentive for utilities to deploy new, costly, often polluting energy sources instead of focusing on energy efficiency and smart-grid applications. One of the first places in the world to successfully begin to decouple profits from large-scale generation was California—and it therefore represents one of the best opportunities for companies and investors interested in the next-generation grid.

Chuck McDermott is managing partner of Boston-based VC firm Rockport Capital Partners and chairman of the GridWise Alliance, a consortium of public and private stakeholders who have joined together to support the U.S. Department of Energy's vision of a transformed national electric system. He's both wary of and optimistic about the smart grid. "The biggest barrier to change is not technological but regulatory," he says. "In the U.S., markets are all regional with no consistent policy—ratemaking is the purview of the individual states. Unlike telecommunications, which was deregulated with a stroke of a pen in 1984, generation and distribution have been deregulated herky-jerky, state by state."

This patchwork quilt of regulations has set up roadblocks to the adoption of new technologies because there is no consistent federal policy. And notoriously failed deregulation efforts in California and elsewhere, in which flawed deregulation policy only exacerbated the problem, have made state-by-state deregulation problematic. Pile this on top of utility rates that don't reflect investments in energy conservation and slow adoption rates by utility customers for new technologies, and many investors and entrepreneurs are hesitant to get involved.

AN OPPORTUNITY OF MASSIVE PROPORTIONS, IF . . .

But the opportunities for companies, investors, governments, and entrepreneurs are still considerable. "Right now the grid is held together by bubblegum and paper clips," says McDermott. He believes, along with many others, that the current grid needs significant investment and a coordinated push by a visionary leader, most likely from a visionary president in the White House. "The example that's become the most telling for me is the interstate highway system in the U.S.," he says. "President Dwight

Eisenhower used his political capital to build out the interstate highway system. This was done for national security, in order to evacuate cities in the case of nuclear attack, and to spur the economy. I believe there are a lot of parallels between the interstate highway of the 1950s and building out the smart grid today."

A range of smart-grid advancements, including new smart meters, remote sensors, energy-management systems, better transmission lines, and advanced storage technologies that serve to optimize electricity generation, dissemination, and usage, are all attracting investments, even without a consolidated federal push. Recent examples include investments in such companies as CURRENT Communications, Comverge, EnerNOC, and GridPoint (all of which are discussed in this chapter). But until the smart-grid movement reaches critical mass and receives more support from the federal government, we are likely to see incremental changes at the regional level first.

The Canadian province of Ontario, for example, is requiring that smart meters be in place throughout the entire province by 2010. Other regions aren't far behind. The Pacific Northwest has been touted as a leader in smart-grid technologies. According to the report *Powering Up the Smart Grid* by nonprofit group Climate Solutions, based in Olympia, Washington, the region is already home to 225 smart-energy enterprises, resulting in annual revenues of $2 billion.

Itron in Spokane, Washington, is North America's leading provider of advanced data metering and management for electric and water utilities. Its automated meter reading (AMR) devices let utilities collect advanced metering data accurately, efficiently, and more frequently—often using wireless communication networks. Utilities can then use the data to support a wide variety of customer-service and energy-delivery applications, such as time-of-use rates, demand response, and utility asset management.

Itron is a leader in helping customers produce what clean-tech guru Amory Lovins of the Rocky Mountain Institute calls negawatts and negaliters—the electricity and water that you *don't* use. "In a world of growing demand, limited supplies, and ever-increasing prices, utilities need to better manage their negawatts and negaliters," says Itron CEO Leroy Nosbaum. His company has tens of millions of smart meters installed around the world to help do just that. Multinationals such as GE and Siemens are now active in the AMR space. Itron's revenues have more than tripled from $180 million in 2000 to $644 million in 2006.

Other innovative smart-grid companies are taking aim at this growing market that many industry watchers believe is on the verge of a tipping point. Silver Spring Networks in San Mateo, California, is leveraging open standards in its race to bring cost-effective solutions to the smart-grid market, and Hunt Technologies of Pequot Lakes, Minnesota, already offers advanced metering infrastructure services to hundreds of customers worldwide. Even IBM is getting in on the game. It's been testing a system with PNNL and the GridWise Alliance in Washington and Oregon to help consumers track, monitor, and control their energy usage. By giving users access to real-time information, the goal of the project is to develop future products and services that help utility customers better manage their own electricity consumption.

BREAKTHROUGH OPPORTUNITY

Automated Meter Reading

Automated meter reading, or AMR, has been around for some time, but it's only recently begun to gain significant traction and see large-scale rollouts starting to happen. The Canadian province of Ontario, for example, recently became one of the first utility regions in the world to require the installation of smart meters for all customers by 2010. And in 2006, California's PG&E (Pacific Gas & Electric) got approval to launch the largest advanced metering infrastructure rollout in U.S. history, some 9 million gas and electric meters. The fast-growing AMR market offers opportunities for investors and job seekers alike looking to capitalize on the shift to a smart grid. UtiliPoint, a research firm that tracks the electric utility space, forecasts that the market for AMR data management alone should grow from $25 million per year in 2005 to more than $200 million annually by 2015.

Other companies, such as Comverge in East Hanover, New Jersey, offer a suite of services to utilities, including load and voltage control, full-scale metering and monitoring, and grid-management services. Comverge, which was voted a top 100 company in 2005 by *Red Herring*, a business technology magazine, and selected by *Newsweek* as one of the top 10 most ecofriendly companies in North America, runs on an innovative business model in which it takes the risk of implementing new technologies away from the utility. Comverge deploys the latest in information technology and utility controls to reduce customers' energy usage. Rather than needing to build new, expensive power-generation facilities or purchase expensive power during peak usage, Comverge provides "virtual peak power" to the utility by tweaking participating customers' thermostats on the highest-demand days and aggregating this saved electricity.

POINT OF USE

Another company, GridPoint in Washington, D.C., is enabling residential and industrial customers to store backup energy during times of peak energy demand and unexpected outages, as well as to provide demand-response, energy-conservation, and load-shaping solutions to utilities. GridPoint sells a unique appliance, about the size of a refrigerator, that provides both traditional and renewable-energy users with instant, automatic plug-and-play backup power with a unique software-controlled, battery-based technology. The company's intelligent energy-management system could be just what consumers are looking for in an easy-to-install system that can reduce energy costs and itemize energy consumption. The system lets homeowners lower their energy bills by tapping the grid for electricity when it's inexpensive and using backup power when electricity is expensive. It can also easily integrate renewable-energy sources such as solar PV, and sell excess power back to the utility. "Our aim is to empower consumers," says Peter Corsell, president and CEO of GridPoint. "Our system allows users to participate in the emerging smart grid and become more proactive in making energy choices." Corsell likes to say that his product is the TiVo of energy management.

In another reflection of the heightened interest in clean-tech companies by high-tech pioneers, one of GridPoint's earliest investors and board members is computer visionary Esther Dyson, publisher of the high-tech newsletter *Release 1.0* and organizer of the annual PC Forum conference. GridPoint "does for the utility grid what the Internet did for the telephone infrastructure," writes Dyson. "It allows it to grow smarter and to scale easily by putting the intelligence at the edges, instead of attempting to impose centralized control." In other words, assuming that regulators and utilities buy into the model, consumers could gain more control and participate more fully in a distributed-energy future.

THE ENERGY HIGHWAY

Although this chapter's opportunity deals primarily with distributed and decentralized forms of energy, there's also a move toward ever larger clean-energy resources—which poses its own unique challenges to a smart-grid infrastructure. Similar to the Internet backbone that can carry billions of bits of information every second, the modern energy system needs to be able to carry massive amounts of electricity on its lines efficiently and effectively over long distances. The current grid has actually done this task pretty well for the last century but is in desperate need of upgrading. And unfortunately, the current grid isn't always located near the best renewable-energy sources.

New onshore and offshore wind farms, for example, are approaching sizes of 400 MW of generating capacity, equal to an average coal-fired power plant. A range of new concentrating solar technologies promise to deliver sun-powered generating plants of a similar large size. To tap the solar rays of the southwestern deserts and the wind power of the Great Plains, we'll need investments in new electric transmission lines, not just smarter grid management.

Some investors, inventors, and entrepreneurs are looking at ways to reinvent the way we transport electrons altogether. In one futuristic but very plausible arena, technologists are working on developing transmission lines that lose significantly less power. As noted earlier, the late Richard Smalley, the 1996 Nobel laureate in chemistry known by many as the father of nanotechnology, envisioned a future in which wires made of carbon nanotubes would carry electricity farther and more efficiently than today's copper wires.

These "quantum wires" have the potential to transform today's electric power grid. Smalley's team at Rice University in Houston is continuing his work, recently embarking on a NASA-funded 4-year, $11 million effort to create a prototype. These wires theoretically could conduct electricity up to 10 times more efficiently than traditional copper wire and weigh one sixth as much. While this development could take years to reach commercialization, it could have significant impact. "If we succeed, we'll be able to rewire the world, permitting a vast increase in the capacity of the nation's electrical grid," Smalley once said.

BREAKTHROUGH OPPORTUNITY

Superconductors

Nanotechnology could enable the grid of the future with so-called quantum wires, but another breakthrough could occur with superconductive materials used for both energy storage and transmission and distribution wires. One company, American Superconductor in Westborough, Massachusetts, has been developing high-temperature superconductor wires for a variety of applications, including power cables, motors, generators, and specialty magnets. And in 2005, 3M installed the first commercial superconductor wire for an overhead power line in the United States for Xcel Energy in Minnesota. Superconductors are still years away from extensive use in the utility industry, but they could provide significant advantages if costs drop and manufacturing technology improves.

All of these developments are moving the current grid into the digital realm. The new smart grid will be one that's self-healing and more compatible with both distributed and centralized clean-energy sources. It will have sensors to anticipate disruptions, circuits to redirect spiking currents, and intelligent systems that will automatically power down noncritical devices such as dishwashers and daytime lighting during times of peak demand. It will be more efficient and operate increasingly like today's Internet.

And there's another parallel between the smart grid and the growth and expansion of the Internet. The servers that power the world of search engine queries, online purchases, instant messaging, and streaming video require massive amounts of electricity. According to author and futurist George Gilder, the five major search engines alone used nearly 5 GW of energy in 2006. "That's an impressive quantity of electricity," Gilder wrote in the October 2006 issue of *Wired* magazine. "Five gigawatts is almost enough to power the Las Vegas metropolitan area—with all its hotels, casinos, restaurants, and convention centers—on the hottest day of the year." The need for this massive amount of energy to power and cool data centers has caused Google to locate its most recent server farm (and 30-acre campus) next to a hydroelectric dam on the Columbia River Gorge in The Dalles, Oregon. Other big Web companies, including Microsoft and Yahoo, have followed suit, with data centers located in similar low-cost hydroelectric service territories. With so much at stake, we believe that Web companies will begin looking seriously at how they can conserve energy with smarter devices and computers, gain access to clean electricity, and guarantee a twenty-first-century grid that can support their mission-critical applications and services.

OPEN SESAME

Another striking similarity between the grid of the future and the Internet of today is the need for standards. The growth of the Internet relied on standard protocols to enable worldwide data dissemination and proliferation. Various governing bodies, such as the Internet Engineering Task Force and the World Wide Web Consortium, established the rules that provided this infrastructure and base.

The smart grid will require similar planning and comparable protocol-making entities. EPRI's IntelliGrid Consortium, with founding members such as ABB, the Bonneville Power Administration, Con Edison, Électricité de France, and Hitachi, is working to establish an open standard for smart-grid interoperability. Similarly, the GridWise Alliance, under the guidance of the U.S. Department of Energy and the PNNL, is developing supportive open standards and guidelines. And in Europe, the European Smart Metering Alliance is working to develop smart-metering standards there.

As part of this standards development, the shift to open source (in which a set of standards is developed and shared freely among users) could be gaining traction. In a shift not dissimilar to the information technology industry's current move away from proprietary Microsoft products to open-source Linux platforms, regional governments around the globe could play an increasing role in the migration to an open and distributed grid. Some major German cities, including Munich and Mannheim, are moving to open-source software solutions for their government servers and desktop computers. The state of Massachusetts recently joined this trend, stating that it would move away from proprietary Microsoft products in favor of OpenOffice. These same governments may end up devising similar policies for the grid of the future, calling for open and interoperable standards for utilities.

Currently, no single entity is leading this march toward utility-based open standards, but the issue is being widely discussed and debated. Most utilities and regulators know it's a matter of when, not if. As standards develop, investment and entrepreneurial opportunities should increase commensurately.

A NEW ENERGY ORDER

"Energy is a $3 trillion a year industry," says Adams of the Smalley Institute. "By some estimates we'll spend $10 trillion to $20 trillion over the next ten to twenty years on energy infrastructure globally. So there's money to spend on shifting our energy future."

In the new energy order highlighted in this chapter, you'll have nodes and distribution networks akin to the Internet. In this model, no single terrorist attack, accident, natural disaster, or heat wave can bring the whole grid down. Instead, you'll have a system in which most everyone is producing, storing, distributing, and sharing energy. In Smalley's vision of the distributed storage-generation grid, for example, individual homes might have 3 to 5 days of energy storage on-site to help during downtimes, peak energy usage, and major disruptions, or to serve as distributed "power stations." Battery packs in hybrid electric, all-electric, or fuel-cell vehicles could also be used to store and feed electricity into the grid when not being used for transportation (most cars sit idle 95% of the time). A number of innovators have called this latter vision the V2Grid (vehicle to grid).

What's so compelling about these new visions of the grid is that you remove one of the greatest obstacles to the mass adoption of renewable energy: its intermittent nature. While coal, natural gas, and nuclear plants can produce electricity any time of day or night, as long as they have fuel, many renewable-energy technologies are constrained by Mother Nature. Solar power can be produced only when the sun is shining, wind power only when a sufficient breeze is blowing, and tidal power only when waves and currents are flowing.

To overcome this obstacle, you need to have three things. First, a power grid that can support and accommodate the two-way flow of electrons from distributed sources, such as solar panels on a rooftop, small wind turbines, or hydrogen-powered fuel cells. With this basic capability, homes and businesses can be both producers and consumers of energy. Second, you need to be able to carry electrons over long distances from far-flung resources, such as massive wind farms in the Great Plains or solar farms in the deserts of the Southwest. It's been estimated, for example, that if you placed solar generators in the Southwest desert in an area 100 miles wide by 100 miles long, you could produce enough PV power to meet all of the electricity needs of the entire United States. Finally, you need a networked system that can store energy for use during times of outages or when demand is higher than generation, mainly peak energy usage times such as hot summer days when air conditioners are taxing the grid.

The quantum wires being developed by the team at the Smalley Institute could theoretically be a critical building block of this new, vastly more efficient and capable smart grid. However, the quest to create conductive nanomaterials for large-scale electricity transmission and distribution will take time. The best-case scenario for such breakthroughs in nanowires is 5 to 10 years, and it could take decades to commercialize the technology and fully transition from our current grid to one based on nanotechnology. But change is coming much sooner in other guises: products such as advanced lithium-ion batteries for backup power storage; smart advanced meters, appliances, and wireless devices that help better manage the flow of electrons; advanced stationary fuel-cell systems that efficiently produce both electricity and heat for homes and small businesses (also known as combined heat and power) and can provide electricity on demand; and superconductors for more efficiency in transmission.

California alone plans to add up to a million solar roofs by 2020 via its $3.2 billion California Solar Initiative, the most aggressive subsidy program ever initiated in the United States. A majority of today's new solar PV installations, in the United States, Japan, Germany, and elsewhere, do not include on-site backup power storage—they simply generate solar electricity for the home and feed excess electrons into the grid. But on-site energy storage is tantamount to the vision of a distributed storage-generation grid where tens of thousands of systems can feed into the grid on demand at any time of the day. It's a huge opportunity. With current technology, an average home would need a small vented room full of batteries costing more than $10,000 dollars to guarantee a 2- to 3-day supply of on-site reserve energy. But nano-enabled battery solutions could dramatically change the equation, enabling days' worth of backup and peak power to the home or grid, in a device the size of a small refrigerator, at a fraction of the current cost.

As we've seen, a smart-grid transformation is upon us in ways both large and small. But perhaps more than any opportunity addressed in this book, the development and implementation of a smart grid will require significant cooperation and coordination between technology developers, policy makers, companies, entrepreneurs, and investors. In the United States, utilities are a highly regulated but disaggregated business. A hodgepodge of regulations are used in different utility districts at the regional and state level, with no single unifying force at the meta level. "Nothing short of a president," says Rockport Capital's McDermott, "needs to come in with leadership and solve some of these transmission issues, like Eisenhower did with the interstate highway system."

It might not take an action that drastic, but until the utility industry can establish standards, with systems and protocols that can be applied across the system, the vision of a next-generation smart grid will be incremental at best. Like the interstate highway and information highway before it, the smart grid will rely on government funding and federal and industry standards to flourish. Indeed, it will take a Texas-sized vision. But with smart and visionary teams like those at the Houston-based Smalley Institute, along with hundreds of other research organizations, companies, and forward-thinking policy makers in the United States and abroad, we will likely see the current grid, much of it envisioned in the late nineteenth century, finally move into the twenty-first. Therein lies one of the greatest clean-tech opportunities of our time.

THE CLEAN-TECH CONSUMER

Smart meters. You can't go out and buy a smart meter—a device that helps manage the flow of electrons into your house by providing detailed information on energy usage and real-time pricing—on your own, at least not yet. But tens of millions of smart meters are now in operation around the globe, and that number is projected to increase dramatically as utilities start to deploy more of them. Two utilities in California alone plan to install more than 6 million smart meters by 2010. Consumers will need to rely on their utilities' upgrading their systems in order to get one—but we see that trend on the rise. Remember, the cheapest and cleanest energy is the energy that you don't use. And smart meters will help in that mission immensely by giving consumers the tools to monitor and control their energy use. Think negawatts.

Energy in a box. One of the biggest issues with our electricity system is that most of us have no backup power readily available. If the grid goes down, so does the electricity in our homes, stores, and offices. One trend that could change that is advanced distributed backup energy systems for your home. And we're talking not about dirty fossil fuel–powered generators but about a new breed of electricity-storage devices that can provide power when the grid goes down, as well as better manage your flow of electrons and help lower your utility bill throughout the year. GridPoint, which is highlighted in this chapter, is the first company to offer a comprehensive plug-and-play clean solution for backup power, but a number of other companies are likely to offer "energy in a box" products as battery and control technologies improve. But these plug-and-play systems don't currently come cheap. GridPoint's basic system starts at about $10,000. For those with less ambitious needs, companies such as computer accessory maker Belkin are now offering small systems to keep your computer and other accessories running during a brief blackout.

TEN TO WATCH

BPL Global

Pittsburgh, Pennsylvania
www.bplglobal.net

The promise of the delivery of BPL has been around for some time—with marginal success to date. But the real traction for BPL has to do with electric grid management: the use of broadband capabilities to carry information critical to a new class of smart-grid applications. BPL Global, a leader in software design and systems integration to make that happen, closed more than $25 million in Series C venture financing in late 2006 from a consortium of mostly Kuwaiti investors. While BPL Global's primary customer to date, local utility Duquesne Light of Pennsylvania, is based in the United States, the company sees significant opportunities in the Middle East, where electricity efficiency efforts are gaining ground and broadband services are still scarce.

Comverge

East Hanover, New Jersey
www.comverge.com

A Red Herring magazine top 100 company and selected by *Newsweek* as one of the top 10 most ecofriendly companies in North America in 2005, Comverge offers a unique business model for large-scale automation. Instead of charging a utility up front for its suite of smart-grid products and services, the company makes a profit off the electricity costs that it *saves* its customers. Customers include such utilities such as Rocky Mountain Power, ISO New England, and PPL. In October 2006 the company filed with the U.S. Securities and Exchange Commission to go public, with Citigroup Global Capital Markets Inc. as the lead underwriter.

CURRENT Communications

Germantown, Maryland
www.current.net

CURRENT is the leading BPL provider in the United States. In May 2006 the company announced that it raised an additional $130 million, from new strategic investors such as TXU Electric Delivery, GE, and EarthLink, along with existing investors such as Goldman Sachs, Google, and Duke Energy. The company has strong support from these high-pedigree investors and a unique technology platform. But high costs, technological hurdles, and entrenched interests mean that while the company's prospects are promising, CURRENT will face continued challenges as it helps to invent an entirely new sector.

EnerNOC
Boston
www.enernoc.com

EnerNOC has earned its share of accolades, including winning the Platts 2006 Energy Pioneer Award and being named one of the 100 fastest-growing new companies in the United States in the June 2006 issue of *Entrepreneur* magazine. Although demand response is nothing new, EnerNOC has created something unique—its trademarked Negawatt Network of distributed-energy resources. The company's system monitors and controls customers' energy assets, such as lights, HVAC, and generators, in real time and dispatches these assets remotely in times of peak demand. The company's goal: to preempt blackouts and lower wholesale energy prices for its customers.

Electric Power Research Institute (EPRI)
Palo Alto, California
www.epri.com

EPRI—the Electric Power Research Institute—isn't really a company per se, but its influence is wide reaching. Perhaps more than any other organization, this nonprofit consortium of utilities and companies has the power and influence to move the utility industry toward a smart grid. Its members produce more than 90% of the electricity generated in the United States. EPRI acts as both a think tank and an R&D shop for the utility industry, publishing reports, convening meetings, and testing and developing a range of technologies that enable a smart grid—continuing to push the envelope on smart-grid developments.

GridPoint
Washington, D.C.
www.gridpoint.com

With backing from top investors, including Goldman Sachs, GridPoint hopes to reinvent the grid with its small refrigerator-sized appliances that fit easily in people's basements. The appliances, simply speaking, can provide consumers with three things: renewable-energy integration (such as from solar power on rooftops), online energy management, and battery-based backup power. According to the company, during periods of peak demand for electricity, a single utility that has deployed 100,000 GridPoint products across its service territory could draw up to 500 MW of stored capacity, equivalent to the amount of electricity generated by an $800 million coal-fired power plant. The company's "intelligent energy management" systems are gaining traction, but the company will need to deliver a business model that results in tens of thousands of systems, not hundreds, being installed successfully on-site.

Hunt Technologies

Pequot Lakes, Minnesota
www.hunttechnologies.com

A leader in advanced metering infrastructure leader, Hunt Technologies doesn't have the reach that Itron does, but it currently serves about 500 utilities around the world with its AMR technology solutions. In March 2006 the company was acquired by Bayard Group, an Australia-based global investor in energy-measurement and energy-efficiency technologies. While Hunt remains an independent operating unit, the investment by Bayard could provide synergies for the company. Bayard has committed more than $1 billion to the energy-measurement and energy-efficiency sector worldwide, and it counts Landis+Gyr, one of the world's largest electricity-metering companies, and Cellnet, another AMR leader, as part of its holdings.

IBM

Armonk, New York
www.ibm.com
New York Stock Exchange: IBM

IBM is applying its computing and consulting expertise to smart-grid developments. In early 2006, the company joined with the U.S. Department of Energy (through its PNNL) to test a system that enables residential consumers to track how much energy they're consuming, in real-time prices, and thereby help them adjust their usage and potentially save money. IBM has been acting as the systems integrator for the project, deploying its WebSphere Application Servers to track and serve up real-time data to consumers. IBM is also involved in a number of other smart-grid developments, including BPL. With its significant war chest and deep networking experience, IBM might be one of the big players to help bring utilities into the computer age.

Itron
Liberty Lake, Washington
www.itron.com
NASDAQ: ITRI

Itron, which started out in 1977 with the goal of making AMR an industry standard, is now North America's leading provider of advanced data metering and management for electric, gas, and water utilities. The company serves about 3,000 utility customers and has more than 40 million of its smart metering devices in use around the world. Itron has been on an acquisition spree of late, picking up such competitors and smart-grid leaders as Schlumberger Electricity Metering and Flow Metrix. The company, with $644 million in revenue in 2006, has solid strategic partnerships, significant market traction, and leading technology that could propel continued market growth.

SmartSynch
Jackson, Mississippi
www.smartsynch.com

SmartSynch has differentiated itself by focusing on wireless AMR solutions for commercial and industrial markets. The company recently began its foray into the residential marketplace, garnering a contract to deploy tens of thousands of wireless meters for Hydro One of Canada and working with Itron to integrate its solution into Itron meters. The company has been a leader in developing wireless AMR solutions based on an open-systems architecture. In October 2006, the company announced that it would be providing Itron with a public wireless communications technology component for Itron's latest advanced metering infrastructure platform, which was due out in 2007.

7

MOBILE TECHNOLOGIES

Powering a World on the Go

In the rugged mountainous region along the border of Afghanistan and Pakistan, in an area often referred to as a "lawless frontier," a U.S. military special forces unit is on a mission to help locate and track Al Qaeda operatives. It's risky business. The soldiers must travel dangerous and inhospitable roads and camp out far from central-command support. These "dismounted" soldiers will be on their mission for days on end. Their backpacks, which carry all the food, tents, and artillery they need for the mission, weigh an average of 120 pounds. As part of the load, each soldier also carries a collection of mission-critical electronic devices, including radio communication units, GPSs, and infrared night-vision binoculars—and the primary and rechargeable batteries needed to power them all.

But on this mission, something is different. Instead of hauling in additional primary batteries or packing heavy, loud, exhaust-belching generators to keep the command's battery packs charged, much of the equipment is powered quietly and efficiently by the sun. The soldiers carry lightweight, backpack-sized devices that easily unfurl into a small array of flexible, camouflaged solar panels. These photovoltaic panels provide power to recharge the lithium-ion batteries required for many of the unit's electronic devices. And unlike diesel generators, which create heat, noise, and pollution, the solar panels are completely silent and have a low "thermal signature," meaning that enemies can't easily identify or track the troop's location.

This isn't science fiction but science fact. Manufactured by United Solar Ovonic in Auburn Hills, Michigan, the Uni-Pac portable solar power system is just one of a handful of portable solar products now being developed or shipped for battlefield operations by companies such as Global Solar Energy, Iowa Thin Film Technologies, and Konarka.

Meanwhile, in a much more peaceful part of the globe, a young couple whiles away a sunny afternoon in a Los Angeles park. Like millions of others around the globe, they're listening to music on their Apple iPods. The low-battery icon comes on and they're miles from their wall-socket charger at home, but no worries. They've brought along a small device called Soldius1, a solar-powered charger from Soldius in Veendam, the Netherlands, that fully recharges an iPod battery in 2 to 3 hours of direct sunlight.

Clean energy, on the go. From battlefields to backpacks, real warriors to road warriors, our increasingly untethered world is turning to portable applications of clean technology to power its mobile energy needs. To meet the challenge of portable energy sources that are safe, clean, and reliable, innovators large and small are ramping up efforts in sectors ranging from lithium-ion batteries to embedded, thin-film solar cells to mobile "power stations" packaged in a standard shipping container. Beyond the huge potential markets of portable power for consumer electronic devices and the military, mobile clean tech is also finding growing applications in disaster recovery and relief, national security, and off-grid power in the rural villages of the developing world.

This wide-ranging sector of clean tech presents growth and investment opportunities for both large and small companies and their investors. Batteries in the United States alone were predicted to constitute a $14 billion market in 2007, growing to $17 billion in 2012, reckons the Freedonia Group, an industry research firm in Cleveland, Ohio. As for battery chargers, look no further than the iPod; Apple was projected to sell 50 million of them in 2006. Then add in the billions of cell phones, personal digital assistants (PDAs), BlackBerry devices, Game Boy players, and myriad other items carried by consumer armies from Shanghai to Stockholm, and you've got some idea of the opportunity for advances in portable energy-storage devices.

As we'll detail later in the chapter, the U.S. military is at the forefront of funding and innovation in this sector—something that any entrepreneur seeking backers or customers should know. Many technologies initially developed for the military—the ultimate power user, you might say—are being adapted for civilian use in disaster-recovery areas, refugee operations, and a range of other commercial applications. Some of these, such as pilotless solar-powered airplanes that act as broadband communications platforms for disaster-stricken areas or unwired rural villages, are a few years away from commercial use. Others, such as solar PV panels or micro-wind turbines delivered and housed in shipping containers for ready deployment, are already viable commercial niches today.

The U.S. military's desire for clean tech on the battlefield is not far in the future—it's here today. In July 2006, U.S. Marine Corps Major General Richard Zilmer, commander of forces in the tumultuous Al Anbar Province in western Iraq, sent a top-priority memo requesting solar and wind power for his troops. Not only was he concerned about the thermal signature of diesel generators tipping off the enemy but he also knew the security risks of the massive tanker-truck convoys required to haul in the diesel fuel (from as far away as Turkey) to run them.

United Solar Ovonic is just one of a growing number of companies seeking to cash in on the specialized yet very large potential military and civilian markets for clean-energy sources that are easily transportable. Former GM chairman and CEO Robert Stempel, now boss of United Solar Ovonic's parent company ECD Ovonics, says that the market for Uni-Solar products is booming and that the company plans to up its solar manufacturing capacity to 300 MW by 2010. That would represent a more than tenfold increase in production from 2005. Stempel's company has shipped thousands of the Uni-Pac portable solar units, with more than half of them being used by defense organizations in the United States and around the world.

ENERGY STORAGE: BATTERIES AND BEYOND

Whether military or civilian, a big key to successful portable energy technology is energy storage. Very often that means batteries, which don't constitute clean tech in and of themselves—they've been around since the nineteenth century and can be extremely harmful to the environment. Basic rechargeable battery technology has moved from lead-acid to nickel-cadmium to NiMH, but until recently batteries remained relatively heavy for the amount of energy they're able to store. Advanced batteries on the market today and the innovations of tomorrow, however, bring battery technology decisively into the realm of clean tech. An ultracapacitor storage device that can be charged in seconds or minutes rather than hours, and recharged hundreds of thousands of times instead of just hundreds or thousands, could dramatically cut the use of both energy and materials—or replace toxic materials such as heavy metals with cleaner, nanotechnology-based innovations. And because of its long life, it could also greatly reduce the solid-waste problems caused by conventional primary and rechargeable batteries. Billions of batteries often containing toxic chemicals are discarded each year, causing an environmental nightmare.

Some of those advances are still in the laboratory stage and at least a decade away from widespread commercial use, but today's nano-based innovations are also addressing a more recent, high-profile issue that laptop computer users worldwide are well aware of: battery safety. In 2006, Sony was forced to recall 9.6 million lithium-ion batteries powering the laptops of the world's leading computer makers, including Dell, Apple, Lenovo, and Sharp. A small number of the batteries overheated during computer use, a phenomenon known as thermal runaway, and videos of some of these hair-raising incidents were quickly transmitted across the globe via YouTube.

Dozens of companies are now competing around the world to create advanced, safer, nanotechnology-enabled lithium-ion rechargeable batteries for use in military equipment, power tools, handheld consumer electronics devices of all types, and eventually backup storage. A123 Systems of Watertown, Massachusetts, is one of the current lithium-ion battery leaders. The company, with funding from such heavy-hitter sources as GE, FA Technology Ventures, Motorola, QUALCOMM, MIT, and the U.S. Army's OnPoint Technologies venture arm, is shipping products today based on its nanotechnology innovations. Other small companies working on such breakthroughs include Altairnano in Reno, Nevada; Nanoexa in Burlingame, California; Valence Technology in Austin, Texas; Infinite Power Solutions in Golden, Colorado, and such big guns as 3M and Toshiba.

"Batteries are the new hot topic for investors," noted Silicon Valley entrepreneur-turned-investor Sunil Paul told the *Wall Street Journal* in November 2006. "People have realized that a major advance in energy storage would be a game-changer."

The global energy-storage device market, $48 billion in 2005, will grow 7% a year to $74 billion in 2010, according to Tokyo-based market research firm Global Information. Not all of that is mobile energy storage, but many of the industry's most important tech advances—extending battery life and squeezing more power and/or storage capacity out of smaller, lighter devices—are particularly applicable to portable power.

New materials, such as Valence's Saphion phosphate-based lithium-ion cathode, use less lithium and promise greater stability and less heat risk than the lithium-ion cobalt oxide that's been in standard use since the 1990s. Nano-based energy storage innovations are unlikely to be limited to lithium-ion batteries. Other innovations could include carbon nanotubes used for hydrogen storage or new types of capacitors—small devices that store electrical energy and are used in nearly every imaginable electronic product.

BREAKTHROUGH OPPORTUNITY

Ultracapacitors

Traditional capacitors can't store much energy and are primarily used to supply quick bursts of energy (such as for a flash in a camera), to smooth out electrical power (evening out the peaks and valleys that can occur in power transmission), and to provide computer memory, when they're paired with transistors. But ultracapacitors, also known as supercapacitors, act more like a battery with increased power, storage, and recharge capabilities. Several companies are already active in this growing market, notably Maxwell Technologies, a NASDAQ-traded company in San Diego. Its line of ultracapacitors works in conjunction with batteries to power consumer electronics and automated meter readers at the low end and stationary applications, including controllers for the pitch of a wind turbine, at the high end. But the big breakthrough will likely come from nanotechnology. A team at MIT's Laboratory for Electromagnetic and Electronic Systems, for example, is applying carbon nanotubes onto pieces of silicon to create a new type of capacitor. If successful, the new device could fully replace today's rechargeable batteries. With today's technology, you'd need a capacitor the size of a soda can to power a flashlight for about a minute. But by placing millions of carbon nanotubes onto the surface of the capacitor's electrodes, the MIT team believes it can crack the issue of power density—basically turning a capacitor into a battery. While still in R&D

mode, and perhaps 10 years from mass production, these tiny devices could eventually leverage many of the same manufacturing techniques used in producing microchips—and provide a power-rich, lightweight source of mobile energy storage.

PORTABLE FUEL CELLS: THE NEXT LEAP FORWARD?

Another longer-term opportunity in mobile clean energy is portable fuel cells. Although much attention has been focused on fuel cells in vehicles, as we discussed in the previous chapter on personal transportation, many believe that smaller, portable fuel cells to power consumer devices will be a larger and faster-growing market. Frost & Sullivan predicts that portable power will be a $15 billion market worldwide by 2010. Fuel cells are arguably cleaner than batteries too, using no acids and much less heavy metal.

Yet here again, many clean-tech providers are eyeing military markets first. According to a 2005 report by Fuel Cell Today, a market research organization in the United Kingdom, the U.S. Department of Defense is by far the largest funder of military-related fuel-cell activities in the world. In 2003, the department's spending on fuel-cell developments was approximately $130 million. The firm's *Fuel Cell Market Survey: Military Applications* report states that fuel cells offer an attractive option to the military because of "quiet operation, a lower heat signature, fuel efficiency, [and] possibility of superior acceleration compared to similar diesel or gasoline-powered vehicles, on-board electric power generation supporting communications, surveillance and other electronic equipment."

One company now offering such a solution for military use is Smart Fuel Cell in Brunnthal, Germany. The company's direct methanol fuel cell, dubbed Jenny, could potentially weigh 70% less than traditional batteries on a 3-day mission. The 25-W system is being tested by armies in Germany as well as Finland, the Netherlands, Norway, South Africa, Sweden, Switzerland, and the United Kingdom.

MTI Micro Fuel Cells in Albany, New York, is typical of many portable fuel-cell companies in its strategy of parallel focus on the military (where it can be easier to secure R&D funding) and consumer markets. MTI's first research funding came from the U.S. Air Force Research Laboratory. Like many fuel cells, MTI's Mobion direct methanol fuel-cell device is powered by fuel cartridges containing methanol, also known as methyl alcohol or wood alcohol. So the "recharging" process is instantaneous—plug in a new fuel cartridge, and you're charged. MTI and others see big opportunities in pushing that as an attractive selling point for consumers.

"Despite the dramatic growth of so-called wireless electronic devices," reads MTI's marketing pitch, "most continue to require wires—wires for recharging!" In May 2006, MTI partnered with South Korea's Samsung Electronics, the world's third-largest cell phone manufacturer (behind Nokia and Motorola), in one of the consumer electronics industry's biggest commitments to portable fuel-cell technology. Samsung is funding about $1 million in joint R&D in an exclusive, 18-month deal with MTI. And MTI has lined up a big-name contract manufacturer, Singapore's Flextronics International, to build the fuel cells for consumers. MTI says its first prototypes, delivered to Samsung in November 2006, could deliver a month of cell phone usage or 5,000 digital camera shots on a single charge.

But there's one significant issue that could seriously derail the market potential for fuel cells powering consumer electronics: the safety of methanol fuel cartridges aboard commercial airliners. The International Civil Aviation Organization's Dangerous Goods Panel voted in 2005 to clear such cartridges for passenger carry-on use starting in 2007, but that ruling was superseded by the U.S. Transportation Security Administration's ban on liquids and gels in August 2006. The fuel-cell industry continues to lobby for carry-on permission, and with good reason—it's hard to imagine much of a market for portable laptop or iPod power that you can't use on a long plane flight. It's a critical issue worth watching for any company or investor looking into the portable fuel-cell sector.

Another start-up, Jadoo Power Systems in Folsom, California, has become the world's largest portable fuel-cell provider with the help of blue-chip VC funding from Sinclair Ventures, Venrock Associates, and Mohr Davidow Ventures. Jadoo (a Hindi word meaning "magic") powers its cells with hydrogen; many believe that the market for hydrogen fuel cells in mobile devices will be a much earlier, faster-growing opportunity than the long-hyped "hydrogen economy" focused on vehicles. Jadoo's customers, who range from soldiers powering their telecom equipment to TV camera operators covering breaking news for stations in Sacramento and Oklahoma City. Like MTI and others, Jadoo pursues military and consumer markets simultaneously. In the same week in November 2006 that the company won a design and engineering award from the Consumer Electronics Association, it announced $2.4 million in additional funding in the U.S. Military 2007 Defense Appropriations Bill.

Another key market is emergency first responders; five fire stations in the Sacramento area are beta-testing Jadoo's 100-watt XRT fuel-cell system to run their emergency radios, battery rechargers, portable satellite phones, and other key devices at a fire or medical emergency scene. Later in this chapter, we'll discuss the opportunities for deployment of mobile clean technologies in wide-scale disaster relief efforts after hurricanes, earthquakes, and tsunamis.

THE MILITARY'S DNA

The military, particularly the well-funded U.S. military, is poised to potentially ramp up production and bring new portable clean technologies to market. As an organization heavily reliant on lightweight, dependable, remote power and storage for its tactical operations—and one of the largest consumers of oil and other natural resources—the U.S. military is heavily involved in the clean-tech ramp-up. Not unlike what happened in earlier tech revolutions, the military may end up being the driving force behind the development and mass commercialization of everything from high efficiency solar cells to advanced batteries. Witness earlier tech developments born out of military labs and development programs that have changed the world: semiconductor-based integrated-circuit chips, radar, and the Internet, to name just a few.

In many areas the military is at the leading edge of investing in and deploying a range of mobile clean technologies, including high-efficiency solar cells, portable fuel cells, water filtration, and other advanced technologies in its fight for advantage on the battlefield. This is creating myriad growth opportunities for developers of and investors in these technologies. "Advanced technology is in the military's DNA," says Scott Sklar, former director of the Solar Energy Industries Association and now vice president of SkyBuilt Power, a mobile clean-tech provider in Arlington, Virginia. "Combine that with the military's focus on logistics, and you have a lethal combination."

Among the U.S. military's vast clean-tech arsenal, it isn't just portable power that's transforming the battlefield and military operations. The military also walks the walk in powering some of its own bases, as the U.S. Air Force is the largest consumer of green electricity in the United States. In 2006 the Air Force purchased more than 457 million kWh of renewable energy, mostly wind power. Two bases, Dyess Air Force Base in Texas and Fairchild Air Force Base in Washington State, now receive 100% of their energy from wind or other renewable power sources provided by local utility companies.

That's not to say that the U.S. military should always be considered a great environmental steward. Under the administration of President George W. Bush, the Pentagon has won exemptions from parts of the Migratory Bird Treaty Act, the Marine Mammal Protection Act, and the Endangered Species Act. The Department of Defense continues to seek exemptions from the Clean Air Act and toxic waste laws. This is all the more disconcerting because the military, according to the government's own documents, is the nation's largest polluter and has more facilities on the Superfund National Priorities List than any other organization. The military accounts for more than 10% of the country's top-priority Superfund cleanup sites. (The Superfund National Priorities List contains approximately 1,500 sites deemed in most need of cleanup from the government's Superfund list of more than 40,000 contaminated and polluted sites nationwide. The Environmental Protection Agency administers the Superfund program in cooperation with individual states and tribal governments.)

But despite all of its negative environmental activities, the military continues to impact technology innovation, making it a clean-tech force to be reckoned with. While this may come as unsettling news to many environmentalists, pacifists, and progressives, the military's imprint on tech development can't be denied. It has, and will continue to have, an impact on a number of critical emerging technologies in portable clean energy, water, and materials that have widespread implications for society at large.

CROSSING OVER

"Inside of a decade you'll see [Department of Defense] DOD- and DARPA-funded clean technologies cross over into commercial applications," predicts Jean-Louis "Dutch" DeGay, equipment specialist and outreach program coordinator for the U.S. Army's Future Force Warrior Technology Program Office in Natick, Massachusetts. "The military is a key driver right now for a number of emerging technologies with commercial applications, including high-yield solar technology, portable fuel cells, and solar-powered tent structures."

Lilliputian Systems is a prime example. The Wilmington, Massachusetts, company makes micro fuel cells, originally developed under DARPA sponsorship at MIT, for portable and wireless applications. With more than $30 million in funding from Kleiner Perkins Caufield & Byers, RockPort Capital Partners, Chrysalix Energy Venture Capital, and other high-profile venture capitalists, the firm is working to commercialize a butane-powered fuel cell that could replace rechargeable batteries and dramatically increase operating time for cell phones, PDAs, and other electronic devices. Lilliputian's "Fuel Cell on a Chip" earned a 2007 Technology Pioneer designation for the company from the World Economic Forum.

The Pentagon isn't doing this type of development for altruistic reasons but because it sees development as part of its basic business model. "The military is looking at the cost of fuel, at the cost of all their electricity requirements, and they realize they need to be a leader in energy efficiency and alternatives," says Joseph Edwards, vice president of new ventures at AeroVironment, which is based in Monrovia, California. His company develops pilotless aerial vehicle systems and energy technologies for the armed forces, NASA, and private industry. "The military can afford development that private companies can't," Edwards continues. "Their focus isn't on traditional financial 'payback' but on fuel reduction, weight reduction, efficiency, and enabling mission-critical capabilities."

To be sure, not everyone is so sanguine. The military can have trouble moving fast enough to keep up with commercial developments, let alone lead a new tech revolution. And there are serious issues that companies must consider when taking military funding. These include protecting a company's intellectual property, navigating the military's extensive bureaucracy, and dealing with long lead times. "It is something that many companies might wish to avoid," says one clean-tech company executive. Still, the allure of the military's deep pockets is great and can provide a tempting source of early stage or ancillary funding, as well as an attractive opportunity for product testing and tuning.

The U.S. Army's VC arm, OnPoint Technologies, has been investing in a number of companies that could help achieve the mission of high performance and longer battery life. One of them is A123 Systems, whose advanced lithium-ion batteries promise 5 times as much power and 10 times longer charge life than conventional lithium-ion offerings.

The company's battery has relevance not just on the battlefield. A123 already has an agreement with Black & Decker to provide batteries for the company's high-end line of 36-volt DeWalt power tools, including a hammer drill, reciprocating saw, circular saw, impact wrench, and rotary hammer. Introduced on Memorial Day of 2006, they were the first commercial products to incorporate such nano-based lithium-ion batteries. The tools do their dirty work with twice the power density of standard 18-volt tools and double to triple the run time per charge. DeWalt says this gives building professionals and consumers the power of corded products without the cord.

SECRET SAUCE: MONEY AND NECESSITY

What makes the military seemingly so suited to technology innovation and development? Two factors: money and necessity.

The money quotient is simple. Militaries, especially in the United States, often have more funds at their disposal for technology research, development, and deployment than many other government agencies do. And the military is often willing to take risks where the private sector isn't. In areas where privately held or shareholder-owned companies might find new technology development too expensive and daunting, the military might find the same technology development an *imperative*—literally the difference between life and death. Imagine a military without tanks, GPS-enabled devices, and radar, and you get the picture.

In the case of the military, necessity is indeed the mother of invention.

Depending on how you slice the fiscal pie, the U.S. government spends 20% to 30% of its total budget on military and defense. In a 2005 report (titled *The Defense Industry in the 21st Century: Thinking Global or Thinking American?*), PricewaterhouseCoopers notes that the Pentagon spent a whopping $500 billion in fiscal 2006—an approximately $420 billion military budget in 2006 plus supplemental expenditures of $80 billion for operations in Iraq and Afghanistan. This total expenditure is double the defense spending of all other countries combined. And the United States' insatiable military appetite continues to grow. On the basis of requests by the administration of President George W. Bush, spending in 2007 was likely to exceed $600 billion.

Approximately $70 billion of the U.S. military's annual total budget, or more than 10%, is spent on research, development, and demonstration programs. To put this number in perspective, the military's R&D budget is *larger than all other federal R&D expenditures combined* (energy, space, general science, health, and other), and it's more than twice the officially stated *total* defense budget of China.

While it's impossible to know how much of the military's research dollars go into clean-tech development (and admittedly clean tech represents only a small portion of total military spending), there are dozens of current initiatives in solar, fuel cells, lithium-ion batteries, advanced materials, water filtration, and other clean-tech research and deployment.

Not surprisingly, the list of recipients of U.S. military clean-tech funding programs (through DARPA, the Department of Defense, and so on) reads like a who's who of the clean-tech industry, including Jadoo Power, Konarka, Lilliputian Systems, Nanosolar, Nanosys, United Solar Ovonic, MIOX, MesoFuel, and Zinc Matrix Power. Many of these companies have received military R&D grants of more than $10 million—a considerable sum for companies working to develop and prove their technologies for real-world applications. Such funding brings a caveat emptor for potential investors, as start-up companies that become too reliant on Pentagon grants can run into trouble if subsequent funding dries up. But such money is an important pump-primer for many clean-tech developers and is often a good indication of a technology's commercial market potential.

BREAKTHROUGH OPPORTUNITY

Embedding Solar

If you're over 30, your first encounter with solar PV technology might well have been the small embedded panel powering your pocket calculator. Today's mobile PV applications take that concept to a whole new level of power and sophistication. Many R&D advancements of the past few years, often funded with VC and Pentagon dollars, have brought easily portable, thin-film solar PV technologies to unprecedented levels of high efficiency and low weight. Konarka in Lowell, Massachusetts, has been one of the more visible and investor-attracting companies in this arena; its Power Plastic is a nano-enabled polymer with solar PV "printed" on it. Moving forward, the big game will be figuring out how to best embed technologies like Konarka's into an increasing range of consumer and military devices, whether in the device itself or its accompanying power supply apparatus. And of course, bringing down costs, especially for mass market products. At a more modest end of the spectrum is Voltaic Systems in New York, which embeds small PV panels in $200 to $250 backpacks and shoulder bags to charge cell phones, PDAs, and other small devices on the go. The packs don't yet have enough solar oomph to charge a laptop, but Voltaic is working on that as its next big consumer market opportunity.

CLEAN TECH SPELLS *RELIEF*

Not to sound like ambulance chasers, but there is a huge opportunity for clean, mobile, off-grid sources of power to help meet the basic needs of people dealing with natural disasters in the United States and around the world. These needs became all the more evident in 2004 and 2005 in the aftermath of the devastating Southeast Asia tsunami that killed more than 200,000 people, Hurricanes Katrina and Rita on the Gulf Coast of the United States, and the Pakistan-centered earthquake that killed 73,000 people.

Following this devastating trifecta, the Clean Energy Group, a nonprofit in Montpelier, Vermont, issued a report on how clean-energy technologies, particularly portable ones that can be deployed quickly, can be used by local communities for disaster relief. "Emergency preparedness and effective response depend entirely on the reliability and quality of a first responder's energy supply," the report said. "If primary grid power goes down, so too can 911 and state emergency communication centers, first responder stations, hospitals, control centers, traffic signals, and public transportation, as well as vital infrastructure like water pumping and filtration systems." The report called for evaluating a mix of distributed clean-energy technologies to help overcome such problems in the future. It recommended the installation of new, more reliable forms of on-site electricity generation for mission-critical public facilities.

Daniel Yergin, Pulitzer prize–winning author and chairman of Cambridge Energy Research Associates, echoed this sentiment in an op-ed piece in the *Wall Street Journal* after the twin hurricane disasters in 2005. "Energy security [now] requires . . . more emphasis on redundancy, alternatives, distributed energy, and backup systems," he wrote.

Such voices did not go unheeded, and the relief and recovery efforts from those disasters showcased the promise of quickly deployable clean-energy and clean-water technologies in devastated areas. We believe this will be a significant growth market. Most climate scientists agree that global warming will produce more powerful hurricanes, typhoons, and other storms. It will take quite a few years for clean tech to displace enough fossil fuels consumption to reduce the CO_2 emissions causing the warming, but mobile solar power, fuel cells, and other clean technologies can help victims recover from these storms today.

BREAKTHROUGH OPPORTUNITY

Portable Power Stations

Like the U.S. Army with its venture arm OnPoint Technologies, the Central Intelligence Agency operates a VC fund named In-Q-Tel—the Q pays homage to the James Bond character Q who supplies Agent 007 with his gadgets. A number of In-Q-Tel investments make the connection between security and clean tech. One such company, SkyBuilt Power in Arlington, Virginia, has developed a modular portable energy system, the Mobile Power Station, that can be sent into just about any environment and quickly powered by the sun, wind, fuel cells, generators, and other distributed-energy sources. The In-Q-Tel investment team likes the SkyBuilt solution for its ability to take off-the-shelf technologies and package them into a unique, easy-to-use system—"the Dell of renewable energy systems," says the company. The Mobile Power Station consists of solar PV panels, a micro wind turbine, or other standard components, inside a standard shipping container. The units can be shipped by train, truck, ship, or plane and deployed within a few hours by two people or can even be parachuted into remote areas. The Central Intelligence Agency and U.S. Homeland Security Department, along with the military, could use this capability to set up operations and command centers, medical refrigeration units, or communication nodes or to power hospitals, evacuee centers, police and fire departments, and cell phone towers. In addition to U.S. federal agencies, government officials from Ethiopia and Kazakhstan are considering the product for use in their nations' rural areas. SkyBuilt's solution isn't cheap—around $100,000—but it's a promising entry in a niche with big potential, particularly if SkyBuilt or a competitor can bring prices down.

PORTABLE SOLAR FOR EVERYDAY LIFE

Mobile clean technologies are proving that they can help out in a post-disaster pinch, but what about for longer-term power needs? There are, of course, myriad growth and investment opportunities for mobile clean technologies in the developing world that don't involve disaster recovery. The lighting and power requirements of everyday life lend themselves to simple, portable, low-cost technologies. It's a field where both grant-funded nonprofits and hotshot entrepreneurs can play, with significant financial and social rewards.

A leading example is Noble Energy Solar Technologies (NEST) in Hyderabad, India. NEST has manufactured and distributed more than 65,000 Aishwarya lanterns, powered by solar PV, to replace dirty and potentially hazardous kerosene wick lanterns in the rural villages of the Asian subcontinent. (An infant cousin of NEST founder Dharmappa Barki was fatally burned in a kerosene lamp accident when Barki was 9.) Used to light homes, nighttime buffalo-milking sessions, retailers' stalls, or dozens of other activities, Aishwarya lanterns sell for about $30, but buyers can take advantage of NEST's microcredit offerings. Microcredit, a financial tool with a good deal of buzz since microfinance pioneer Muhammad Yunus of Grameen Bank captured the 2006 Nobel Peace Prize, is often an important component for clean-tech entrepreneurs who want to take advantage of market opportunities in developing nations. Barki's company has begun manufacturing some lanterns in China to cut costs and is now selling Aishwarya lanterns in Pakistan, Sri Lanka, Somalia, and South Africa.

CLEAN POWER FOR THE NEXT GENERATION

In all aspects of our society, mobility is one of the hottest and most fundamental trends of twenty-first-century technology. Consumers and businesspeople, whether shuttling between business meetings in Bangalore or between kids' soccer games in Boston, want information and communication capability whenever and wherever they are. Laptops, cell phones, iPods, PDAs—it's a wireless world and getting ever more so. At the same time, today's military strategists are aiming for many of the same goals of nimbleness and portability in a world where today's enemies bear little resemblance to the traditional regiments of the past. And the very real threats posed by both natural and human-caused disasters are redefining the concept of the battlefield. Planners and logistics experts are thinking not just about how we can better arm the military but also about how we can better "arm" all the frontline personnel working to tackle some of the biggest battles of our time: the fights against disease, poverty, resource depletion, environmental degradation, and climate change.

These trends all demand energy sources that are portable, lightweight, and easily recharged or refueled. Clean tech can help make that happen, in a big way. Portable fuel cells, advanced nano-based batteries, mobile solar rechargers, and the other technologies discussed in this chapter add up to potential multibillion markets in the next few years. And the field remains fairly open for small start-up companies, particularly if they can partner with electronics giants such as Samsung—which is why we see such interest and dollars in this sector from top-tier VC investors.

And the mobile clean-tech sector, more so than others, will continue to benefit from the extensive financial, R&D, and market test-bed support from the Pentagon and other U.S. federal agencies such as the Homeland

Security Department and NASA. We firmly believe that the early adoption of mobile clean technologies by military and space agencies, coupled with applications for national security, disaster, and relief operations, will continue to expand for several years. Although these are not easy markets for entrepreneurs and companies to tap, they can offer a great source of early financing, proof-of-concept opportunities, and big potential markets for clean-tech companies large and small.

THE CLEAN-TECH CONSUMER

Solarize it. The U.S. military is pushing the boundary on solar cells and rechargeable lithium-ion batteries to power everything from night-vision goggles to communication equipment. The objective: to keep remote "dismounted" soldiers powered in the field for days at a time. This research is starting to result in solar cells' being embedded into a range of consumer devices such as personal computers. Think calculators on steroids. These solar-integrated devices may be a few years from store shelves, but for now, there are a growing number of companies, including Solio and Soldius, offering sleek solar battery chargers for everything from cell phones to iPods.

Get gyrating. In the event of a power outage—caused by human error, natural disaster, or terrorist attack—you'll want to have access to electronic devices that can operate for days, if not weeks. One answer: devices powered by hand-cranked dynamos. Quite a few manufacturers, including Eton, Freeplay, and Grundig, now make radios, flashlights, and other consumer devices powered by the simple crank of a handle. Turn the handle a few dozen times and the light or radio will operate for 10 to 30 minutes at a time. We expect the availability of such consumer products to increase.

TEN TO WATCH

3M
Minneapolis
www.3m.com
New York Stock Exchange: MMM

The venerable inventor of Scotch tape and Post-it notes is at the leading edge of advancements in nanotech-based lithium-ion batteries for laptops and other portable electronics devices. Called a "nanotech powerhouse" by investment guide service The Motley Fool, 3M is applying its considerable R&D muscle to develop nano-based batteries that are both more powerful and safer (that is, cooler). And in the battle for contracts to supply the world's largest computer and electronics companies with advanced batteries for mobile devices, 3M's size, stability, and brand cachet can be a big edge over its many start-up competitors.

A123 Systems
Watertown, Massachusetts
www.a123systems.com

A123, spun out from nanotechnology research breakthroughs at MIT, is now a fast-growing, advanced lithium-ion battery provider with an impressive lineup of investors. The funders' roster includes the U.S. Army's VC arm OnPoint Technologies, traditional VC stars Sequoia Capital and North Bridge Venture Partners, and strategic investors GE, Motorola (the world's second-largest purchaser of lithium-ion batteries), and QUALCOMM. A123 has targeted many different application areas for its advanced batteries, including the hybrid car market, but its batteries for portable industrial and consumer devices have shown particular momentum. Providing Black & Decker with portable energy for DeWalt power tools gives A123 a breakthrough deal in a consumer niche often overlooked by other companies chasing consumer electronics.

ECD Ovonics
Rochester Hills, Michigan
www.ovonic.com
NASDAQ: ENER

Also known as Energy Conversion Devices, ECD Ovonics garners more than 80% of its approximately $100 million in annual revenue from its profitable United Solar Ovonics unit. That subsidiary's Uni-Solar thin-film solar cells power a range of mobile energy needs, including those of U.S. soldiers on missions in remote parts of Afghanistan and elsewhere. ECD bears watching as the military expands its use of solar power to replace heavy batteries and fuel-guzzling diesel generators. ECD has quite a management pedigree, with former GM chairman Robert Stempel at the helm and Stanford Ovshinsky, a legendary solar inventor since the 1960s, as cofounder president, and chief scientist.

Jadoo Power Systems
Folsom, California
www.jadoopower.com

Named for a Hindi word meaning "magic," Jadoo has conjured up a growing business in portable hydrogen fuel cells since its founding in 2001. The company has landed blue-chip VC investors Mohr Davidow Ventures, Venrock Associates, and Sinclair Ventures, as well as Pentagon funding, including $2.4 million in the 2007 defense appropriations bill. Perhaps Jadoo's biggest advantage is market versatility. Customers for its 100-W N-Gen and XRT fuel cells include soldiers, consumers, firefighters, and operators of television news cameras.

Konarka
Lowell, Massachusetts
www.konarka.com

Konarka has a long list of blue-chip VC investors in the United States and Europe who have been ponying up some $80 million since 2001, and its gregarious founder and chairman, Howard Berke, is a fixture at solar and clean-tech industry events. Can Konarka deliver on its promise to provide large amounts of low-cost, thin-film solar PV material to power a wide range of mobile and other devices? Production of its Power Plastic PV material, which rolls off a production line like newsprint, was to begin in 2007 at its manufacturing partner G24 Innovations in Cardiff, Wales. Konarka will be watched closely as it moves to commercialization after years of R&D and big financial bets.

Mechanical Technology

Albany, New York
www.mechtech.com
NASDAQ: MKTY

One of Mechanical Technology's two operating subsidiaries is MTI Micro Fuel Cells (www.mtimicrofuelcells.com), a pioneer in portable methanol fuel cells for military and consumer applications. Like others in its field, MTI is moving from its R&D stage to military sales first; it began taking orders for its $14,900 Mobion 30M cells from the Pentagon in late 2006. The cells weigh about 2 pounds, compared with 8 pounds for the 11 batteries whose power they replace. But MTI may have even greater long-term potential in powering consumer devices, thanks to a plum joint development deal with cell phone and electronics giant Samsung. MTI sent prototypes of its Mobion 1 charger, with enough juice for 5,000 digital camera shots, to Samsung in late 2006. The company expects commercialization of that product by 2008.

Noble Energy Solar Technologies (NEST)

Hyderabad, India
www.solarnest.net

NEST is a leading player in the burgeoning market for low-cost, portable solar-powered lanterns in the developing world. Focusing mainly on the India market, NEST's Aishwarya lantern, named after popular Indian actress and onetime Miss World Aishwarya Rai, replaces polluting, fuel-consumptive, and often dangerous kerosene lamps. NEST is a good example of companies that work with microcredit providers to deliver clean-tech products; some 75% of its lanterns have been financed this way. NEST sold some 65,000 solar lanterns between 2001 and 2006 but has only scratched the surface of its home market; an estimated 100 million households in India use kerosene lamps as their main light source.

SkyBuilt Power

Arlington, Virginia
www.skybuilt.com

SkyBuilt delivers portable clean power on a large scale—in a shipping container containing solar panels, small wind turbines, high-capacity batteries, or other technologies specified by the customer. The self-proclaimed "Dell of renewable energy systems" packages such components for delivery to military field operations, disaster-relief areas, or any off-grid location requiring 3.5 to 150 kW of electric power. The innovative concept caught the attention of In-Q-Tel, the Central Intelligence Agency's VC arm, which inked an investment and development deal with SkyBuilt in 2005. SkyBuilt is in discussions with government agencies in Ethiopia and Kazakhstan for potential business. Its challenges ahead are finding a broader range of customers not stopped by its $100,000 price point and attracting additional investors.

Smart Fuel Cell

Brunnthal, Germany
www.smartfuelcell.de

The U.S. Department of Defense is not the only military looking to lighten soldiers' battlefield loads with lightweight portable fuel cells. Smart Fuel Cell's 25-W methanol fuel cell is being tested by armies in Germany and seven other European nations, plus South Africa. But the company also wants a piece of the world's biggest defense budget and so partnered with DuPont Fuel Cells to win initial Department of Defense approval of its product in December 2006; it's hoping for U.S. military deployment by 2008. Smart Fuel Cell is also very active in consumer markets and in mid-2006 was able to cut the price of its EFOY ("Energy for You") fuel cartridges by 40%, thanks to manufacturing improvements. That's tough competition.

Soldius
Veendam, the Netherlands
www.soldius.com

Why recharge your twenty-first-century iPod with last century's wall socket? That's the pitch from Soldius, maker of solar-powered chargers for today's don't-leave-home-without-your-earbuds crowd. Funded by private investors, the company makes the pocket-sized Soldius1 device, selling for about $100. It charges up iPods as well as BlackBerry devices and more than 250 models of cell phones. The only downside, compared with the wall socket, is time; it takes 2 to 3 hours of direct sunlight to fully recharge an iPod battery. But the "power anywhere" pitch is compelling, and hooking your clean-tech fortunes to one of the world's fastest-selling consumer products isn't a bad strategy.

8

WATER FILTRATION

Turning Oceans, Wastewater, and Other Untapped Sources into Pure Water

In remote rural Indian villages such as Korukollu, located in the state of Andhra Pradesh, women provide water for their families as they have for generations—by gathering water at a shared community site and carrying it back to their homes. But in this village, something is changing. The water in Korukollu is purified using a technology developed by Dr. Ashok Gadgil at the Lawrence Berkeley National Laboratory in Northern California. His company, WaterHealth International, is on a crusade to solve one of the biggest problems facing humanity by deploying its solutions in India and elsewhere—and to make money doing it. The company's technology uses low-voltage ultraviolet light to purify water. The system's energy needs are minimal, and the purification meets or exceeds some of the most stringent criteria for the removal of waterborne pathogens—including those of the World Health Organization and the U.S. Environmental Protection Agency.

Clean water in Korukollu and elsewhere can play a life-or-death role in the health of the villagers. It's been estimated by the World Health Organization that nearly 2 million people die each year because of unsafe drinking water, inadequate sanitation, and insufficient water for hygiene. Other estimates put the annual global death toll from waterborne pathogens at 3 million to 5 million—a crisis on par with the global AIDS epidemic. Clean up rural water supplies, the thinking goes, and you could eradicate a majority of the diseases that kill millions of people in the developing world: cholera, typhoid fever, dysentery, and diarrhea.

"In villages, there is no tap water, so options have often traditionally been contaminated well or surface water or very expensive bottled water," says WaterHealth International's president and CEO Tralance Addy. "A one-liter bottle of water costs upwards of twenty cents in India. Our technology allows us to deliver twelve liters of clean water for about two cents—putting it within easy reach of people who earn as little as two dollars per day. We fill a void for reliable, high-quality, healthy water."

Sounds like a promising recipe for success, but it's historically been very difficult for companies, including multinationals, to figure out how to make money by serving the markets of the developing world. There just aren't many role models for the successful build-out of profitable businesses, with decent returns, serving the poorest people on the planet.

But in the water business, a growing number of large and small companies are turning to innovative clean technologies, and equally important new business models, in an effort to change that. In both the developing and developed world, they are using a range of new technologies, including desalination, reverse osmosis, nano-based membranes, and ultrafiltration, combined with new financing schemes and service offerings, to capture their piece of the approximately $400-billion-a-year water market.

WaterHealth International is one player making significant headway. In November 2006 the company received a $7 million investment from Dow Venture Capital, the investment arm of the global chemical giant. It also forged a relationship in 2006 with India's largest private bank, ICICI Bank, to help finance the installation of the company's water purification and disinfection systems. The company said it was on target to set up 50 new village-based water purification systems per month in 2007, mostly in India. In addition to village water systems, the company has developed and shipped units for relief after disasters like the 2004 Asian tsunami and for urban centers in the developing world. Eventually, it will target individual households.

WaterHealth International, whose technology received recognition from *Discover* magazine as a "best of the decade" invention in 1999, believes it can deliver on its ambitious promise by embracing a developing world-centric business model. That means being involved in the entire water supply and purification process from end to end, including design, product manufacturing, financing, servicing, and hiring locals to operate and run the company's systems.

If companies such as WaterHealth International can beat the odds, rural development and disaster relief will offer a huge viable market—but those sectors still represent just the tip of the water iceberg. Access to clean, safe, reliable, and affordable water is proving just as critical in day-to-day operations in the industrialized world. From office towers to factories to homes, the need for clean water has never been greater. For this reason, clean water, like clean energy, is becoming big business.

Since the mid-1990s, a number of multinationals have positioned themselves as leaders in the water industry. Companies such as Danaher, General Electric, ITT, and Siemens have captured a significant share of the filtration, purification, and processing markets. Other multinationals, such as RWE, SUEZ, and Veolia Water, control a majority of the world's private water utilities. Since 2002, GE alone has spent more than $3.5 billion acquiring smaller water companies such as ZENON Environmental, Ionics, Osmonics, and BetzDearborn. Other significant acquisitions include Siemens's purchase of water-technology company USFilter for nearly $1 billion in 2004 and 3M's acquisition of water-filtration company Cuno Inc. for $1.35 billion in 2005.

One reason for the corporate consolidations and investments is that water is becoming an increasingly profitable business. GE's investments, for example, seem to be paying off—with a division that now exceeds $2 billion in annual revenue. Water also outperformed oil as an investment sector over a period of nearly 3 years, starting in 2003, according to a Bloomberg report in June 2006. The article reported that "the lack of usable water worldwide has made it more valuable than oil. The Bloomberg World Water Index of 11 utilities returned 35 percent annually since 2003, compared with 29 percent for oil and gas stocks and 10 percent for the Standard & Poor's 500 Index."

We believe that the insatiable thirst for water, in both the developing and developed world, will translate into continued opportunities for multinationals and their acquired companies, as well as for some smaller private companies that develop and deploy unique technologies and business models. Picking the winners won't be easy, and consolidation will make placing bets even more difficult, but there will be unique opportunities for entrepreneurs, investors, and those seeking new and challenging work as the need for clean water expands and underserved markets are exploited.

In this chapter we'll explore the key drivers behind the need for new, advanced filtration and purification technologies, uncover some of the leading companies and innovators, and look at how both large and small companies, and investors, can play a part in this growing sector.

A MARKET OF MASSIVE PROPORTIONS

One major factor driving the growth of the clean-water industry is sheer demand. While the earth has plenty of water, it simply doesn't have a ready supply of clean, fresh water. As most elementary schoolchildren can recite from memory, approximately three quarters of the earth's surface is covered by water. The issue: about 97% of this abundant water is salty, making it undrinkable for humans and unusable in most commercial and industrial applications.

The other stumbling block: billions of people now live far from clean, potable sources of water, as regional supplies dry up. China, for instance, has 7% of the world's freshwater but represents 21% of the global population. Equally pressing, China's water supply is concentrated in the southern half of the country, far from its two largest cities of Beijing and Shanghai. Four hundred cities in China have problems supplying enough clean water to their residents, according to the Beijing office of Greenpeace.

This is all happening at the same time that demand for water is rising dramatically around the world. The growth of industry, not to mention expanding agricultural and household needs, is playing a significant role in the increasing demand for water. The U.S. Environmental Protection Agency estimates that the average American uses more than 100 gallons per day. As China, India, and other nations expand their middle classes, the need for water supplies, and the distribution systems to get water to end users, will expand exponentially.

The global water market is currently valued at around $400 billion annually, trailing only electricity and oil in market size. "Demand is the big driver," says Evan Lovell, principal of Texas Pacific Group Ventures, which manages $35 billion in global capital, including Aqua I, a private equity fund dedicated to water-technology investments. "There's a fundamental supply–demand imbalance—people just don't have access to enough."

Wars have historically been waged over resource constraints, most recently over oil. In the future, if humans don't acquire the knowledge and deploy the technology to purify and filter dirty and salty water supplies inexpensively and on a large scale, water could become the next oil. We estimate that nearly half of the world's population will face severe water shortages by 2035 if new technologies are not deployed—raising the specter of escalating violence.

"Water crises could come in 'sudden shocks' in the future," says Laura Shenkar, a water-technology consultant based in San Francisco. "Global phenomena such as global warming, population growth, massive increases in the use of water for agriculture and manufacturing, and increased pollution will put mounting pressure on current and future water supplies."

In addition to dwindling supplies and increased demands, water requires vast amounts of energy to pump, filter, purify, distribute, and recycle. In many localities around the world, the water system is the single largest consumer of energy. Reciprocally, the production of energy—electric power generation, and petroleum refining to a lesser extent—is the number two consumer of water in the United States, trailing only agriculture. The water–energy confluence, sometimes referred to as "watergy," has the attention of big-league investors such as William K. Reilly, who ran the U.S. Environmental Protection Agency for President George H. W. Bush. Reilly now heads Aqua International Partners, a San Francisco investment firm with about $250 million in water-technology investments worldwide. "Energy uses water and water uses energy, and I'm focused on both of them," he says. "Water prices are going to go up, and that will make many technology improvements possible."

While no consumer likes to see higher prices, water pricing that is more in sync with market realities could provide industry with the right incentives. Industry analysts like to point out that consumers currently consider water a nearly free resource. Until we change that equation, they say, we won't see as much investment in new technology. But with ever-dwindling supplies of clean water—and the pressing need to accommodate growth in both the developing and developed world—the equation is indeed finally changing.

"Water is still one of the least technologically influenced industries on the planet," says Shenkar. "We've seen the advent of some desalination, ultrafiltration, new membranes, and biomimicry—but it's still very nascent. But looking forward, since technology adoption is still relatively new, water could provide profit opportunities even greater than clean energy."

BIG ANSWERS IN SMALL PLACES

Nanotechnology offers one of our best hopes to solving some of these significant hurdles—not only with potentially cheap power sources for the energy-intensive desalination process but also with membranes that can trap impurities, toxic waste, bacteria, and other pollutants. In fact, basic nanotechnologies are already being applied to water filtration around the globe. In addition to companies making advances in the United States, Europe, and Japan, nations such as Israel and Singapore are aggressively applying nanotechnologies to desalination. The key to these advances lies in the ability of nanotechnology to use membranes with pores that are small enough to filter out a range of impurities but offer better flow—more water filtration per minute—than conventional filters.

"Nano-based water purification technologies are leading the way in getting to market quickly," explains Scott Mize, nanotech consultant and former president of the Foresight Institute for Nanotechnology. "Everyone is doing something different, but the developments center around creating nanostructures that can trap impurities out of a stream of water. Some are focused on killing biological stuff, some on removing metals or other pollutants. They all have their own particular twist."

ZENON Environmental, which was acquired by GE in June 2006 for more than $680 million in cash, has been a pioneer in ultrafiltration (water filtration using microporous membranes and nanotechnology). ZENON, with headquarters in Oakville, Ontario, Canada, should add significant capabilities to the GE Water & Process Technologies division, bringing the largest diversified manufacturer on the planet together with a world leader in nano-scale membrane technology.

There are dozens of emerging companies working on a number of different breakthroughs. Argonide, based in Sanford, Florida, deploys aluminum oxide–based nanofibers for its water-filtration technology. The system has been used by NASA for extracting bacteria and even viruses from water and is applicable for more down-to-earth applications such as purification of industrial effluents and wastewater treatment. Seldon Laboratories, located 30 minutes down the river from Dartmouth College in

Windsor, Vermont, has developed a nano-based technology that removes microorganisms from fluids, without the use of heat, ultraviolet radiation, chemicals, or significant pressure. The company's water-filtration technology is currently being field-tested by the U.S. Air Force. A company in Providence, Rhode Island—eMembrane—is developing nanoscale brushes that can capture and remove heavy metals, bacteria, and other pollutants from water.

"Everyone says water is the next oil, but that hasn't hit the American consciousness yet," explains Wall Street veteran and nanotech investor Scott Livingston of the Livingston Group, an investment and advisory firm based in New York. "Americans take for granted turning on the tap and getting water. Many people see this as a developing-world issue—right now it dovetails with the economic development crowd, United Nations, and intragovernmental agencies more than it does with business-driven venture capital." But that is likely to change soon. The U.S. Department of the Interior's own estimates show that parts of the United States could run out of adequate supplies of water by 2020 if action isn't taken now to avert disaster.

BREAKTHROUGH OPPORTUNITY

Nano-Based Membranes

Membranes are materials that separate unwanted molecules, particulates, and pollutants from liquids. They have transformed the water industry since the mid-1990s, providing a low-cost solution to water filtration and purification. Membranes, which allow water to flow through but block out unwanted contaminants, can work at different scales, ranging from microfiltration (algae, bacteria, and parasites) to ultra- and nano-filtration (viruses, organic compounds, and pesticides) and reverse osmosis (salts). Companies active in this arena include giants such as GE and emerging start-ups such as eMembrane, as well as university labs. In November 2006, the University of California, Los Angeles, announced that it had developed a new class of nanocomposite material—a membrane that uses a "uniquely cross-linked matrix of polymers and engineered nanoparticles." The university researcher who invented the membrane, Professor Eric Hoek, is working with NanoH2O, LLP, an early-stage partnership, to develop the "technology into a new class of low-energy, fouling-resistant membranes for desalination and water reuse." He has estimated that the company's membranes would be commercially viable by about 2008. Nano-based membranes are still relatively uncharted territory and, we believe, offer a materials science breakthrough opportunity for university labs, corporate behemoths, and entrepreneurs alike.

The path to success, however, will require foresight and careful navigation.

"The real game-changing opportunities that have the largest upside are also the most difficult to deploy," says Matthew Nordan, president and director of research at Lux Research, a nanotech research and consulting firm in New York. "With water and energy, we're talking about major infrastructures that will change over decades, not years."

Nordan sees opportunity for companies to develop technologies that plop into existing infrastructure—the rare "drop in" like nano-enabled lithium-ion batteries or industrial water-filtration systems that can leverage existing infrastructure. The other option, says Nordan, is for companies to tackle big issues that require drastic changes in infrastructure. To succeed in this high-risk, high-reward realm, a company must learn how to navigate its growth from low-volume, high-cost applications (where you have customers who are willing to pay a premium) to high-volume, low-cost mass deployment. This can be a very difficult and tricky path to navigate for entrepreneurs, let alone large and established companies.

Emerging companies will need to devise smart licensing strategies and/or develop strong distribution channels to survive and thrive in this environment. Many of the early players will be acquired by larger multinationals (ZENON Environmental provides a great example) or better-funded competitors. But however the markets unfold, we believe that nanotech could play an increasingly significant role in the transition to a clean-water future and offer a range of opportunities to investors, companies, and entrepreneurs.

THE DESALINATION DILEMMA

No water processing technology is more intertwined with energy use than desalination—the conversion of seawater to freshwater for drinking and other uses. Operating in more than 100 countries, desalination plants consume vast amounts of power for high-pressure pumps and other equipment. Desalination is common in the energy-rich and water-poor Middle East; Saudi Arabia alone accounts for 24% of the world's desalination use. About half the world's desalination plants use reverse-osmosis membrane technology, in which salt water is "pushed" through a semipermeable membrane to remove the salt. It's big business; GE paid more than $1.1 billion in 2005 to acquire Ionics of Watertown, Massachusetts, the world's leading supplier of membrane-based desalination systems.

Recent tech breakthroughs in reverse osmosis have the potential for significant energy reductions. The Affordable Desalination Collaboration, comprising 22 water tech companies and water agencies, is testing an "ultra-efficient" reverse osmosis system at the U.S. Navy's Seawater Desalination Test Facility in Port Hueneme, California. Using a more energy-efficient pressure exchanger from Energy Recovery in San Leandro, California, the Affordable Desalination Collaboration reported a 35% power use reduction, compared with earlier forecasts, in an early 2006 test. Energy Recovery's PX line of pressure exchangers has only one moving part, a ceramic rotor, to trim energy use.

BREAKTHROUGH OPPORTUNITY

Desalination Plants Powered by Renewable Energy

Desalination makes a lot of sense. More than three quarters of the earth's surface is covered with water, and the bulk of this water is salty. While there are some environmental concerns surrounding desalination, such as what to do with the salt that's extracted from the water, the biggest issue facing large-scale implementation is *cost*. In fact, outside of the oil-rich Middle East, desalination plants currently "have the capacity to provide just three one-thousandths (0.3%) of total world freshwater use," according to the Pacific Institute, a research organization focused on global water issues. To bring down costs, a number of innovators are looking to apply renewable energy sources to the desalination process. In Australia, for example, a team of researchers at RMIT University in Melbourne plans to demonstrate a desalination plant that uses solar thermal technology to heat water and evaporate water from salt. Israel's solar concentration company Solel says it could apply its technology to desalination applications as well. In 2004 the very first wind-power plant on the Arabian Peninsula came online. Its purpose? To power a seawater desalination plant. And in late 2006 researchers at Texas Tech University and GE announced a collaboration to pair up wind power and desalination. Considering the cost of desalination, we expect to see much more activity in the marriage of water purification and clean energy.

Notable desalination plants under construction using Energy Recovery's PX technology include a $350 million facility in Perth, Australia, and the Yuhuan facility in China's Zheijiang Province, the largest in mainland Asia. Built by CNC Technologies in Beijing, the Yuhuan plant will supply freshwater to produce steam for turbines in the new electric power plants going up to meet China's burgeoning power demands. Those are the two sides of the "watergy" equation—using less energy to produce the freshwater needed to generate more energy.

DISTRIBUTED WATER

Much like the shift that's taking place in the energy sector—away from centralized production and toward distributed generation—the water industry is going through a similar transformation, especially in the developing world. As WaterHealth's Addy puts it, "We've taken the same approach that distributed energy is taking. Rather than developing large centralized plants that are suitable for large cities, we've developed systems that are optimized for developing-world villages."

This is a critical development, considering that 1.2 billion people on the planet do not have access to clean, potable water and many are not connected to water-distribution infrastructure. The opportunity in countries such as India, China, and throughout the rest of Asia and Africa is immense, but few have been able to capture the opportunity effectively. In the developing world, building a business has just as much to do with servicing and financing as it does with technology creation. Looking at other industries can help provide ideas and inspiration for the water industry. With the right models, markets can not only succeed but thrive in the developing world.

The pioneering work of U.S. business school professors C.K. Prahalad of the University of Michigan and Stuart Hart of Cornell University has helped transform the world's view of the so-called Base of the Pyramid—the world's poorest 4 billion people—from a global charity case to a true market that can be served profitably. A classic example is Grameenphone in Bangladesh, an offshoot of microcredit pioneer Grameen Bank. The bank provides microloans to rural village women to buy cell phones; the women then sell phone time to villagers. Grameenphone, with 6 million subscribers, now makes about $80 million profit on revenue of $500 million.

Grameenphone founder Iqbal Quadir is now embracing clean tech. He's teamed up with Segway scooter inventor Dean Kamen in an effort to propagate Kamen's biomass-powered (usually by cow dung), 1-kW electric generators and Slingshot water purifiers throughout rural Bangladesh and ultimately elsewhere in the developing world. Quadir formed Emergence Energy in Cambridge, Massachusetts, to license the technologies from Kamen's DEKA Research and Development Corp. in Manchester, New Hampshire, and he's now seeking $30 million in venture capital to fund manufacturing of the devices in Bangladesh. The Slingshot vaporizes contaminated water, separating out the contaminating solids or sludge and shooting them through a plastic tube—thus the name. Kamen's goal is to couple the Slingshot with the generator and sell them together, powering the water-filtration device with the generator's waste heat.

"Water and power efforts usually start from the top down—that model is borderline ridiculous," says Kamen. "Why don't we make little boxes that take *any* water source, wherever you are, and purify it right there?"

Water needs in poor nations have hatched some other innovative clean-tech solutions. In South Africa, Mozambique, Swaziland, and Zambia, nearly 1,000 communities get drinking water via the PlayPump, a combination of merry-go-round and water pump from British company Roundabout Outdoor. For less than $10,000, usually funded by global agencies such as UNICEF and the World Bank's International Finance Corporation, the PlayPump harnesses a tremendously renewable power source—kids' energy—to pump underground water into a 30-foot-high tank for community use. The pumps are often located at schools, helping boost school attendance with the enticement of play. Funders include the Case Foundation, the grant maker of AOL founder-turned-healthy-lifestyle company CEO and clean-tech investor Steve Case. Roundabout also sells ad space on some of the PlayPump devices. "It's an interesting business model," says Case. "In serving this vast market, my hope is that the lines between nonprofits and businesses will increasingly blur."

BREAKTHROUGH OPPORTUNITY

Water from Air

Hundreds of gallons of water extracted from thin air? It sounds fantastical, but a number of companies are trying to solve the issue of providing water in extreme conditions, including disaster recovery and war zones, and they are looking to some unlikely sources. The cost to ship and supply water to remote and hostile environments today can run tens of dollars per gallon. Aqua Sciences, of Sky Lake, Florida, is one company making progress in trying to provide an alternative that runs closer to 30 cents per gallon. The company's water-harvesting machine was awarded a *Time* magazine "Best Inventions 2006" award and can extract 600 gallons or more of water per day in just about any environment on the planet. Its company's president and CEO, Abe Shear, acquired global rights to the technology from an Israeli firm and has contracts with the U.S. military. The company doesn't like to give details on the technology, but Shear likens it to the effect of a grain of rice in a salt shaker—which pulls moisture out of the salt. Shear points out that the earth's atmosphere contains trillions of gallons of water at any given time in the form of water vapor. Now that's a potential resource for him and others to tap.

A FRESH CUP OF SEWAGE, PLEASE . . .

People are used to the concept of recycling newspapers into packaging and plastic bottles into fleece jackets, but what about recycling wastewater and turning it into drinking water? Most people's initial reaction is one of disgust. The notion of drinking old sewage, no matter how clean and safe once purified, is enough to make many people sick. But the conversion of municipal sewage, which is made up of approximately 75% water, into potable water is exactly what's happening in a number of regions that have limited supplies of freshwater. Singapore stands out as a shining example and is becoming home to an increasing number of companies and research organizations that could end up, literally, hydrating the world.

Hyflux, a Singapore-based provider of large-scale, highly efficient water systems to Singapore, China, India, and Dubai, is a case in point. The company is part of a used water-recovery technology developed in Singapore called NEWater. The process uses microfiltration, reverse osmosis, and other processes to convert wastewater into drinking-quality water. The city-state of Singapore launched the NEWater project in 1998 and now is using water produced at three NEWater facilities for both industrial applications and for mixing into reservoirs for drinking water. Singapore is targeting up to 2.5% of its municipal water supply from reclaimed wastewater by 2011.

In addition to Singapore, the United States and Israel have been water-reuse leaders. In the United States, a number of communities in Southern California, Washington, D.C., and elsewhere have discharged high-quality reclaimed water into underground aquifers and surface reservoirs (which then get filtered again) for drinking water. The technique, while still not widely adopted, is called indirect potable reuse. Israel, the water reuse leader, currently processes 75% of its wastewater—treating it and reusing it primarily for the nation's vast agricultural irrigation network (not for drinking water). Researchers in Israel are looking at the possibility of turning wastewater into potable water, but they haven't taken the plunge yet.

Turning sewage into potable water may seem like a relatively new idea, and one that many people hope never becomes a common practice, but NASA has been thinking about it for quite some time. For decades, NASA has funded the research and development of technologies that can support life for extended duration in space, with water reuse and purification being a critical example. Successful long-term piloted space exploration requires an ongoing supply of fresh potable water, clean air, and food. Imagine Christopher Columbus sailing to the New World without adequate food and water supplies—his crew never would have made it. Space travel adds similarly unique challenges. To support astronauts on a 2- to 3-year mission, say to Mars, you need to pack everything with you that you'll need during the expedition.

While the focus of recent missions to Mars and other planets has been on pilotless flights, NASA is working on returning astronauts to the moon by 2020, and eventually to Mars and beyond. Its current fiscal budget exceeds $16 billion annually, with a portion going to the study of growing food in space, generating onboard oxygen, purifying water, and other extended-duration needs.

In the 1970s, NASA funded development of a water-filtration technology that's now used on the International Space Station and has been used on every space shuttle mission since its development. Originally designed by UMPQUA Research of Myrtle Creek, Oregon, the technology is now being commercialized for the developing world by Water Security in Sparks, Nevada. NASA originally used the technology to convert human urine and other captured wastes into potable water. "It's whiz-bang technology," jokes Ray Doane, president and CEO of Water Security. The company has added a special filter to the original NASA design, creating a system that can remove up to 99.9% of all waterborne viruses. This company's technology could prove particularly useful in the developing world.

INDUSTRY'S INSATIABLE THIRST FOR WATER

While the need for clean water is critical to people living in suburbs, cities, and villages, residential applications still represent only about 10% of global water usage. According to the United Nations *World Water Development Report*, industry now represents about 60% of water usage in industrialized countries.

"From a business perspective," explains Doug Brown, venture partner at DFJ Element, a venture firm investing in clean technology, and former CEO of water-tech company Ionics, "in the developed world the real opportunity is around supplying high-quality water to manufacturers and industry."

Indeed, one of the biggest uses of water in the United States is for electricity production in power plants, particularly in the cooling process. These power plants prefer water free of debris and percolates, providing a longer life for expensive turbine blades and other components. Other industrial applications are also water hogs and require a high level of purity. These include everything from semiconductor manufacturing and food processing to pharmaceuticals and consumer goods production. The U.S. Environmental Protection Agency, for example, reports that it takes an average of 40,000 gallons of water just to manufacture a new car and its four tires. More than 60,000 gallons of water are needed to produce 1 ton of steel.

Companies that provide filtration technologies, wastewater reuse, and services to industry could continue to reap significant rewards. That's one of the reasons why companies such as GE, 3M, and Siemens have been on buying sprees, picking up the best filtration companies on the market. Christ Water Technology Group, based in Mondsee, Austria, is one of a number of pure-play companies that are also well positioned in this space. Christ Water has won contracts to provide clean water for wafer and semiconductor manufacturers in Asia, formed a joint venture to provide water services to the pharmaceutical and biotech industry in India, and services companies in a number of industries in Europe and the United States.

Israel, with its strong water expertise, is also well positioned to see its nation's companies service the global industrial market. AqWise, Atlantium, and P2W are just a few of the dozens of Israeli companies that may be well positioned to leverage their expertise. Singapore is positioning itself as an international "hydro hub" to garner its fair share of the water business—including industrial applications. GE Water and Siemens recently committed $82 million and $33 million, respectively, to develop R&D centers of their own in Singapore. Whether in Israel, Singapore, Switzerland, or the United States, the market for on-site industrial wastewater treatment and serving the quality water needs of industry is, we believe, positioned for strong growth.

LEAK DETECTION, FLOW CONTROL, AND NEW INFRASTRUCTURE

While the bulk of this chapter is focused on opportunities in filtration and purification, we see opportunities emerging in many other facets of the water-value chain. Water-monitoring and water-saving techniques, for example, will increasingly use highly advanced tech concepts, sometimes borrowed from other fields such as sound engineering and management of the electric power grid. "If you can't measure it, you can't manage it" applies to water as well as electrons, and accurate flow data is critical to improved efficiency.

The Acoustic Doppler Velocimeter, from YSI in Yellow Springs, Ohio, for example, uses radar signals to measure water flow volumes, speed, and direction. Another Ohio company, Fluid Conservation Systems in Milford, makes Permalog remote leak detectors that "eavesdrop" inside water pipes below the streets to catch leaks early. The Las Vegas Valley Water District uses 8,000 of them and saved more than 575 million gallons of water, enough to supply 3,200 homes, in 2 years. The city of El Paso, Texas, has 11,000 Permalog detectors that help save 6 million gallons a day. Sensicore of Ann Arbor, Michigan, develops smart sensors and networks that automate water testing, data collection, and analysis for both drinking and wastewater applications.

Water-usage data accuracy is also the goal of a technology called submetering. It meters individual use within rental apartment buildings, many of which have only had building-wide metering for decades. Without submetering, landlords take the hit when water usage and/or rates go up, and tenants have no incentive to conserve. "Is sub-metering the wave of the future?" asked a 2004 article in *National Real Estate Investor* magazine.

Submetering technology is also used for electricity and natural-gas metering, and not surprisingly, some companies, like Itron in Spokane, Washington, supply meters to all three markets. Itron racked up revenues of $644 million in 2006, with the bulk of that for its core electric utility metering business. The company, however, expects water metering to grow significantly as a percent of total revenue by about 2015. Privately held Wellspring International in San Diego uses wireless radio signals in its ZigBee metering networks for apartment-level water use monitoring. By helping landlords reduce financial risk, Wellspring claims that submetering raises the property value of a building by $5,000 per unit.

Another area of significant opportunity, at least in industrialized nations, is the massive need to upgrade aging and decaying distribution systems. Nothing's less efficient than water-main breaks, and they happen 200,000 times a year in the United States. Even without breaks, some 30% of the water supply leaks out on its journey to the household tap or factory pipe, not unlike the loss of electricity that happens in grid transmission and distribution. "Many Americans get their water from pipes that were laid when Lincoln was president," says general partner Ira Ehrenpreis of venture firm Technology Partners. The estimated price tag to fix and modernize those pipes nationwide is a staggering $500 billion by 2025.

That's likely to send water rates higher than most Americans are used to, creating huge business opportunities in water efficiency. On average, Americans pay less for water than residents of most industrialized countries. In 2005, the average water rate in the United States was 0.23 cents per gallon, according to TechKNOWLEDGEy Strategic Group, a water industry research firm and consultancy in Boulder, Colorado. Only Canada, number one in the world in freshwater supply per capita, has a lower average rate at 0.20 cents. Germans paid 0.84 cents per gallon; Britons, 0.57 cents; the French, 0.53 cents; and the Italians, 0.36 cents.

What's more, big federal water projects, especially in the western United States, have historically freed local municipalities from a realistic share of infrastructure investments, creating artificially low local water rates. Folks living in the desert in Las Vegas, for instance, pay half the rate of wet, snowed-in Bostonians. "Price has little to do with the actual cost today," says Steve Maxwell, TechKNOWLEDGEy's managing director. "Water demand is totally inelastic—it's still so cheap that most people don't vary their usage with a small change in rates. But with the infrastructure improvements we need, and growing demand, it will certainly get a lot more expensive."

WATER SERVICES, INC.

As in the energy sector, changes to the world's water infrastructure will take decades, not years. In the developed world, utilities, governments, and companies have billions of dollars invested in large-scale water-filtration processing facilities that were built to last for decades—and upgrading that system often moves slowly. In the developing world, the issue of up-front capital costs combined with the right technologies and business models provide their own unique challenges. But shifts are starting to happen to the approximately $400-billion-a-year water industry. Not only is the infrastructure old and deteriorating in much of the developed world but also an estimated 1.2 billion people currently do not have easy access to clean drinking water in the developing world. And with a projected increase in world population from 6.5 billion today to 7.6 billion by 2020, the need for new clean water sources will only increase, according to the United Nations.

Some investors and analysts believe that the value of water will continue to appreciate more than oil as governments scramble to serve billions of people who do not have access to clean, potable water. Water shocks and severe shortages of water, the very essence of life, will change market dynamics as we move into the second decade of this century. Indeed, the significant demand for clean water, and the need to deploy new infrastructure, will provide significant profits for clean-tech investors, smart entrepreneurs, and multinationals likely through 2030.

One way to potentially capture market growth and upside is to invest in publicly traded companies or utilities that are in the business of sourcing, filtering, and delivering water services. As reported by Bloomberg, water outperformed oil from 2003 through mid-2006. As in the clean-energy sector, there are a number of water indexes tracking both water technology and utility companies, including the Bloomberg World Water Index, Palisades Water Index, and Dow Jones U.S. Water Utilities Index. At the time of the publication of this book, one index with an associated ETF was the Palisades Water Index's PowerShares Water Resources Portfolio (AMEX: PHO). We expect to see other ETFs that track the water sector in coming years.

The other opportunity for entrepreneurs is to develop products and form companies that serve markets currently underserved by multinationals and utilities. Chief among these opportunities are the very large yet untapped markets for clean water in the developing world and niche markets in the developed world. Entrepreneurs and emerging companies that wish to compete effectively in this environment will need to address not only technology development but also the entire value chain, including installation, financing, and systems maintenance. We call this opportunity "Water Services, Inc."

"It's hard to just sell people a technology in the water space," explains Texas Pacific Group's Lovell. "It's not like selling someone a laptop that's easy to operate—it's more complicated than that. At the end of the day, users want clean water for their application without having to think about the underlying technology."

As we move into the second decade of the twenty-first century, the water industry will look increasingly like the clean-energy sector, with new distributed technologies and business models emerging. Certainly, it will continue to have its share of mergers and acquisitions and be dominated by very large players. But there will still be room for innovators who develop new technologies and deploy service-centric business models that pull water from the air, turn wastewater and seawater into potable water, leverage nanotechnologies for state-of-the-art filtration, and serve the emerging markets of India, China, and Africa. The ability to transform salt water, polluted well and surface water, and wastewater into clean, high-quality water is one of the last great frontiers of human industrialization.

THE CLEAN-TECH CONSUMER

Water on the go. You've seen the ads for them in magazines or perhaps looked at one at a local sports store: small devices that can turn dirty water into fresh potable water. They've been around for decades for campers and those traveling to remote regions in foreign lands. And in the case of an emergency, nothing can beat one of these. Companies such as Katadyne have been selling them for years. Now consumers can have access to the latest in portable water-purification technology to process even larger volumes of water. Developed by MIOX under contract to the military, and available for purchase from MSR (Mountain Safety Research), this system can purify from 0.5 to 4 liters at a time.

Around the water cooler. While the traditional water cooler is best known as a spawning ground for short-lived office romances and tantalizing gossip, it comes with some other unexpected costs. Not only does a water service company need to ship bottles by fuel-consuming trucks but also someone in the office needs to lift that heavy 5-gallon plastic jug (about

40 pounds) every time the water runs dry. A new solution now comes in the form of point-of-use water coolers, which act the same as the old water cooler, except that they tap into a building's existing water supply. These water coolers are great for gyms, offices, and even homes. Companies such as Innowave and Macke Water Systems offer a range of systems to consumers, including water coolers that combine advanced-carbon, reverse-osmosis, and ultraviolet filtration. Maybe that will help clean up some of the dirty office rumors spread around the proverbial water cooler!

TEN TO WATCH

AqWise
Herzliya, Israel
www.aqwise.com

There are dozens of water-technology companies in Israel that are relevant to the broader international market. But in a nation that reuses 75% of its wastewater, and is a global leader in water-tech development, AqWise stands out. The company's simple yet innovative "biofilm reactor" technology can be used in existing wastewater treatment facilities for municipal and industrial applications, giving operators the ability to add capacity without adding new tanks or infrastructure. The "fecal-munching, bacteria-loving" technology (basically polymer-based beads that thrive on microorganisms) is already in use in sewage treatment plants in Israel, Canada, the United States, and Latin America.

Christ Water Technology Group
Mondsee, Austria
www.christwater.com/EN
Vienna Stock Exchange: CWT

Many of the large filtration and purification companies have been acquired by GE, Siemens, 3M, and others. Christ Water Technologies is a publicly traded pure play based in Austria. The company's reach is impressive, with operations and partnerships in Europe, Asia, and the United States. One key area of focus for the company is in the industrial sector, providing water-purification systems and services to the semiconductor, pharmaceutical, and food-processing industries. With its fresh deals in place to provide such systems in China, and its 800 employees in more than 30 locations worldwide, we plan to keep on eye on this player.

eMembrane

Providence, Rhode Island
www.emembrane.com

With its technology still in development, eMembrane is working to prove that tiny "nano brushes" can capture toxic impurities like a hairbrush captures hair in its bristles. The company's technology, licensed from Japan, can be applied to a wide range of materials development and filtration needs, including water purification. In 2004 the company was recognized for its business strategy, winning the grand prize in the fourth annual MIT Enterprise Forum of Japan Business Plan Contest. Membranes can be used for everything from removing pollutants to desalination, with the promise of lower costs. With nanotech developments potentially still years away from mass adoption, we will be looking at eMembrane and others for potential breakthroughs.

Energy Recovery

San Leandro, CA
www.energy-recovery.com

One of the biggest issues facing the water industry is the pure cost associated with the filtration and purification of water. Desalination, in particular, is extremely energy-intensive and in many cases, cost-prohibitive. Enter Energy Recovery. The company can reduce energy costs for water-treatment facilities with its patented, highly efficient process that recovers energy from high-pressure waste stream during the desalination process. Energy Recovery's technology is becoming an industry standard in existing and new desalination plants and is being used on some of the largest reverse-osmosis desalination facilities in the world, including several in China.

GE Water & Process Technologies
Trevose, Pennsylvania
www.gewater.com
New York Stock Exchange: GE (Corporate Operations)

GE's water division has been on a buying spree, acquiring such filtration and purification leaders as ZENON Environmental and Ionics. The company's water division, while still representing a small portion of the corporate giant's spoils, is now generating more than $2 billion a year in revenue. GE's water activities stand at the center of the company's Ecomagination strategy, along with renewable-energy activities, particularly wind, and industrial efficiency. We expect to see GE continue to expand its capabilities via acquisitions and internal R&D—furthering its global leadership in water technology.

Hyflux
Singapore
www.hyflux.com
Singapore Stock Exchange: HYFLUX

Hyflux is a membranes technology company with a core focus on water filtration. In 2001, Hyflux became the first water-treatment company to be listed on the Singapore stock exchange. Hyflux's ultrafiltration membranes, reverse-osmosis membranes, and ultraviolet technologies are used in Singapore's NEWater plants—and are being applied to other wastewater treatment and reuse facilities and desalination plants. In addition to being active in Singapore, the company's operations span into China, India, and more recently, the Middle East.

NEWater
Singapore
www.pub.gov.sg/NEWater_files/index.html

NEWater, a government-backed initiative, is blazing new trails in the world of water reuse. Utilities, notably in the United States, have added treated wastewater into reservoirs in the past (referred to by the water industry as "indirect potable reuse"), but NEWater is pushing the envelope on new technologies and adoption rates. In less than a decade, Singapore plans for up to 2.5% of its potable water to come from treated sewage. Singapore is now becoming a clear leader in water-tech development—attracting new talent, investments, and global R&D centers—and owes much of its success to the NEWater program.

Siemens
Munich, Germany
www.siemens.com
New York Stock Exchange: SI

Siemens is a global industrial giant with nearly 500,000 employees worldwide working in energy, lighting, electronics, and other sectors. But similar to GE, it's also been positioning itself as a leader in water technology. In addition to its acquisition of water-purification company USFilter for nearly $1 billion in 2004, the multinational has been on a buying spree, picking up a handful of other companies. Siemens Water Technologies is targeting not only municipal water filtration but also water reuse, especially for the lucrative industrial markets. Siemens is currently one of the top water and wastewater equipment and service providers in North America, holds more than 1,100 water-related patents, and has estimated annual revenues of about $2 billion.

WaterHealth International
Lake Forest, California
www.waterhealth.com

With more than 1 billion people in the world living without access to clean water, and anywhere from 2 million to 5 million estimated annual deaths from waterborne pathogens, the developing world offers a huge potential market for water service companies. But as we note in this chapter, it's not an easy place to make money. We believe that WaterHealth International, however, has a shot at success. The company's technology, combined with its "end to end" business model, corporate and investment backers, and initial focus on India, could give the company what it needs to build a sustainable market presence.

YSI
Yellow Springs, Ohio
www.ysi.com

A number of companies are applying new technologies to bring visual data and sensing capabilities to water-quality management—but YSI shows particular leadership and vision as a company. The company provides a range of instruments, software, and data-collection platforms for monitoring water quality and safety, including optical sensors that can detect blue-green algae in drinking-water reservoirs, giving water managers a chance to attack algae problems before they get out of hand. The employee-owned company's goal is to do nothing less than "develop solutions for the growing burdens on our planet's natural resources." As part of that mission, YSI has announced its intention to apply the company's sensor technologies not only to water-quality management but also to tracking air and land quality as well.

9

CREATE YOUR OWN SILICON VALLEY

Jobs, Growth, and Economic Potential

Most of *The Clean Tech Revolution* focuses on specific technology sectors and individual companies that present the best prospects for business and financial growth in the burgeoning clean-tech industry worldwide. But there's another key opportunity that should not be overlooked: the potential for cities and regions to become world-renowned hubs or clusters for clean-tech companies, R&D activities, and showcases for the region itself to walk the walk in its use of clean energy, transportation, and water technologies.

The payoffs can be varied and lucrative. They include high-end job creation and long-term workforce development, overall economic growth, greater investment at all levels, and the chance to completely overhaul a city or region's image into a place that attracts more conventions, more tourism, and more people who want to live there. We'll discuss two prime examples of that phenomenon, the city of Chicago and the state of Pennsylvania, in detail later in this chapter. This opportunity mirrors efforts of the 1980s and 1990s to build high-tech clusters—the various Silicon Forest, Silicon Prairie, and Silicon Glen development initiatives around the world—but with a significant new twist. In clean tech, cities and regions can *lead by example* in their own activities—buying or generating a cleaner energy mix, using fleets of HEVs or FFVs, or constructing solar-powered green buildings, to name just a few.

We believe that by 2020, dozens of clean-tech clusters will flourish around the world. Already, cities as diverse as Austin, Copenhagen, and

Shanghai are competing to lead in various clean-tech sectors. How are these cities and regions positioning themselves to be the next Silicon Valley of clean tech?

While some people will argue that the invisible hand of the market should guide growth and development of industries and that governments should stand aside, we believe the reality is far different. Governments—in partnership with the business and financial community—must take an active role in supporting local clean-tech initiatives if they wish to fully take part in the next great industrial transformation.

Energy, transportation, water, and materials markets, by their very nature, are highly governed sectors. They are highly regulated, subsidized, and often operated by public agencies at various government levels. As we like to say, there is no "subsidy-free" or policy-independent energy source on the planet. All conventional energy industries, from coal, natural gas, nuclear, and oil to the transmission and distribution of electrons, are guided and impacted by governmental and quasi-governmental bodies. Equally, the global water industry, a core utility service, is sanctioned by thousands of governing bodies, including utility boards and ratepayer advocates. Transportation similarly faces mandates and receives supports to lower emissions, increase mileage, incentivize mass transit, and guarantee safe products and services.

We believe it's naive to think that clean technologies do not require, or deserve, similar supports to what has fueled the conventional fossil-fuel industries. The issue is not *if* clean tech should get support but *how rapidly* governments will shift their focus from conventional industries to emerging, high-growth clean-tech sectors. We believe that those countries, regions, and cities that embrace the growth and development of clean technology—that embrace policies and programs to speed up the transition—will lead and win in the twenty-first century.

In this chapter we take a close look at how governments, in particular regional ones, can play a critical role in the transition to a clean-tech future and be at the forefront of investing in change. We look at how governments around the globe are competing to create the next Silicon Valley of clean energy, water, advanced transportation, and materials—and provide a blueprint to get there. In particular, we look at cities and regions that stand to gain the most by attracting new industry, high-paying jobs, and carbon-free or carbon-neutral industries.

CLEAN-TECH CENTERS OF EXCELLENCE

As a business legend in Vancouver, British Columbia, since the 1960s, John MacDonald has seen the city transform from a timber, fishing, and mining port to a major center of technology creation and innovation. So when the cofounder of spacecraft information systems pioneer MacDonald Dettwiler and Associates (now MDA Corporation) decided to end his retirement and enter the clean-tech industry in 2001, there was no doubt in his mind where to locate. He started up Day4 Energy, raised $10 million mainly from local angel and venture investors, and hired about 20 people from as far away as Germany. Commercial-scale production of the company's proprietary high-performance solar PV modules was slated to begin in the summer of 2006 in the Vancouver suburb of Burnaby.

"Thirty years ago, who the hell would have expected the Canadian space industry to be based in Vancouver?" MacDonald laughs. "Now, it's renewable energy and clean tech. What it is, I think, is that the lifestyle here attracts creative people. It's that simple. People with new ideas, people willing to be entrepreneurs—the kind of people we want to hire. Even though real estate is expensive, they keep coming!"

Day4 Energy and thousands of other pioneering clean-tech companies like it present a huge economic development opportunity that Vancouver, and dozens of cities and regions across the globe, are moving to embrace. Like high tech, biotech, and other industries before it, clean tech offers localities the promise of skilled, well-paying jobs, an expanding commercial tax base, and the cachet of innovation and modernity.

But unlike most other industrial development, clean tech gives cities and regions the opportunity to integrate locally produced technologies *into their own operations and activities*—to walk the clean-tech walk themselves. Big-city governments construct and maintain hundreds of buildings, consume vast amounts of electricity, burn thousands of gallons of fuel in public and city-employee transportation, treat and supply water for thousands or millions of people, and sometimes own and run their own municipal electric and/or gas utility. So a city or region can be a test bed for new, cleaner, more efficient energy and water technologies and sell itself as a true clean-tech mecca, not just the site of a slick new industrial park housing companies in the business.

"We feel like we can see what success in this area would look like," says Jennifer Entine Matz, deputy director of San Francisco mayor Gavin Newsom's Office of Economic and Workforce Development. "We build, we travel, we use energy. So the city is a major actor that can really influence the community."

San Francisco and other cities with a long-standing reputation for greenness (such as Seattle; Vancouver; Portland, Oregon; and Burlington, Vermont) are aggressive participants in the twenty-first-century competition to lure clean-tech players to their doors. But dozens of other places beyond these usual suspects are also jumping in with full force. Chicago. New York City. Lausanne, Switzerland. Pennsylvania. Santa Fe, New Mexico. Copenhagen. Los Angeles. London. Shanghai. Boston. Reykjavik, Iceland. Melbourne. Freiburg, Germany. Albany, New York. And not least of all Austin, Texas, which, in the heart of oil and gas country, boldly calls itself "the clean energy capital of the world."

Whatever the merits of Austin's Texas-sized claim, and there are many, this will not be a single-winner, zero-sum game. Far from it. Clean-tech capitals and wannabes are springing up everywhere, and many have a chance at true staying power and success. Start-ups and large corporations alike are setting up shop in global centers of technology and commerce, accessing the best talent, building out capabilities, and creating new markets for their products and services. And for good reason.

We believe that as 2020 approaches, the clean tech revolution will play out in dozens of places around the globe, not in single epicenters like the Silicon Valley or Route 128 of the 1980s. Consider the proliferation of technical talent in India, China, and other developing nations; the growth of global capital sources; the use of the Internet for round-the-clock worldwide collaboration; and the growing demand for products and services in the developed and developing worlds. That's the context in which the global clean-tech industry is growing up.

PICK YOUR STRENGTHS

One big difference between clean tech, especially clean energy, and other technology-focused twenty-first-century industries: the proximity of natural resources matters. That's another reason why there are already many geographically diverse clean-tech clusters, and why we believe there can be many, many more. There's no way that every city, for example, is going to lead in solar. So it just makes sense to pick your strengths.

Pennsylvania, with strong wind resources throughout the state, is making the attraction of global wind-turbine manufacturers a cornerstone of its clean-tech development efforts. New York City is focused on greening what it has most of: buildings. It claims more green-building square footage than any city in the world. Portland's been a leader in green building for more than a decade, after making a GHG reduction commitment in 1993. Its strong mass transit system, coupled with its proximity to agricultural areas in Oregon and southern Washington, also makes it a model location for regional biofuels production. The San Francisco Bay Area's role as the financial wellspring of high tech since the 1980s is proving to be a pretty smooth segue to clean tech. One of the first dedicated clean-energy venture firms, Nth Power, makes its home there, and VC heavy hitters such as Kleiner Perkins Caufield & Byers, Technology Partners, Draper Fisher Jurvetson, and many others are launching clean-tech or green-tech funds. Then there's the bay itself: Its powerful ocean currents through the Golden Gate offer one of the world's best test beds for the nascent technology that turns the tides into electricity. The city's department of the environment is studying the feasibility of such a system in the shadow of the Golden Gate Bridge.

As clean tech scales up and becomes ever more cost competitive, there will be a growing movement, fueled by political pressure in some cases, to source a greater chunk of a region's energy close to home. As we discussed in chapter 3 ("Biofuels and Biomaterials: Developing Next-Generation Refineries and Feedstocks"), today the United States wants to lessen dependence on Middle Eastern oil; tomorrow, California may want to reduce its need for Midwestern ethanol. Grow your own, and keep the jobs and the revenue at home.

WHAT IT TAKES: THE CLEAN-TECH TOOLKIT

So what does it take to create your own clean-tech mecca? Our company, Clean Edge, has some on-the-ground experience with this. In 2004, the city of San Francisco engaged our firm to help the city create a plan for clean-tech development, which we released in an October 2004 report entitled "San Francisco's Clean Tech Future." Through that work, a subsequent progress report for the city, and other research, we've identified five key elements that cities and regions must offer or feature in order to lure, retain, and develop clean-tech providers large and small. These actions can play a significant role in furthering a city's or region's clean-tech development initiatives. In brief, they are:

- **Access to capital.** No business, clean or dirty, can survive and grow without financial backing. With both public money, and private, or some combination of the two, any area must make financial investment or assistance a major part of its effort to attract and grow clean-tech companies. The state clean-energy funds, for example, are projected to invest a total of $3.5 billion in clean-energy firms between 1998 and 2012, said a 2006 study by the Clean Energy States Alliance and Lawrence Berkeley Laboratory.

  Governments can attract businesses with a range of other incentives. They can be the direct, write-a-check variety, like the city of Austin's 2005 grant of $500,000 to the Clean Energy Incubator at the University of Texas. At least fifteen U.S. states have public clean-energy investment funds that are infusing billions into early-stage companies and clean-tech project finance. The Connecticut Clean Energy Fund, for example, created by the state legislature, offers $21 million in grants to Connecticut businesses, factories, and hospitals that install distributed-generation technology at their sites. Across the seas, the government of Abu Dhabi is providing $100 million to a plan called the Masdar Initiative to develop and commercialize technologies in energy efficiency, renewable energy, carbon management, and water usage and desalination.

  But public money is just one piece of the financial pie. Traditional financial centers such as London, Shanghai, New York, and San Francisco are natural magnets for companies seeking VC or investment bank funding, and clean tech is no exception. Public clean-tech development efforts can help bring potential private funders together with young companies. There are many different ways to prime the financial pump. The Commonwealth of Pennsylvania offers a total of $320 million in low-interest loans and investment guarantees to VC firms that invest in mid-stage companies based in the state. It's open to all industries, but since Pennsylvania has made clean tech a top priority for economic development, much of the capital is flowing into that sector.

  Public employees' pension funds are another funding source with huge potential to help build clean-tech clusters. As in many other areas of the clean tech revolution, California has taken the pole position here. Its two largest public pension funds, the Public Employees Retirement System and the State Teachers Retirement System, commonly known as CalPERS and CalSTRS, respectively, have committed to invest $500 million in clean tech and environmentally responsible companies in the so-called Green Wave initiative. In our work with San Francisco, Clean Edge has advised the city to consider committing 0.2% of its managed pension fund assets, or $20 million, to private equity investments in clean tech (but vetted for maximum return as with any other investments). For San Francisco or any other city, pension fund investments offer a great opportunity to show its commitment to the clean-tech sector with real financial muscle.

- **R&D support.** Government or university research labs with dedicated clean-tech programs can be a cornerstone of a region's clean-tech business development. They foster the collaborative work that can cause big technology breakthroughs, hatch start-up companies to commercialize such breakthroughs, and provide a ready source of engineering talent. Sacramento's efforts to become a clean-tech hub, for example, got a big boost in April 2006 when the California Clean Energy Fund chose the nearby University of California, Davis, for its $1 million grant to house the state's major energy-efficiency research center.

  Top technical universities are spawning an increasing number of clean-tech start-ups. Two of the leading advanced lithium-ion battery companies, the Boston area's A123 Systems and Lilliputian Systems, were both founded by MIT grads to commercialize research that started in MIT labs. Beyond serving as a new-company breeding ground, universities and research labs can provide firms in their home cities with testing and tech expertise.

  SustainLane, a San Francisco–based online marketplace for green products and services, rates U.S. cities on their performance each year in sustainable policies and clean industries development. One of its rating metrics, called Knowledge Base, includes data on the extent of a city's collaboration with at least one major research university or federal research lab. But the institutions need to collaborate with one another other, and the city should play an active role in coordinating their clean-tech efforts to get maximum bang for the buck.

"Partnering with other research resources is absolutely critical," says SustainLane chief strategy officer Warren Karlenzig. "Cities can't take this on by themselves. For the city government, those partnerships are a much lower cost way to push all of this forward."

At the University of Texas in Austin, for one, doctoral candidates and engineers from the university's engineering and petrochemical departments work with start-ups at the city's Clean Energy Incubator (partially sponsored by the university) to help hone their products for technical and market viability. Students from the campus's McCombs School of Business in the master of business administration program help the companies vet business plans and financials before they seek venture funding. Entrepreneur Dave Weddle plans to move his start-up Effenergy, which converts municipal solid waste to low-cost electricity while separating carbon, from Southern California to Austin in 2007 because of such university support. "Austin has the public university, the public utility, and the city in partnership to support clean energy," he says. "To me, that shows the depth of their commitment."

Up in the Big Apple, at least four academic institutions—City University of New York, Bronx Community College, Pratt Institute, and Pace University School of Law—have started clean energy or sustainable-planning programs in recent years. "All of our big schools are jumping on this," says Ariella Rosenberg, senior project manager at the New York City Economic Development Corporation.

In the high-tech heyday of the 1980s, business incubators sprouted around the United States and the world to provide R&D support and other beneficial collaboration to nascent hopefuls in software, microchips, telecom, and other tech businesses. The concept has proved popular in clean energy and clean tech as well, and cities seeking to build clean-tech clusters should encourage the starting of an incubator. Although there's no standard model, incubators may provide office space, mentoring, consulting, R&D support, access to funding sources, or in some cases early-stage investments themselves (although just 10% of U.S. incubators do that).

The United States leads the developed world in business incubators mainly or solely devoted to clean energy with 40, according to a 2006 report by British investment research firm New Energy Finance. Some of these are in unexpected places like Tulsa, Oklahoma, and Huntsville,

Alabama. Among other leaders, the United Kingdom follows with 14, Germany has 13, Israel has 8, Spain and France have 7 each, Italy has 5, and Canada has 4.

Solar power is the most common sector represented among the 217 "incubatees" in the developed world, with 55 solar companies involved. Other leading categories are fuel cells (33 companies), biofuels (28), generation efficiency and power storage (23 each), and wind energy and user efficiency (21 each). In the United States, 78 early-stage companies in 11 incubators commercialized 52 clean-energy technologies from 2002 to 2005, according to the National Alliance of Clean Energy Business Incubators. An incubator can help start-ups bridge the so-called valley of death between technology development and initial funding.

The newest devotee of clean-energy incubation, not surprisingly, is China. Although many of its more than 500 innovation centers and university technology parks are basically just transferring former state-owned enterprises into the private sector, New Energy Finance identifies 163 Chinese incubators earmarked for work under China's landmark 2006 national renewable energy law, which calls for 15% of the country's gargantuan electricity needs to come from clean sources by 2020. Many leading Chinese technical institutions are intimately involved. Shanghai's Tongji and Jiaotong Universities, for example, are working on the NRDC's sustainable transportation project in that city, helping develop fuel-cell technology for scooters and other vehicles, and helping cultivate start-up companies to provide it.

- **Workforce talent.** Clean-tech companies need the right people—entrepreneurial, managerial, and technical—to lead and staff them. Most cities and regions that have had success luring or incubating clean-tech companies have major universities, business schools, and/or research labs that are turning out well-qualified people to work in those companies. But once again, the biggest key to attracting talent, as in any twenty-first-century industry, may well be the quality of life that the region offers. "Talent in demand is not going to come to a dirty, unattractive, dangerous place," says Katy McGinty, secretary of the environment for the Commonwealth of Pennsylvania, whose cities had that grungy reputation not long ago. But with a big push for clean tech–

based economic development under McGinty and her boss, Governor Ed Rendell, Pennsylvania moved from forty-sixth to fifteenth among U.S. states in new job creation and beat out Austin and other hopefuls to land the U.S. headquarters and manufacturing plants of Spanish wind-turbine maker Gamesa.

Since universities and business schools are such obvious sources of the technical and managerial talent, regions should encourage them to develop and hone programs in clean-energy technologies, advanced materials, and other relevant areas. But they're not the only source. Today, much of the best "entrepreneurial DNA" to lead clean-tech firms comes from other, more established industries that value innovation, creativity, and speed. High tech, biotech, and increasingly agricultural technology (for biofuels) are providing the right talent fit for aspiring clean energy, water, and materials providers.

"There aren't too many 'clean-tech management experts' so far, but there are a lot of parallel-type industries providing relevant skills," says Rich Amato, former director of Austin's Clean Energy Incubator. "The knock on clean tech used to be that there's not enough management talent in the field, but I'm seeing more and more high-quality people coming in. The other day I got a call from a fifty-something guy taking an early retirement package from Anheuser-Busch who wants to get into biofuels. We're able to draw from that type of talent pool now."

- **Supportive policies.** These include both "walking the walk" city-operations directives such as procurement policies—buying ethanol or biodiesel, say—and economic development levers such as tax incentives or targeted exemptions. Steering a city's, county's, or state's procurement budget toward clean tech can greatly expand market demand to help grow local industry sectors. Another key aspect of the policy toolkit is addition by subtraction—removing often arcane regulatory *barriers* that may be in place. For San Francisco, Clean Edge recommended that the city hire part-time legislative analysts to identify key regulatory obstacles, such as a state law limiting solar rebates to a total of 1 MW per year for all projects within a city.

In one telling example in a 2004 survey in California, 79% of venture capitalists (representing more than $7 billion in private funding) said that current public policy in that state factors heavily in their clean-tech investment decisions. The NRDC and Environmental Entrepreneurs (E2), a nationwide coalition of businesspeople that lobbies for environmental policy on economic grounds, jointly conducted the study. The venture capitalists ranked policy as their number two reason for investing in clean tech in California, and 91% said favorable public policy is a key driver for clean-tech business and investing.

Policies relevant to clean-tech development include traditional business-friendly incentives such as targeted tax breaks and relocation deals. But they also include more recent policy innovations specific to clean tech, such as renewable energy standards, green building mandates, and energy-efficiency directives. And as mentioned above, governments can have a huge impact on clean-tech business development with the policy choices they make in their own activities, such as electricity and fuel use, product procurement, and building construction, maintenance, and operations.

Case in point: New York City's new construction ordinance. Starting in 2007, all new city-owned buildings or renovations in New York with capital budgets over $2 million must meet the U.S. Green Building Council's LEED Silver criteria or better. That will affect some $12 billion worth of Big Apple construction. "We're putting our money where our mouth is," says Rosenberg of the city's economic development corporation. "It creates tremendous demand, and is a great vote of confidence for the growth and maturity of green building design and materials. And for the city, our analysis shows that it won't cost us more, and will save a lot of energy costs in the long run."

One of the most visible policy trends in clean tech in the United States has been statewide renewable portfolio standards, often known as RPSs. Most U.S. cities and regions that we consider clean-tech business leaders are located in states with an RPS, which requires a specified percentage of the state's electricity to be generated from renewable sources by a specific target year. Since Iowa enacted the nation's first RPS in 1991, more than 20 other states and the District of Columbia (comprising well over half of the U.S. population) have followed.

RPS targets range from the very aggressive (California's 20% of power from renewables by 2010) to the modest (Maryland's 7.5% by 2019). But large or small, an RPS gets utilities looking for clean-energy sources to meet the mandated targets, and that means demand for providers of clean-energy technology and services. On the flip side of the coin, business-advantage arguments have sometimes been used to get the renewable standards implemented in the first place. "In many instances, any climate benefits are deemed ancillary to a variety of economic advantages seen as accruing from an RPS," University of Michigan public policy professor Barry Rabe wrote in a 2006 report on state RPS trends for the Pew Center on Global Climate Change. "Many RPS states have emphasized particular economic development advantages as a rationale for action."

Policy levers come in a variety of flavors. In 2005, San Francisco's Board of Supervisors passed a 7.5-year payroll tax exemption for renewable energy companies that do research, development, or manufacturing in the city. For residential and commercial developers that build green, Chicago offers an expedited permitting process (30 days instead of the usual 100) and a free design review, which can normally run $5,000 to $50,000. Seattle is one of several cities running public buses on at least 5% biodiesel; King County Metro Transit aimed to have all 1,200 of its buses using a biodiesel mix by the end of 2006.

- **Vision.** It may be true for any initiative aiming for a significant impact on a city or region's future, but we can't overemphasize the importance of a clear, compelling, and inspiring vision from political and community leaders to make clean tech happen. Figures such as Pennsylvania's Governor Rendell and mayors such as Austin's Will Wynn, Chicago's Richard Daley, Seattle's Greg Nickels, San Francisco's Gavin Newsom, and Dieter Salomon of Freiburg, Germany, have all made clean-energy growth and sustainable development a priority, and the key actors in their communities know it. "Part of our success in clean energy is policy, part is the image of Austin, and a big part is leadership from elected officials like Will Wynn and (city councilor) Brewster McCracken," says Jim Butler, manager of creative industries development, whose purview includes fields like film and digital media as well as clean tech.

This direct vision, action, and involvement is what separates the winners from the losers. Many cities have lots of players who *want* to see clean-tech companies and policies flourishing locally, but lack of an overall unifying vision can lead to efforts that don't capture synergies or even work at cross-purposes. As much as the enviro crowd loves grass-roots movements, a full-blown effort to make a city or region into a clean-tech center really needs top-down leadership.

Chicago's Daley has done a good job communicating and proving the economic development payoff from the city's increasingly green reputation, not just in attracting clean-tech firms (where Chicago's actually had some setbacks) but in luring other big companies such as Boeing, conventions, and tourists. A big step was hiring Sadhu Johnston, the then 29-year-old executive director of the Cleveland Green Building Coalition, as assistant to the mayor for green initiatives in early 2004 to implement Daley's vision on a regular basis. "People throughout the Heartland are really looking to Mayor Daley for leadership in this area," says Johnston, who was promoted to environment commissioner in July 2005. "People expect green leadership from San Francisco, Portland, or Seattle, but Chicago (like Cleveland) has bad winters, lots of snow, and a big industrial base with union issues. Other places can look at us and say, 'If Chicago can do it, we can too.'"

Developing a national or global reputation for leadership doesn't hurt, either. Seattle's Greg Nickels was one of the first mayors to say his city would follow the GHG reduction dictates of the Kyoto Protocol, and more than 320 other cities around the United States have now taken a similar pledge. Austin's Wynn heads the energy committee of the U.S. Council of Mayors and is probably the nation's leading politician promoting plug-in hybrid car technology. Freiburg's Salomon, a member of Germany's Green Party, had his city of 200,000 host the International Council for Local Environmental Initiatives conference in 1999. San Francisco was the first U.S. city to host the United Nations' annual World Environment Day in 2005, where Newsom led mayors from some 50 cities worldwide in signing Urban Environmental Accords for more sustainable development.

Civic leaders' words and actions are important, but a city should also have at least one tangible, visible, high-profile clean-tech project—a physical manifestation of the vision. In Chicago, City Hall used to be synonymous with Daley's father, political machine boss Richard J. Daley, who ruled a gritty town with an iron fist for two decades. Today, the grassy green roof atop a new city hall built in 1995 is a perfect symbol of the city's transformation. New York will boast the world's tallest green building when the 54-story Bank of America Tower opens at One Bryant Park in 2008, a good showcase of the city's efforts to lead the world in green square footage. Philadelphia's green mavens can point to their National Football League (NFL) team, the Eagles, and not just for the team's uniform colors. The Eagles and their Lincoln Financial Field home stadium lead the league in energy efficiency, recycling, and the purchasing of wind power. In 2005, the Eagles and St. Louis Rams played the first NFL game in which the teams purchased offsets for all the CO_2 produced by the game operation and related travel by the teams, fans, and support personnel.

BUILDING A CLEAN-TECH CLUSTER: A HOW-TO GUIDE

Under these key elements, there are several specific actions that a city or region should take as it launches an effort to join the ranks of centers of clean-tech development. Here are some of our top recommendations:

- **Assess current clean-tech assets.** What industries are already there, in energy, water treatment, materials manufacturing, high tech, and other areas, that fall under the clean-tech umbrella? What natural resources are in close proximity—such as wind, tides, and river currents, or farmland for biofuels feedstocks—that the city can leverage to attract companies with the technologies to exploit them?
- **Identify leaders.** The mayor and prominent city council members are critical to lead a clean-tech effort. But cities should also look for business innovators who understand green development and local environmental leaders who are realistic about business needs.
- **Create a magnet clean-tech institution.** EcoTrust's Natural Capital Center in Portland, the Saratoga Technology and Energy Park (STEP) outside Albany, New York, the Sohrabji Godrej Green Business Centre in Hyderabad, India—these are all hubs for public and private-sector clean-tech businesses and related activities. Such magnets come in many varieties—they can be business incubators for early-stage companies, workforce development and training centers, or showcases for clean-tech products. The building itself should embody clean-tech principles too. Some call Sohrabji Godrej the greenest building in the

world—it was the first outside the United States to receive the highest LEED rating of platinum in 2004.

- **Create a high-profile project.** A project of major importance and magnitude helps galvanize industry, the public sector, and the overall community by providing a visible, central focus. Think solar panels on a major public building, a hydrogen or biodiesel fueling station in a prominent location, or (for coastal cities) a state-of-the-art, energy-efficient water desalination plant.
- **Involve local utilities.** A city or region's electric power providers are a huge factor in encouraging or *blocking* clean-tech developments. We believe that cities with municipally owned utilities, among them Austin, Sacramento, and Seattle, have a huge advantage here. Public utilities tend to be much more aligned with city government policy goals and can both test and purchase local companies' clean-energy technologies. Private-sector, investor-owned utilities have a far more mixed record on cooperation in local and regional clean-tech efforts. But if they're brought in early on planning and strategy efforts, they're less likely to resist clean-tech development efforts as competitive.
- **Form a clean-tech advisory council.** Pull together key players from business, government, the financial community, educational institutions and research labs, and relevant nonprofits to advise policy makers and business leaders on the best steps to take to attract and retain clean-tech industry.

These represent just a handful of strategies that a city or region can deploy to harness human capital and build a clean-tech base. While each city or region has its own unique qualities, all of them need cooperation and coordination among the key players in industry, government, and academia. Whether a region features solar power, biofuels, or green buildings, the most important resource of all is human capital, with appropriate leadership steering it in the right direction—combining diverse elements toward a common goal of clean-tech development and prominence.

THE JOB CREATION DIVIDEND

We believe that clean tech will be one of the best creators of well-paying, high-skill, high-quality new jobs in the decades to come. Its potential is now widely recognized by a diverse array of politicians, labor leaders, government officials, chambers of commerce, and business captains, as well as the traditional advocates of green and sustainable business. The Apollo Alliance, a nonprofit group formed in 2002 to push for clean-tech jobs, has united leading unions from the automobile, mining, and steel industries with environmental groups like the Sierra Club, Greenpeace, and the National Wildlife Federation. No mean feat, considering their traditional animosity. Under the banner "Three Million New Jobs. Freedom from Foreign Oil," Apollo (named for the NASA program that fulfilled President John F. Kennedy's 1961 inaugural pledge to land a man on the moon in a decade) is lobbying for $300 billion in federal investment to greatly expand U.S. domestic clean-energy production.

Although its funding goal may be quixotic, the alliance has helped bring the clean tech–as-job-creator theme into the forefront of local economic development. "Far from being antagonistic to heavy industry, our clean-tech effort is putting us back on the map as a manufacturing state," says Pennsylvania's McGinty. "It's also helped us take the mask off the myth that 'environmental' jobs are just service-sector jobs, tour guides, and the like."

Clean tech, and clean energy in particular, also benefits from something called the "jobs multiplier effect." Very simply, this means that power generation from solar, wind, biomass, and other clean-energy sources create more jobs per comparable output than electricity produced from coal, natural gas, or nuclear plants. Studies by a wide range of government agencies, labor statisticians, and advocacy groups bear this out. The New York State Energy Research and Development Authority says that wind power creates 27% more jobs per kilowatt-hour than coal plants do and 66% more jobs than natural gas plants. For the Union of Concerned Scientists, the calculation of wind versus coal or natural-gas jobs is 2.4 times more jobs during construction of wind farms and 1.5 more times during ongoing operation and maintenance. The California Public Interest Research Group estimates that 5,900 new megawatts of renewable energy in the Golden State would create 120,000 person-years of employment over 30 years, whereas the same output from natural gas plants would produce just one fourth as many jobs (29,000).

Job creation, development and expansion of innovative industries, local economic growth, thriving universities and research labs—they're all positive attributes that any city or region, and the business and political leaders who run them, should want to embrace. Then add the cleaner air and water, greener buildings, and improved quality of life that come with actually using clean-tech products and services. That's the promise of a "clean-tech Silicon Valley," but the hurdles to getting there can be formidable. Following the lessons laid out in this chapter should help executives, entrepreneurs, officeholders, civic leaders, and active citizens move their communities down the path toward seizing the growth opportunities of the critical twenty-first-century industries of clean energy, transportation, water, and materials.

TEN TO WATCH

So who's out in front in the race to create clean-tech Silicon Valleys? Let's take a closer look at some of the cities and regions around the world that are making clean tech an important part of their economic future.

Austin: Making All the Pieces Fit

In mid-2005, the Austin culture guide Web site Austinist.com ran the headline "Austin: ~~Live Music~~ Clean Energy Capital of the World?" Clean tech may have a way to go before it topples Sixth Street's clubs as the city's leading feature of global renown, but Austin is one of the world's best models of bringing all the pieces of a successful clean-tech cluster together.

The Austin Clean Energy Incubator, partially sponsored by the University of Texas, has 10 member companies who've come from as far as Oregon and California to take advantage of its consulting expertise, financial referrals, resources such as a shared part-time virtual chief financial officer and close ties to university energy research. Mayor Will Wynn, city councilor Brewster McCracken, and Austin Energy deputy general manager Roger Duncan provide leadership and vision. Solar- and wind-energy resources abound. Austin Energy, the municipally owned electric utility, is the nation's leader in selling green power, with locked-in rates that can make it cheaper than conventional electricity. The utility's commitment to clean power makes it an attractive test bed and potential customer for the renewable energy, efficiency, and grid management technologies of Clean Energy Incubator members and other local start-ups. "Without Austin Energy's support, we probably wouldn't even exist, or at least we wouldn't have had the type of success that we've seen," says former Clean Energy Incubator director Rich Amato. With city funding, the Austin Chamber of Commerce even hired a full-time director of economic development, Lara Valentine, specifically devoted to seeking and supporting clean-energy companies. In March 2007, SustainLane named Austin the number one clean-tech city in the United States for its combination of capital, R&D, and market opportunities for field testing and prototyping.

Chicago: From Grit to Green

The most famous greenery in baseball is the ivy on the outfield wall of Chicago's Wrigley Field, but it's the 150 types of plants and grasses on the roof of Chicago City Hall that symbolize the new green image that the Windy City is quite literally cultivating. Chicago leads the world with more than 2.5 million square feet of green roofs, which have tangible, money-savings benefits beyond their scenic value. They insulate better than most conventional roofs to save energy and heating and cooling costs, capture rainwater, and cut long-term maintenance and repair expenses.

As with all of Chicago's clean-tech efforts, the driving force is economic. Environment commissioner Sadhu Johnston cites arcane stats such as people buying 12% more of any given product when they shop in a district with mature trees, and more obvious numbers such as Chicago now generating $9 billion a year in convention and tourism business. "It's hard to precisely quantify, but we know that [the city's greening initiatives] have had a huge impact on economic development," he says. Chicago is also home to the Chicago Climate Exchange, founded in 2003 as the world's first voluntary but legally binding carbon-trading system. Its 100-plus members include IBM, Bayer, Baxter International, American Electric Power, Dow Corning, DuPont, Rolls-Royce, Motorola, and Ford.

Freiburg, Germany: Sun City

Freiburg, a city of 200,000 on the edge of the Black Forest in southwestern Germany, is the solar capital of the world's top solar energy country. The

Germans are number one in the world in solar energy use and production, with 150 factories producing PV panels and related equipment, and Freiburg is the industry's spiritual center. Home to the International Solar Energy Society, the Fraunhofer Institute for Solar Energy Systems (Europe's largest solar research organization), and many related groups, Freiburg also walks the walk itself with a city council-mandated renewable energy target of 10% of the city's power by 2010.

Led by Green Party member Dieter Salomon as its mayor, the city markets itself as SolarRegion Freiburg and may be the only place with a city-published SolarGuide (in German or English) for visitors to tour its numerous PV installations. If you're downtown, that would be a walking tour: Freiburg's central area is car-free. Needless to say, solar manufacturing is a growing, job-creating local industry led by Solar-Fabrik, a 200-employee, $100 million solar module and system components producer (it recently also entered into solar cell and wafer manufacturing via acquisitions) whose Freiburg factory is Europe's first zero-emission solar fabrication facility. Talk about practicing what you preach (or sell): Solar-Fabrik powers the whole factory from renewable energy sources, including a rapeseed oil–fired combined heat and power unit, passive solar heating, and PV panels on its roof and walls.

New York: "Advantage by Tonnage"

To many, *New York* and *clean* don't often live in the same sentence or book chapter. But the Big Apple is actually the nation's leader in one key aspect of sustainability: limiting personal vehicle use. Less than one quarter of Manhattanites own a car; the national average is 92%. New York is the king of mass transit ridership and urban housing density and was named the American city best prepared to weather an oil crisis (defined as oil at $100 a barrel) by SustainLane. New York is also the capital of big buildings and has many aggressive public and private sector efforts to be a world leader in green building. "We have twenty million square feet of LEED or green building projects—that's bigger than Portland's entire central business district," says Saul Shapiro, vice president for client coverage at the city's economic development commission. "I like to call it New York's advantage by tonnage. And each one of those square feet contributes to job growth in green building and clean tech."

The city landed $224 million over 3 years in state funds for energy efficiency and clean, on-site generation targeted to save 675 MW of power demand over the next 5 years. Showcase projects include a 40-kW solar PV array on the Whitehall terminal for the Staten Island Ferry in lower Manhattan, and a pilot effort with Verdant Power to install underwater tidal-powered turbines in the East River. Add an increasingly clean tech–focused financial community, led by Goldman Sachs and VC firms such as Ardour Capital Investments and SJF Ventures, and you've got a lot of fiscal and intellectual muscle to complement all the green tonnage.

Vancouver: Fuel-Cell Heritage

As patriarchs of its tech industry family tree, Silicon Valley has HP and Fairchild Semiconductor, and Vancouver has Ballard Power Systems. Launched by Geoff Ballard as Ballard Research in 1979, Ballard Power was one of the world's first developers of fuel cells, a technology that's fallen short of its hype but has still become a billion-dollar global business. Like those from Fairchild and HP before it, Ballard alumni have moved on to start or work for a number of fuel-cell companies, making Vancouver arguably the world's leading fuel-cell cluster.

It's also a place where 20% of the workforce arrives by bicycle (the highest percentage in a major North American city). Vancouver's building a "hydrogen highway" to the Whistler ski resort in time for the 2010 Winter Olympics, and even some local car washes use ecofriendly products and donate a piece of their profits to local food banks. Add in the stunning natural beauty of the forests, mountains, and water that surround it, and it's a good recipe for clean-tech development.

"Our lifestyle attributes definitely contribute to people's passion for the clean-tech business," says Paul Zimmerman, CEO of Angstrom Power, a maker of micro fuel cells that power cell phones, PDAs, and other consumer devices. Angstrom typifies Vancouver's clean-tech industry strengths. Its director of business development, Olen Vanderleeden, is an 8-year Ballard Power veteran and the company's backed by several local clean tech–focused venture funds including Ventures West and Chrysalix Energy Venture Capital. Angstrom grew out of research at the nearby University of Victoria, which along with the University of British Columbia and Simon Fraser University give Vancouver a critical mass of relevant academic expertise and support. "For early-stage innovation, good educational institutions are almost always a necessity," says Zimmerman. "You have to have a critical mass of people, money, and ideas."

Hyderabad, India: A Research and Development Tradition

Bangalore is the Indian city best known in the West as a technology haven, but Hyderabad, capital of the south central state of Andhra Pradesh, has a long-standing academic and research tradition that it's now steering into clean tech, especially solar power. Home to more than 100 biotech companies in "Genome Valley" and a new 350-acre nanotechnology industrial park, India's sixth largest city (population 6 million) knows how to parlay its universities' intellectual capital into commercial successes. It's home to a variety of growing solar companies including solar-power lantern maker NEST and Photon Energy Systems, a seller of solar hot-water systems known in India as solar geysers. NEST founder Dharmappa Barki named his product the Aishwarya Solar Lamp, in homage to Bollywood bombshell and former Miss World Aishwarya Rai; "both have beauty and brains," he says on the company's Web site. NEST's Hyderabad factory cranks out 100,000 solar cells a year to power the $30 devices, which replace polluting and hazardous kerosene lamps in rural villages.

Hyderabad's also taking aim at the biodiesel industry, as Andhra Pradesh is home to India's largest biofuels initiative. In a $9.4 million, 10-year project, BP and the influential Indian nonprofit Energy and Resources Institute will plant 8,000 hectares of jatropha, an oil-producing tree with high hopes as a next-generation biofuels feedstock. But the crown jewel of Hyderabad's clean-tech collection is the Confederation of Indian Industry's Godrej Green Business Centre, one of the highest-rated green buildings in the world. The center offers consulting and research on green building design and energy efficiency, and plays regular host to international conferences on those topics.

Copenhagen, Denmark: Wind and Water

Followers of the global wind-power industry know that Denmark is the world leader in wind production per capita, with wind turbines supplying some 30% of the nation's electricity. But they may not know that the world's largest offshore wind installation three kilometers outside Copenhagen Harbor, the 40-MW Middelgrunden Windmill Farm, is half owned by a local wind-energy cooperative of nearly 9,000 people, most of them Copenhagen residents.

That's pretty typical for this picturesque city of 1 million, whose goal to be known as the environmental capital of Europe places it against much larger cities such as Stockholm, London, Barcelona, and Turin. Local utility Copenhagen Energy is a key supporting player; it owns the other half of Middelgrunden and has been a world leader in the use and growth of wind power. And the local clean-tech job market is vibrant. Copenhagen and its nearby communities are home to the corporate headquarters and research labs of both Vestas Wind Systesm, one of the world's largest wind-turbine manufacturers, and Novozymes, a biotech pioneer whose enzymes are used in the production of ethanol and biodiesel around the globe.

Portland: The Sustainability Payoff

Portland, Oregon, perhaps for longer than any other U.S. city, has taken its role as a leader in clean tech and sustainability very seriously. It's a big part of what makes Portland Portland. It was the first U.S. city to make GHG reduction a city policy goal in 1993, and that type of leadership continues. New York may have more total green-building square footage, but the much smaller Portland leads in the number of green buildings and certified green architects and designers per capita. Rated America's most sustainable city by SustainLane in July 2006, it became the first U.S. city to require that all vehicle fuel sold in the city contain biodiesel (5%) or ethanol (10%) starting in 2007. Portland is home to a host of nonprofits and other groups advocating a clean-tech economy, including the Bonneville Environmental Foundation and the EcoTrust Natural Capital Center, and to clean tech–focused investment firms like Portfolio 21.

Perhaps because of this heritage, Portland sets the bar high for itself. The city would like to land more big, job-creating clean-energy companies like Vestas, the Danish wind-turbine pioneer that chose the Rose City for its U.S. headquarters in 2002. But more than 80% of the city's businesses (of all kinds) employ 50 or fewer people. The city's Office of Sustainable Development now works more closely with private sector business boosters such as the Portland Development Commission, honing strategies that can translate the city's well-deserved green prominence into a thriving industry. Says Stephanie Swanson, the office's communications manager: "We're looking at how the work that we've already been doing can be an economic development tool." The strategy tallied a victory in early 2007 when Germany-based Solar World Group announced plans to turn a semiconductor chip factory in the Portland suburb of Hillsboro into the United States' largest solar PV manufacturing facility, creating up to 1,000 new high-paying jobs.

San Francisco: Money and Mind-Set

The City by the Bay, like Portland, only recently began leveraging its traditional green-minded reputation and policies into clean-tech job creation and industry growth. "We looked at our very progressive policies based on the precautionary principle, our solar bonds, our recycling mandates," says Jennifer Entine Matz, deputy director of the Mayor's Office of Economic and Workforce Development. "We realized that we hadn't been thinking of the power those could have in driving workforce development."

Now that effort is under way in full force. As noted in this chapter, the city contracted with our company, Clean Edge, in 2004 to help identify strategies and initiatives to grow the local clean-tech industry sector. San Francisco clearly has all the potential elements. There's a robust community of venture capitalists and investment bankers, in the city and nearby Silicon Valley, looking to fund The Next Big Thing. There's a rich array of world-renowned university and government research labs, and a storied tradition of tech innovation and entrepreneurship. There's a great potential source of clean-tech financing in the mayor's energy conservation account, which receives $5 million to $15 million annually in revenue from sales of water from the city-owned Hetch Hetchy Reservoir near Yosemite National Park. And there are several high-profile projects already under way that showcase the payoff of clean tech, including 60,000 square feet of solar panels on the roof of the Moscone Convention Center, another solar roof on a wastewater treatment plant, and a pilot project literally testing the waters for the feasibility of electricity from the power of tidal currents in and out of San Francisco Bay through the fabled Golden Gate.

"Clean tech here is where biotech was 20 years ago—a nascent industry with many disparate parts," says Matz. "If it's nurtured and given some attention, it could really explode here. There's a real sense that this country's economic future is going to be built around this industry. It's time to put real money and commitment around it, or someone else is going to do it."

Shanghai, China: The Clean Side of Hypergrowth

Can one of the world's fastest-growing cities also be a model for clean-tech and sustainability? The answer may come shortly on Chongming, the Yangtze River island that's home to Shanghai Pudong International Airport and soon, the world's largest "eco-city" of Dongtan. Designed by U.K.-based global engineering consultancy Arup, Dongtan aims to house 500,000 people and dozens of schools, high-tech manufacturers, and public facilities by 2040 in a series of communities that will produce all of their own energy, much of it from clean sources such as the GE wind turbines at a nearby Shanghai wind farm. The first community of 80,000 is slated for completion in time for the Shanghai World Expo in 2010.

The Dongtan plan, partially funded by Shanghai Industrial Investment Corporation, may be utopian. But it's part and parcel of a vibrant, cosmopolitan, can-do city with increasing dreams of becoming China's clean-tech showcase. Shanghai is home to the Shanghai Clean Energy Research and Industry Promotion Center, a showcase of new efficient appliances and building products run by China's first nonprofit energy-efficiency advocacy group. And the city government, exemplifying the collaboration among key players that we've emphasized throughout this chapter, is working with the Shanghai Economic Commission, two local universities, and the Shanghai Municipal Science and Technology Commission on a NRDC sustainable transportation initiative to promote FCV use and build local businesses to supply the necessary technology.

As a growing location for R&D operations of companies from around the world, Shanghai has great potential to lead in clean-tech innovation. At GE Energy's China Technology Center in Shanghai, more than 100 professionals are devoting increasing efforts to commercializing innovation in solar, small hydroelectric, wind, and biomass sources of energy. Like the developers of Dongtan, GE's research managers hope that their work can be a model not only for the rest of China but also for the entire world.

10

CLEAN-TECH MARKETING

Five Key Lessons

Long Island City, New York, is the home to the nation's largest fortune cookie factory and to Silvercup Studios, where HBO filmed scenes of *The Sopranos*. This drab, industrial Queens neighborhood may be best known as the place you pass through to get onto the 59th Street Bridge into Manhattan. Yet here, sharing a parking lot near the East River with 325 yellow New York taxicabs, are the 80 silver Toyota Prius sedans and five Lexus RX-400h SUVs of OZOcar—New York City's first all-hybrid hired-car service.

There are more chauffeured cars and limousines (20,000) in New York than taxis (13,000), and OZOcar's cofounders saw a business opportunity in the growing market sector of "eco-chic"—making the clean, environmentally friendly choice the hip one as well. OZOcar's rates are comparable to those of the gas-guzzling black Lincoln Town Cars that dominate the local industry, and its passengers get more than a cleaner, more fuel-efficient ride. To help make OZOcar's value proposition hip, fun, and practical, each car comes equipped with Sirius satellite radio, Wi-Fi access, and a spare Mac laptop in the seat pocket if you didn't bring your own computer. And instead of a two-way radio squawking from the dashboard, drivers are dispatched via BlackBerry devices.

"In order to reach more people, we have to make it fashionable to be green," says cofounder Jordan Harris. Harris, a former music industry executive, worked with Toyota to help create the recent "Green Car to the Red Carpet" tradition of Hollywood stars such as Harrison Ford and

Charlize Theron arriving at the Oscars in hybrids and electric cars. "The environmental movement has often been righteous and judgmental, and that limits the reach of the message by alienating people. Our motto at OZOcar is style, service, and sustainability."

The OZOcar service is not just about cool, even if it did launch at New York's Fashion Week in fall 2005 (first passenger: Victoria's Secret supermodel Angela Lindvall). It's competitively priced. It's as simple or easier to use than its conventional counterpart—a few Web clicks, a phone call, or a corporate account does the trick for a reservation. The Wi-Fi and satellite radio are perks, with a practical business benefit (the Wi-Fi, anyway) that competitors don't offer. So the "feel good about doing good" aspect of the OZOcar experience is actually pretty far down the benefits list. The point is that for OZOcar, and anyone else selling a cleaner, more energy-efficient product or service, green for green's sake isn't enough. "We're showing that the environmental choice does not have to be how it's been traditionally perceived: less comfortable, less cool, less fun, and too earthy," says OZOcar cofounder Roo Rogers.

So far, it's working. OZOcar's business, growing 13% a week, became profitable in early 2007, just 18 months after starting up. The bulk of its business is its 150 corporate accounts that include blue-chippers such as Goldman Sachs, Sony, Time Warner, and Condé Nast—"both the pinstripes and the fashionistas," says Rogers. The company has plans to expand its service with franchises in London, Washington, D.C., and Chicago in 2007.

OZOcar's success is one of the many indicators that clean tech has moved from niche to mainstream, but it also illustrates the fact that to break out of the "green consumer" niche and sell to a widespread, mainstream audience, it's not enough to have a great product: The world also needs to know about it and be ready to receive it.

As large companies and entrepreneurs alike develop new clean-tech products and services, an equally important focus is now shifting to effective marketing tactics. It's the critical "last mile" to any successful product introduction—reaching the customer. In this chapter, we'll explain what it takes to bring clean-tech products and services to mass markets in the twenty-first century. We'll examine current clean-tech marketing success stories and lessons from the failures of the past and present. We'll discuss several marketing dos and don'ts, and discuss why clean or green, on its own, is not enough to move beyond the tree-hugger niche. Financial value, ease and convenience, and a certain hipness factor can be just as or more important for widespread, mainstream acceptance and adoption. Marketing clean tech, to some degree, is not that different from selling soap suds, sports cars, or financial planning services: how you frame the message can be just as much of a success or failure factor as the product or service itself.

CLEAN-TECH MARKETING 101: FIVE KEY LESSONS

Let's take a look at some lessons for selling clean tech in the mainstream. Below are five recommendations for successful marketing—a critical component to most any company that wants to thrive and excel in a brave new environment. Many of the following lessons apply to business-to-business marketing as well as mass consumer markets. While not every lesson is relevant to every product or service, we believe that together, they form the core of what clean-tech companies large and small must keep in mind as they set about building loyal, far-reaching, and lasting mainstream markets.

Lesson 1: It's All About Cost

In a sense, we could paraphrase the real estate industry's favorite line of "location, location, and location" and call this the three most important factors of clean-tech marketing: cost, cost, and cost. Beyond the hard-core greenie, do-the-right-thing niche, it's very tough to convince mainstream consumers to pay significantly more for a cleaner, more efficient product or service. As we pointed out in the introduction and throughout the technology chapters, *clean tech cannot go mainstream if it's viewed as a premium item.*

Indeed, today's clean tech revolution must overcome the historical perception of environmentally friendly products as elitist—a pricey perk for those with discretionary income. Environmental benefits can be *part of* an overall luxury package that commands a premium—witness the brisk sales and long waiting lists for the $45,000 hybrid Lexus RX 400h SUV (the answer to the question "What would Al Gore drive?"—he owns one) and hybrid Lexus GS 450h sedan. We'll get into the "luxury sell" for clean-tech products in a moment. But as a basic rule of thumb, the surest way to keep clean tech confined to a niche is to consistently charge a premium for it.

There's a raft of clean-tech marketing lessons in the phenomenal, industry-changing sales success of Toyota's Prius hybrid. It's now Toyota's third-best–selling car, and it passed the half-million mark in worldwide sales in April 2006. One lesson is simply that the model is quite affordable for a mainstream audience, with a base list price in mid-2006 of less than $22,000—cheaper than the popular Honda Accord. In China, 200 million people in 40 million homes heat their water with solar power, and it's not because they decided to do something about global warming. It's because the heaters in the world's biggest solar hot water market sell for as little as $160.

On the flip side of the pricing coin—what *doesn't* work so well—take the case of green power. These are programs in which homeowners and businesses can purchase wind-generated electricity and other clean energy from utilities and third-party marketers, almost always at a rate premium. Dozens of utilities across the United States offer green-power options and their popularity has steadily increased, but it's decidedly still a niche; even a 5% customer participation rate lands a utility on the Department of Energy's Top 10 green-power sellers list.

Things changed in late 2005 and early 2006, however, when two of the larger programs, those of Xcel Energy in Colorado and Austin Energy in Texas, reversed the equation and became *cheaper* than the utilities' regular conventional power. That occurred mainly because natural-gas price spikes sent conventional electric rates higher, but consumers didn't spend much time pondering the reasons. Both programs experienced a run-on-the-bank flurry of customer sign-ups, became fully subscribed, and had to start waiting lists. Suddenly, "doing good" was a money-saver, and the market came knocking.

Austin Energy maintained the rate advantage of its GreenChoice program because of its 10-year price lock-in for clean-energy customers. But Austin Energy is the exception to the rule, and its price lock-in is a big reason why that utility is the top marketer of green power in the United States, selling 435 million kW of wind and landfill gas-powered electricity annually. That's 28% more than the number two seller, Portland (Oregon) General Electric, according to the U.S. Department of Energy. Austin Energy's customer participation rate is less than 3% but would be higher if it had more supply to offer and some of its green-power options weren't sold out.

Xcel's experience is more typical of most green-power marketers. Natural-gas price drops sent Xcel's conventional power rates back down by June 2006 so that its Windsource program was slightly more expensive again. But then the utility applied to state regulators for a 13% rate increase for Windsource. "This is a premium price program [that was] never designed to be competitive with traditional generation," Xcel spokeswoman Ethnie Graves told the *Denver Post.* We disagree, and believe that Xcel failed to heed the market message. As a subsequent *Denver Post* editorial said on June 30, 2006, making wind permanently more expensive than natural gas power (a possible result of such a rate increase) "would run afoul of common sense as well as market economics."

If Xcel wants to be a leader in growing the wind-energy market, it can't make wind a premium product and price it accordingly, which unfortunately is what most green-power pricing programs do now. We project that if left to market forces, wind will be price-competitive with fossil-fuel electricity in hundreds of regions worldwide by 2010. As that happens, utilities should view wind as a mainstream power choice, with the advantage of stable rates not subject to natural-gas price gyrations, and market it accordingly. It should be seen not as a premium-priced option but instead as a stable price hedge against fluctuating fossil fuel prices.

Lesson 2: Don't Lead with the Environment

Performance. Superior, state-of-the-art technology. Innovation. Financial savings and high resale value. Those are pretty good selling points for any product, and in fact performance and innovative technology were a big part of the Toyota's original marketing of the Prius. "You'll help save the planet" was not on the list, and for good reason. It's an emotional pitch, appealing to altruism or even guilt, rather than touting the tangible benefits of the product worthy of a buyer's hard-earned money—that's Marketing 101 in just about any industry.

"At the end of the day, being clean isn't enough—these have to be *better products,*" says Joel Makower, founder of online information resource www.greenbiz.com (and a cofounder of Clean Edge) who's consulted to the likes of GE, GM, HP, and Nike on their sustainability and green marketing strategies. "No one ever said build a *greener* mousetrap and the world will beat an eco-friendly path to your door."

In other words, those who are marketing clean-tech products and services need to sell them on many different positive attributes. Environmental benefits can be one of them, but those should be well down on the list, below tangible, recognizable advantages for consumers. And even the environmental benefits issue, as we'll discuss shortly, has evolved from a cleaner-air-and-water goal to a much more multifaceted picture involving geopolitics, economics, and global climate change.

In consumer markets, the most successful clean-tech products *are* better. *Motor Trend* magazine bestowed its coveted Car of the Year honor on the Prius in 2003 and on Honda's Civic and Civic Hybrid two years later. Energy-efficient appliances from makers such as Bosch, GE, Haier, and Whirlpool get consistently high marks for quality from *Consumer Reports* and other product-rating outfits, as do long-lasting compact fluorescent lightbulbs.

Homebuilders such as Lennar of Miami and Clarum Homes of Palo Alto, California, are moving aggressively into the market of solar-powered, zero-energy homes, with other environmental attributes such as cleaner paints low in volatile organic compounds and the use of recycled building materials. Lennar is building the largest solar community in the continental United States (more than 600 homes) in the Sacramento suburb of Roseville; completion was scheduled for 2008. But all the green stuff isn't high on these companies' marketing lists. Clarum's Enviro-Homes are "priced right, and in good locations," says Clarum project development consultant Aaron Nitzkin. "Cost and location are still number one, and we recognize that. Solar power is almost never high on the priorities for most people buying a home, but it goes way up later on the reasons why they *like* their home. It becomes bragging rights when their neighbor's electric bill is three hundred dollars and theirs is twenty dollars."

Of course, there will always be early adopters of the latest and greatest technology, be they part of the exploding crop of young middle-class consumers in China and India or good old gadget-crazed Americans. Within the next few years, having the latest-model iPod or laptop won't be enough—they'll want one powered by a micro fuel cell or a long-lasting, state-of-the-art lithium-ion battery. The large market of early adopters will go for fuel cells or better batteries because they're the latest thing and provide longer run times; the environmental benefits will be secondary.

And don't be fooled by opinion surveys that say people would gladly make the clean and green choice—actual market behavior proves otherwise. "Since the first 'green consumer' study in the late 1980s, seventy percent consistently say they'd buy the green product, but it has never panned out," says Makower. "I've been following this for almost twenty years, and the gap between green concern and green consumerism is pretty vast."

Lesson 3: Framing and Naming Are Critical

In the past few years, Dr. George Lakoff, renowned linguistics professor at the University of California, Berkeley, has become popular in political strategy circles for his study of the "framing" of national issues with language. Now-classic examples include Republican strategists' renaming the estate tax "the death tax" and referring to cutting taxes as "tax relief," both of which helped achieve political goals.

Language is critical to the successful marketing of clean tech as well. SmartPower, a nonprofit based in Hartford, Connecticut, promoting clean energy, did its own naming-and-framing research in a nationwide poll and focus groups in 2002 and 2003. The firm first learned of market confusion. There were too many different names for clean energy in the marketplace: clean, green, renewable, alternative. "It's almost Marketing 101, but it seemed to have missed this entire industry," says SmartPower president Brian Keane. "Coke waited almost one hundred years for Diet Coke, so as not to confuse the customer. But those marketing clean energy had too many different labels."

Then there were consumer perceptions of those labels. *Renewable,* SmartPower found, was too inside-baseball, considered a term for industry experts, unclear in meaning. *Alternative* implied that you had to make a lifestyle change, and people weren't comfortable with that at all. And *green* got the lowest marks of all. Respondents connected it with the Green Party and Ralph Nader, whose 2000 presidential campaign still rankled many people 2 to 3 years later. *Clean* had the best perception, although SmartPower found many still had doubts that clean energy was as reliable as electricity from fossil fuels.

After the initial research, SmartPower ran a public information campaign in Rhode Island, including TV spots narrated by actor Peter Gallagher spotlighting clean energy–powered houses, hospitals, and factories with the tagline "Clean energy: It's real. It's here. And it's working." To emphasize clean energy's reliability, the campaign also noted that the number one buyer of green power was the U.S. Air Force. The result? A thousand new customers switched to the local utility's green-power option within 100 days, and the number of people who agreed that clean energy is as reliable as fossil fuels jumped from 40% to 51%. Since then, the cities of Hartford, New Britain, New Haven, Stamford, and more than 30 other Connecticut communities have joined SmartPower's Clean Energy Communities program, pledging to receive 20% of their power from clean sources by 2010.

Framing and naming clearly relates to the previous lesson of selling multiple benefits, and putting the eco-friendly pitch aside, or at least making it secondary. Sales of Philips's compact fluorescent lightbulbs were sluggish, for example, when the product carried the name Earth Bulb. Sales took off when Philips renamed it the Marathon Bulb, placing the emphasis on its life span, something of tangible, easily recognizable benefit to the consumer.

"Telling people about environmental benefits just doesn't rally them in a big way," says Terry Swack, founder and former CEO of the Beam, an online marketplace for clean-tech consumer products slated to launch in 2007. "Take the phrase 'lifestyle simplification'—how unappealing is *that?* Does that mean I have to give up my TV, my car? Conserving implies limitations, and Americans don't like that. We're not called *consumers* for nothing. Marketing has to include or imply that you don't need to change the way you live or what you do."

Lesson 4: It Has to Be Easy, Accessible, and Convenient

Again here, it's back to marketing basics. Whether it's a hybrid car, a rooftop solar PV system, tankless hot-water system, efficient front-loading washer-dryer, or a hand-cranked or solar-powered radio, the same precepts as any other consumer product apply to clean tech: price, ease of use, convenience, service, and reliability. "Can I get it where I already shop, use it like the one I already use, know that it will work as well?" asks Makower.

Since the 1970s, the answer to those questions for many clean-tech products has often been no. They were rarely available at Home Depot or

Wal-Mart, relegated to the "specialty products" niche sought out only by serious environmentalists and counterculture types. Or they required special skills and equipment appealing mainly to hard-core techie tinkerers. It's no surprise that Toyota's early mainstream ads for the Prius hyped the fact that "you never have to plug it in." Although the plug-in hybrids now being developed (as we discussed in chapter 5, "Personal Transportation: Designing Ultra-Efficient, Low-Emissions, High-Performance Vehicles") get considerably better gas mileage, Toyota knew that hybrid cars would never reach the mainstream sales results that they have if they required such an unusual procedure that people weren't used to. And even so, the earliest Prius drivers were surprised how many of their friends still confused hybrid with EVs and asked them whether the (nonexistent) plug-in requirement was a pain.

Nothing succeeds like success, and the more Toyota Priuses and Camry hybrids, Honda Civic hybrids, and other models show up in America's neighborhood garages, the more they clear up mainstream misperceptions about ease and convenience. They do, after all, have all the features of regular cars. Hybrid SUVs such as the Lexus, Ford Escape, and Mercury Mariner take that effect a step further. "People now see that you don't have to get rid of your dog or your children to drive a hybrid," jokes Christine Biondi, former marketing manager for the Escape Hybrid SUV at Ford.

Convenience can be not only an attribute that makes the clean-tech choice as easy as its conventional counterpart—it can also be the cornerstone of a clean-tech business idea. Take the burgeoning industry of carsharing services, now offering residents in most major U.S. cities the ability to use a car (often a hybrid) for errands and short trips. With self-service key pickup at many locations around town, it's much easier than traditional car rental. Fast-growing private start-ups Zipcar and Flexcar (the latter with high-profile investors such as Steve Case and Lee Iacocca) have moved into a market pioneered by nonprofits such as I-GO in Chicago and City CarShare in the San Francisco Bay Area. The order of attributes on Flexcar's Web site is telling: *convenience*, *affordability*, and *reliability* come before *sustainability*.

"While some Americans will make the right choice, no matter how hard or inconvenient, the fact is that most won't," says Case, whose investment firm Revolution LLC owns a controlling interest in Flexcar. "It's incumbent upon us to make sure they don't have to."

Lesson 5: Remember the Cool Factor

Is green the new black? Many think so. Increasingly, especially for younger consumers, purveyors of clean tech can pitch their products as something unheard of in this market years ago: hip and trendy. The scraggly back-to-the-land types from the 1970s must surely be chuckling at the sight of Hollywood glitterati such as Cameron Diaz, Salma Hayek, Harrison Ford, and George Clooney zipping around town in hybrid cars (or in Clooney's case, the two-seat Tango electric sports car). A-list rock stars such as R.E.M., the Dave Matthews Band, and Pearl Jam are on board too. Pearl Jam donated $100,000 in 2006 to groups like the American Solar Energy Society and Washington Clean Energy Initiative in a "carbon portfolio strategy" to help reduce GHGs.

As a longtime music industry exec and the founder of Virgin Records in the United States, OZOcar's Jordan Harris knows about trends and hipness (and his wife Julie is a clothing designer, to boot). "I've seen how entertainment and fashion can rapidly shift lifestyles and consumption choices," he says. "Somehow, with SUVs, driving trucks got to be fashionable. If we can shift that to more fuel-efficient driving—without demonizing SUV drivers—I think we can really drive a business opportunity and cause significant change."

And if your "cool" cachet is high enough, you may be able to command a premium price for a clean-tech product. That's the vision of Martin Eberhard, a Silicon Valley high-tech inventor who cofounded Tesla Motors in 2003 to build the Porsches and Ferraris of electric cars. Talk about a cool factor—the Tesla Roadster, powered by some 7,000 lithium-ion batteries similar to those in a cell phone or digital camera—does 0 to 60 mph in 4 seconds (almost silently) and can hit 130 mph. The Roadster was due on the market in 2007 at a list price of about $92,000. It's not exactly a mainstream price point, but if it gets buzz going among the Ferrari crowd, that could drive wider sales of Tesla's electric sedan, rumored to debut in 2009 for around $50,000. Tesla's aiming to be the exception that proves the rule of clean-tech pricing (don't charge a big premium) and cash in on what Andrew Shapiro, founder and CEO of green marketing consultancy GreenOrder, calls the Grey Goose vodka effect. That is, consumers will embrace certain products *because* they cost more. Time-honored consumer marketing goals such as cachet and status symbol can apply to clean tech as well.

An early test driver of the Tesla Roadster was noted Hummer and motorcycle enthusiast Governor Arnold Schwarzenegger of California. Tesla's investors include a who's who of Silicon Valley tech success: Google's Larry Page and Sergey Brin, PayPal's Elon Musk, and eBay's Jeff Skoll, as well as clean-tech investment pioneer Vantage Point Venture Partners. Where auto industry mavericks Preston Tucker and John DeLorean failed (they never were able to break into a market dominated by industry giants), Eberhard may succeed. High-end cars will become increasingly high tech—built on computers and with clean-tech innovations such as lithium-ion batteries and advanced carbon-composite materials—and have nothing to do with the 100-year-old-plus internal-combustion engine. So what better place to create a new vehicle than in the heart of Silicon Valley?

Eberhard, like all high-tech entrepreneurs, is also well aware of an important component of the cool factor: design counts. His design team comes from British race car icon Lotus. The Roadster is not dorky-looking, to say the least. Neither is the Toyota Prius. But the same can't be said for the most fuel-efficient hybrid on the road, the two-seat Honda Insight. It gets 66 miles to the gallon, but its bullet-shaped looks have invited comparisons to the Miele vacuum cleaner, and its sales, compared to the Prius, were minimal. Honda stopped making the car in 2006.

Design is a key factor in any clean-tech product, not just cars. In New York City's former Brooklyn Navy Yard where nineteenth-century tech pioneer Robert Fulton launched the steam frigate *Fulton* in 1815, a start-up called IceStone makes high-end kitchen countertops from recycled materials such as glass and concrete. IceStone couldn't possibly compete with the industry standard material of granite if its designs didn't look as good; renowned architect Maya Lin has called them "beautiful." The solar PV industry has worked hard to develop panels, called BIPV, that blend much better into residential and commercial walls or roofs than the traditional panels mounted on racks. Most BIPV is about 10% less efficient, "but most home buyers would trade efficiency for esthetics in a heartbeat," says Nitzkin of Clarum Homes.

The cool factor should emphasize innovation, even if you're selling something as obscure, intangible, and altruistic as carbon offsets, whereby customers buy certificates to fund renewable energy projects that offset a specified amount of CO_2 produced by the buyer's driving or other activity.

Carbon-offsets purveyor TerraPass, which went from a class project at the Wharton School of the University of Pennsylvania in 2004 to a small but growing, nationally publicized business with a joint marketing deal with Ford in mid-2006, is proof of that.

"We felt that fear and guilt—'your car is a significant contributor to climate change'—wouldn't work for us," says Tom Arnold, chief environmental officer of TerraPass in Menlo Park, California. "Instead, it's a message of innovation, how you can help support clean-energy development. Plus, it can be hot and hip, like the Lance Armstrong bracelet, with 52 million sold."

TerraPass membership fees range from $30 to $80 and fund clean-energy projects like a wind farm in Nebraska and a biomass methane digester in Minnesota. TerraPass members are 65% male (a greater percentage than the audience of the NFL, Arnold likes to note)—a demographic feat that'd be unlikely to happen with a guilt-based, think-of-future-generations approach. "Innovation, technology, change, and hope—that's what motivates someone to take action," says Arnold.

Back to Basics

Buyers are motivated by low cost, value, the "cool" factor, reliability, ease of use, performance, convenience—all the things we've focused on in our clean-tech marketing lessons in this chapter. As we noted at the beginning of the chapter, not all of the lessons apply to every clean-tech sector. But one overall precept holds for all: For mainstream consumers, the marketing of clean tech is not fundamentally different from the basic marketing concepts for any other product or service.

Forget about telling your potential customers what they "should" do. Instead, focus on attributes that appeal to their sense of value, hipness, style, technology savvy, or simplicity. "Decades of so-called green consumerism have never really moved the needle in this market," says GreenOrder's Shapiro. "Now, mixing in other factors like global geopolitics and oil prices is shifting things, and I think we're at an inflection point. I've heard from so many people who say things like 'my father-in-law's a Republican who's never done anything environmental, but he just bought a Prius because he's so pissed off at high gas prices.' That's a whole new way of thinking about green."

The more that companies selling clean energy, water, and materials follow the lessons outlined in this chapter and the rules of mainstream marketing, the more mainstream clean tech will become. In many sectors, it's already there or well on its way. Having people like Steve Case on board doesn't hurt. A featured speaker at the annual LOHAS Forum business conference in Santa Monica, California, in April 2006, Case said that at AOL, he'd know that the Internet was truly mainstream when people dropped the *e* and said simply, "Have you checked your mail?" "And I'll know this sector is mainstream," he said, "when there's no more need for a LOHAS conference. It won't be a segment; it'll just be the way that business is done."

11

CONCLUSION

Leading the Way

The clean tech revolution is upon us. It represents the greatest economic and technological shift in modern history: the move from human reliance on fossil fuels to clean-energy sources such as solar, wind, waves, and biofuels; the advent and embrace of clean water-filtration and water-purification technologies to alleviate global water distribution inequities and shortages; the development and deployment of a new class of transportation technologies that are ultra-efficient, carbon neutral, and optimized for a rapidly expanding global population; and the flourishing of a materials science revolution that eradicates pollutants, replaces fossil-fuel feedstocks with renewable ones, and increases efficiency and performance.

If companies, governments, and individuals choose to move down this path with conviction and resources, as many pioneering individuals and organizations have already begun to do, then we will be able to tackle the most pressing global issues of our time while building our economies, increasing our collective security, and guaranteeing brighter prospects for future generations. If we do not aggressively pursue clean technology but continue down a "business as usual" path, we will overtax the earth's ability to support its growing population; see increasingly violent wars over energy, water, and materials; and face other unprecedented security and environmental threats.

The purpose of this book, however, is not to use scare tactics and create widespread despair. That's something that many earnest but misguided environmentalists and sky-is-falling alarmists have done for years. Nor is it our aim to stubbornly ignore the challenges facing us and paint an unrealistic view of the world—one in which environmental and economic issues somehow exist separately, as a small but powerful group of politicians and corporate interests have contended. Instead, our goal is to shine a light on the most dramatic industrial shift in more than a century—the clean tech revolution—and highlight the business and investment opportunities and challenges that come with it.

A POSITIVE TRANSITION

We firmly believe that a transition to a clean-tech future will not harm or hinder our economy, as some entrenched interests and critics would like you to believe. On the contrary, clean tech is serving as the next great generator of high-paying jobs, technological innovation, and global competitiveness. We embrace what we call a "pragmatic optimism" that outlines realistic and achievable pathways to change by deploying the best emerging technologies, the most effective government policies and initiatives, and the most proven financial and market-based solutions.

For more than four decades combined, the authors of this book have tracked and probed the inner workings of the world of technology, from computer chips and consumer electronics to telecommunications and the Internet—and since 2000, clean tech. We remain unabashed believers in the power of technology to play a central role in solving seemingly insurmountable problems. Such daunting issues include the end of cheap oil and other fossil fuels; growing resource constraints as hundreds of millions in China, India, and other nations join the ranks of the world's resource-voracious middle classes; and environmental degradation of epic proportions in the form of global climate change and massively polluted cities, air, and water. There is no silver bullet, of course, but there are thousands of solutions and millions of variations, both large and small, that can be and are being deployed.

From such unlikely quarters as oil-rich Abu Dhabi and the resource-poor villages of West Africa, the clean tech revolution is well under way. By pulling the three key levers of technology, policy, and capital—and exploiting the growth of clean technology among stakeholders as varied as the U.S. military, farmers' cooperatives, and entrepreneurs developing "the next big thing" in a suburban garage—we believe that we can build a world that supports economic growth and sustainability at the same time. In fact, it is financial growth—the creation of wealth around current and future business opportunities in clean energy, water, and materials—that will build a sustainable world. Technology markets, in partnership with supportive capital and the right policies and incentives from governments at all levels, will be the engine that drives this critical business revolution.

We live at a unique time in history when the interests of future generations are finally aligning with emerging technologies and the best opportunity for near- and mid-term profit and economic gain. As GE CEO Jeffrey Immelt says, "'Green' is green." The traditional "choice" or trade-off between the economy and the environment is a false dichotomy.

The opportunities to serve the needs of a growing human population are astounding and staggering in their sheer size. But huge shifts in the energy and water sectors happen not in weeks or months but instead over years and decades. That is, in fact, the big difference between this revolution and the computer and Internet sectors. The transition to obtaining 25% to 50% of our total global energy from renewable sources and efficiency will take at least 20 to 30 years. Earlier in the book we highlighted how many Japanese corporations, and now some Western companies, are in leadership positions today (Sharp in solar power, Toyota in HEVs, GE in wind energy) because of their embrace of long-term business plans and strategies, in some cases reaching out decades. This long-term thinking is one of the most important aspects of the clean tech revolution.

INVENTORS, FINANCIERS, AND ENTREPRENEURS

"The future belongs to those that believe in the beauty of their dreams," said First Lady and activist Eleanor Roosevelt more than half a century ago. That might sound more like social idealism than traditional business advice, but think again. Anyone who's watched the creative forces at play behind the growth of high technology knows that innovation is central to success. It takes nothing less than dreamers and visionaries to make new industries happen and flourish. It requires a "fire in the belly" within policy makers, captains of industry, lab scientists, and entrepreneurs that can come only from people who believe fiercely in the importance of their visions.

Those people are here now, with many more joining them every day. Think about the many pioneering people, and their efforts, outlined in this book. Dean Kamen, the wealthy and accomplished inventor who's developed a potential solution to the twin issues of clean water and electricity in villages throughout the developing world in the form of the Slingshot. Martin Tobias, the ex-Microsoft exec and serial entrepreneur who's refining biodiesel to power vehicles and heat buildings. Harish Hande of Solar Electric Light Company, who's combining the economic innovations of microfinance with the latest PV technology to bring clean, affordable solar power to cities and villages in India and other developing nations. Andy Ruben, the young Wal-Mart executive starting to turn chairman and CEO Lee Scott's vision of a clean-tech, energy-efficient retail giant into reality. And current and former policy makers and government officials, from former Central Intelligence Agency director James Woolsey to Pennsylvania secretary of the environment Katy McGinty, whose actions and advocacy are spawning local clean-tech industries and reducing dangerous dependence on foreign supplies of oil and natural gas.

The clean tech revolution, like other tech revolutions that preceded it, will require leaders who can shepherd us through new territory and overcome inevitable resistance from many quarters; clarion voices who can communicate the mission and vision; and an army of dedicated soldiers working to make clean energy, transportation, water, and materials the norm, not the exception. Farmers and scientists will need to collaborate to turn nonfood crops and agricultural wastes into ethanol and biodiesel. Countries will need to focus on turning the earth's abundant but salty ocean water into clean, potable water with reverse osmosis and other water-filtration technologies. Large companies and emerging entrepreneurs will need to beat down the cost of solar power and deploy it widely on home and factory rooftops, and in large photovoltaic power plants in countrysides and deserts.

INVESTING IN CLEAN TECHNOLOGY: A SIX-POINT ACTION PLAN

Below is our six-point action plan that brings together the actions of companies, entrepreneurs, investors, communities, and other key stakeholders in investing in our collective clean-tech future. We believe the following plan, if fully implemented, would enable the build-out of a robust clean-tech future.

Point 1: Grow Commitments for Venture, Project, and Corporate Investment

There are already many signs of a big financial push from large investors to develop clean technologies, bring down their costs, and deploy them in large-scale implementations. But more venture firms, corporate venture arms, and project financiers will need to join the push. In energy technology alone, the International Energy Agency, an intergovernmental body focused on energy policy, projects an estimated $16 trillion will need to be spent between now and 2030 to meet the growth in projected demand for new electricity and fuel sources worldwide. If a third of that went toward clean technologies, the annual influx of capital would be about $200 billion a year. We call on corporate boards, pension funds, major banks, governments, developers, and other financial players to look at the opportunities and rewards of clean technology, consider the consequences of not pursuing a clean-tech path, and design investment programs that capture and embolden clean-tech innovation.

Point 2: Build Regional Clean-Tech Clusters

Unlike the computer-chip industry, which primarily emanated from one place in northern California, the clean tech revolution will be highly dispersed and will grow out of a diverse set of locations. For local governments to capture their fair share of the clean-tech pie, regions will need to assess their strengths and assets, develop policies and programs to support regional development, and find the right champions to clearly communicate their visions. There's much that a city, region, state, or multistate collaborative can do to attract business and grow its clean-tech base, including regional renewable portfolio and renewable fuel standards, tax incentives, and local government procurement of clean-tech products and services, From green-building and wind-energy development firms taking root in Portland, Oregon to venture finance and solar PV clusters developing in the San Francisco Bay Area to the fuel-cell and advanced-battery industries growing up around Boston, each region can attract its fair share of clean-tech spoils by developing policies and programs to attract and keep businesses.

Point 3: Shift Subsidies from Conventional Energy Sources to Clean Tech

Skeptics and naysayers have traditionally dismissed clean-energy technologies like solar and wind by arguing that these technologies "can't compete on price without public subsidies." The problem with this argument is that there is no such thing as subsidy-free energy, and there never has been in the modern world. The history of coal, oil, natural gas, large-scale hydroelectric, and especially nuclear power—a subsidy all-star if there ever was one—makes it clear that all these industries' growth occurred partly with the direct and indirect financial support of governments that wanted to encourage them. There's nothing inherently wrong with that, but don't ask other energy sources to compete on the same playing field without comparable support.

With policies and incentives, governments decide what they want to encourage most. We strongly believe that governments need to shift many of those subsidies away from mature and established industries and toward high-growth sectors in clean energy, water, and materials. In the United States alone, according to the Congressional Research Service, the public policy research arm of the U.S. Congress, the federal government spent $74 billion to support R&D for nuclear and fossil fuels from 1973 to 2003. Nuclear-energy R&D accounted for nearly $50 billion of this expenditure. During the same time frame, renewable-energy technologies and energy efficiency combined received just $26 billion. At a time when oil companies are reporting record profits, the U.S. federal government is still offering the industry billions in incentives, and more than half of the U.S. Department of Energy's fiscal 2006 R&D budget went to nuclear energy and atomic defense activities. In 2006, the Department of Energy's R&D budget for fossil fuels (coal, oil, and gas) was twice that of renewable-energy sources. A shift must be made to level the playing field and to support the growth sectors of the future: solar, wind, biofuels, and more.

And just as important, subsidies and incentives need to be reliable, long term, and consistent, as they have been for decades for conventional fossil fuels. The wind industry, for example, currently has a PTC in the United States that has catalyzed industry growth. But it comes up for renewal every 2 to 3 years. This doesn't give the industry a long-term, consistent policy on which to depend. Many have started to call for a 5-year, 10-year, or even permanent term for the PTC, and with GE, Goldman Sachs, utility giant FPL, and others seeing multibillion-dollar annual revenues from their wind-energy efforts, the potential for some kind of long-term extension looks promising.

We believe that rebates, subsidies, and incentives must be designed intelligently and with an eye on bringing down costs—not simply as large giveaways to companies. In Germany, for example, the solar rebate equates to approximately 60 cents per kilowatt-hour, considerably more than the prevailing cost of electricity in Germany. This "rich" subsidy has made Germany the leading solar industry in the world today, but it's neither sustainable nor smart. Instead we recommend subsidies that enable cost parity between an emerging technology (such as solar and wind) and prevailing prices for conventional sources (such as coal or natural gas)—and that then decline over time. The goal is not to simply shift subsidies from one special interest to another but to use government incentives to quickly grow self-sufficient, competitive markets and to bring down costs.

Point 4: Support Emerging Economies With a Multibillion-Dollar, Multiyear Clean-Tech Fund

The World Bank estimates that two-thirds of the increase in world energy demand through 2030 will come from the developing world. It will cost trillions of dollars to build infrastructure and provide for the needs of the 2 billion people without access to electricity and the 1.2 billion people without easy access to potable water. To solve this serious resource inequity, we believe in the need for development funds to focus on building clean energy and water sources in the developing world.

The Clinton Global Initiative, the foundation headed by former U.S. president Bill Clinton, is working to raise funds from major donors to tackle such pressing issues as climate change, global poverty, and ethnic and religious conflict. Since 2005, Clinton has garnered hundreds of commitments valued at more than $8 billion. Among the commitments are pledges for solar, wind, and biofuels developments by nonprofits, governments, and corporations.

Another former president, ex-Soviet head Mikhail Gorbachev, now leads Green Cross International, a global nonprofit environmental organization. Gorbachev and Green Cross have called for the creation of a $50 billion Global Solar Fund over 10 years. The fund, according to Green Cross, could be raised by cutting subsidies for fossil fuels such as oil and coal. The money would fund the installation of solar PV equipment around the planet, thereby driving down the price of photovoltaics and creating a mass market for a clean-energy technology.

In early 2006, U.K. finance minister Gordon Brown called for rich nations to spend $20 billion to help finance developing nations' clean-energy projects. Others, such as award-winning journalist and author Ross Gelbspan have proposed even larger commitments. Gelbspan has called for the creation of a $300 billion clean-energy fund for developing countries through a tax on international currency transactions.

It's uncertain whose programs will gain traction and which will be long forgotten a decade from now, but a number of great minds are already thinking about how to fund clean-tech development in the developing world.

Point 5: Implement "Sin" Taxes and Carbon Trading Schemes

For any significant shift to clean technologies to occur, we will need more aggressive public policies and innovative market mechanisms to place a greater value on activities that reduce GHGs and other pollution while punishing companies and technologies that increase them. Many places in the world today have so-called sin taxes on cigarettes and alcohol. So why not tax our other great addiction: fossil fuels?

It's already being done in places such as Sweden, which is seeking to become oil-free by 2020. We know the "T word" is a third-rail issue in American politics today. But sin taxes have been more palatable because they tap revenue from the "public bad" (tobacco) and shift it to the public good (cancer research and health care). We'd like to see a similar sin tax, for example, on the most fuel-inefficient vehicles—Hummers and very large SUVs—with the revenue then funding technologies for vehicle efficiency and cleaner fuels.

In electric power, California, Oregon, Washington, and other states already collect what's called a system benefit charge (deftly avoiding the T word). In California it's a modest monthly utility bill surcharge that funds energy efficiency, clean-energy R&D, residential and industrial programs, rebates, and education throughout the state. That's helped make California the nation's efficiency and clean-energy leader, and that will likely continue as the California Public Utilities Commission funds $2 billion in efficiency programs by utilities from 2006 to 2008, the largest such program in industry history.

Carbon trading will likely be a huge financial growth area through 2020. It's the leading example of what's known as a clean development mechanism—a market-based scheme that places an economic value on reducing GHG emissions. It's a complicated, challenging and often far from perfect mechanism, but the underlying theory is simple enough: companies that reduce GHGs earn credits that they can sell to companies that do not. In other words, there's a direct, tangible, predictable cost penalty for producing CO_2 emissions, and an immediate economic incentive for reducing them.

The United Nations Climate Change Secretariat says that the clean development mechanism set up under the Kyoto Protocol will help reduce more than 1 billion tons of GHGs, or the current annual emissions of Spain and the United Kingdom combined, by 2012. The incentive to earn credits has helped initiate more than 800 clean-energy projects around the world, including wind farms in India and power plants in Brazil that burn sugar cane waste, says the secretariat.

Some environmentalists condemn clean development mechanisms as a "license to pollute." But we believe that if properly set up, implemented, and enforced, such schemes effectively bring the power of marketplace economics to global environment issues and will be a significant and welcome driver of clean-tech investments.

Point 6: Encourage and Support Clean-Tech Education and Collaboration

A nation is only as competitive as the students that it produces. Clean technologies will require great scientists, mathematicians, engineers, marketers, engineers, policy makers, and others that can build the technologies of the future. This will require educational programs from kindergarten through grade 12 that prepare students for a wide range of opportunities arising out of the intersection of the economy and the environment. It will necessitate cooperation among universities and academic institutions within states and regional governments, as well as at the national level.

In addition to traditional education, the Internet can be used to share information and promote clean-tech collaboration among people, companies, and governments. The Canadian province of Ontario, for example, has published maps of clean-energy sources within its borders—enabling developers and businesspeople to more easily scope and cite wind projects and other developments. Others have created Web sites with information on how to "hack" a Toyota Prius to turn it into a plug-in hybrid. The opportunities for education and collaboration are nearly limitless but require a concerted effort by educators of all stripes to focus on the most effective curricula and information sharing.

THE CHALLENGES AHEAD

We believe these six actions alone would go far in guaranteeing the success and growth of the clean tech revolution. As in any revolutionary shift, however, significant challenges remain in the transition to a clean tech–driven economy.

Entrenched interests will fight to hold on to a business-as-usual scenario—working to protect their livelihood and incentives. Some groups will continue to vehemently deny human impact on climate change, even in the face of incontrovertible evidence. Others will be so busy building up their economies they won't realize the detrimental impact to their people and society in the form of disease and pollution caused by fossil fuels. Supply constraints will create momentary stumbling blocks to clean-tech development in the form of shortages of critical materials like processed steel and silicon. Investors, at times, may exhibit irrational exuberance—running up the prices of stocks with valuations that outstrip their real value. Venture capitalists, too, may fall prey to this behavior, with too many dollars chasing too few deals resulting in a herd mentality and overvalued private offerings. And when demand outpaces growth, we will see occasional increases in pricing for certain clean-tech goods and services.

But overall we find that the confluence of forces—the six "Cs" we described in the first chapter—is so great, and the support among diverse groups so coherent, that the clean tech revolution represents one of the best unifying opportunities of a generation—and the greatest promise for wealth creation, sustainable economies, and quality of life for billions of citizens around the world. Of course there will be winners and losers, as there are in any dynamic industrial shift. A rising tide does *not* lift all boats, but it can often lift those with savvy management, reliable products and services, strong market positioning, and effective marketing strategies. While some observers, and we partly agree, are concerned that some clean-tech sectors may be overheating or some company valuations may be too high, we believe in the fundamental strength of this ongoing opportunity. It is the next big growth and investment opportunity, not for years but for decades to come.

LEADING THE WAY

We are in the midst of one of the greatest shifts in human history. Within 50 years, we'll look back at the beginning of the twenty-first century and see it as the tipping point for clean technology. And as a human race, we will wonder how we ever operated without considering the twin concerns of balancing economics and the environment.

We therefore believe the choice for investors, companies, governments, and individuals is simple. Be part of one of the greatest business and economic shifts in recorded human history or become extinct like the dinosaurs whose fossils fueled the last great industrial revolution. The opportunity for wealth creation stands on one side of the equation and the very real threat of the collapse of civilization as we know it on the other.

To borrow the words of former president Ronald Reagan: "If not us, who? And if not now, when?" These words ring true today for the great challenge we face in serving the needs of a growing population and ensuring our long-term environmental and economic survival. We hope you'll join us in the clean tech revolution. It offers the promise of untold profits for companies, investors, governments, and individuals, and we believe it is the most exciting and important revolution of our time.

NOTES

INTRODUCTION

Much of the introduction draws on our research and reports at Clean Edge, all available for download at www.cleanedge.com. These include *Clean Tech: Profits and Potential, Clean Energy Trends 2005, Clean Energy Trends 2006,* and *Clean Energy Trends 2007*. The latter three include important data from Nth Power and Clean Edge on VC investments in clean-energy technologies. Several key reports provided clean-tech and overall industry statistics, including the International Energy Association's *World Energy Outlook 2005* (www.iea.org/Textbase/npsum/WEO2005SUM.pdf); Renewable Energy Policy Network for the 21st Century's (REN21's) *Global Status Report 2006*, www.ren21.org/globalstatusreport/issueGroup.asp; the Global Wind Energy Council's *Global Wind 2005 Report,* www.gwec.net/index.php?id=49; and the U.S. Environmental Protection Agency, Top 25 Green Power Partners data, www.epa.gov/greenpower/partners/top25.htm.

Interviews with a wide range of industry experts and participants produced valuable information, insight, and quotes for the introduction. From the investment world, these included Ira Ehrenpreis, Technology Partners; Sunil Paul, private investor; Nancy Floyd, Nth Power; Nicholas Parker, Clean Tech Capital Group; Colin le Duc, Generation Investment Management; Chris Moran, Applied Ventures; Gary Rieschel, Qiming Venture Partners; G. Bickley "Bic" Stevens, Ardour Capital; and Diana Propper de Callejon, Expansion Capital Partners. Key corporate executives interviewed were Ray Anderson, Interface; Ron Kenedi, Sharp; Gregg Semler, ClearEdge Power; and Thomas Werner, SunPower. We spoke with a variety of industry analysts and consultants, including Amory Lovins, Rocky Mountain Institute; Jim Harding, former director of Seattle City Light; R. James Woolsey, Booz Allen Hamilton; Donald Aitken, Union of Concerned Scientists; Christopher Flavin, Worldwatch Institute; Chris Raczkowski, Azure International; Dan Carol, Apollo Alliance; Jeff Goodell, author of *Big Coal: The Dirty Secret Behind America's Energy Future* (Houghton Mifflin, 2006); and Mark Trexler, Trexler Climate and Energy Services.

Several references and quotes came from speakers at various industry conferences that the authors attended in 2005 and 2006. These presenters included Steve Case, Revolution LLC; John Doerr, Kleiner Perkins Caufield & Byers; William Reilly, Aqua International; Mark Little, GE Energy; Matthew Simmons, Simmons & Co.; Henry Groppe, Groppe Long

& Littell; Peter Schwartz, Global Business Network; and Win Neuger, AIG. Articles referenced include several pieces covering the Trojan nuclear power plant demolition in the *Oregonian*, May 22, 2006; John Doerr's essay "California's Global Warming Solution," *Time*, September 11, 2006; and "Super Shoppers," *U.S. News & World Report*, May 1, 2006.

CHAPTER 1

This chapter is based on conversations and interviews with solar industry executives and experts, including Dave Pearce, Miasolé; Dan Shugar, PowerLight; Suvi Sharma, Solaria; Ron Kenedi, Sharp; Bill Gross, Energy Innovations; Brad Hines, Practical Instruments; Charlie Gay, Applied Materials; Thomas Werner, SunPower; Jesse Pichel, Piper Jaffray; Jigar Shah, SunEdison; Alan Barnett, University of Delaware; Bob Freling, Solar Electric Light Fund; Christine Peterson, Foresight Institute; and Scott Mize, nanotech entrepreneur. Additional inspiration and insight was gleaned for this section through attendance at a range of relevant conferences, including Solar Power 2004, 2005, and 2006. A number of reports were instrumental in the development of this chapter, including *Our Solar Power Future*, September 2004; *A Vision for Crystalline Silicon Solar Cells*, by Richard M. Swanson, June 2004; and *Study of Potential Cost Reductions Resulting from Super-Large-Scale Manufacturing of PV Modules*, by M.S. Keshner and R. Arya, final NREL Subcontract Report 7 August 2003–30 September 2004. Web sites and online newsletters of value that provided information to the authors for the solar chapter include www.renewableenergyaccess.com, www.solarbuzz.com, and www.cleanedge.com. For readers looking for additional reference material, we recommend an earlier report by Clean Edge and the Solar Catalyst Group titled the *Solar Opportunity Assessment Report* (SOAR), which can be downloaded online at www.solarcatalyst.com and www.cleanedge.com.

CHAPTER 2

Key interviews for this chapter were conducted with Donald Aitken, Union of Concerned Scientists; Roger Duncan and Elizabeth Kasprowicz, Austin Energy; David Frost, Energy Unlimited; Nick Brod, Vestas Americas; Ted Bernhard, Stoel Rives; Craig Garcia, Advanced Micro Devices; and Peter O'Donnell, San Francisco Department of the Environment. Articles referenced included Naazneen Karmali, "Wind Man," *Forbes*, June 19, 2006. Several Web sites provided important industry statistics and growth trends, including those of the American Wind Energy Association (www.awea.org), Canadian Wind Energy Association (www.canwea.org), European Wind Energy Association (www.ewea.org), and the Earth Policy Institute (http://www.earth-policy.org/Indicators/Wind/2006.htm). Much of the information about wind industry opportunities in China came from interviewees and presenters at the Renewable Energy Finance Forum China conference in Beijing in March 2006, including Josu Arlaban Gabeira of Acciona, Josh Bradshaw of Roaring 40's, and Eric Martinot of Tsinghua University. Other conferences with useful resources were AWEA's Windpower '05 in Denver in June 2005 and Pacific Growth Equities' Clean Tech Investing Conference in San Francisco in November 2006. The U.S. Environmental Protection Agency's green-power Web site at www.epa.gov/greenpower contains valuable data on green-power providers, purchasers, and usage trends.

CHAPTER 3

This chapter is based on conversations and interviews with biofuel and biopolymer industry executives and experts, including Martin Tobias, Imperium Renewables; Eric Bowen, Sigma Capital; James Woolsey, former Central Intelligence Agency director; Toby Janson-Smith, Conservation International; Thomas Endicott, SeQuential Biofuels; Dan Kammen, University of California, Berkeley; and Rhys Roth, Climate Solutions. Additional inspiration and insight was gleaned for this chapter through attendance at a range of relevant conferences, including Harvesting Clean Energy Conference VI, the Second Annual Clean-Tech Investor Summit, and the 2006 National Biodiesel Conference and Expo. A number of reports assisted in the development of this chapter, including *Impacts on U.S. Energy Expenditures of Increasing Renewable Energy Use*, by Mark A. Bernstein et al., published in 2006 by the RAND Corporation; *The New Harvest: Biofuels and Windpower for Rural Revitalization and National Energy Security*, by Patrick Mazza, et al., November 2005, the Energy Foundation; *Henry Ford, Charles Kettering and the "Fuel of the Future,"* copyright Bill Kovarik, Ph.D., 1998, http://www.radford.edu/~wkovarik/papers/fuel.html#-introduction; and *Growing Energy: How Biofuels Can Help End America's Oil Dependence*, principal author, Nathanael Greene, published December 2004 by the NRDC. Web sites that provided additional information to the authors for this chapter included www.wikipedia.org, www.eere.energy.gov/biomass, and www.ethanolrfa.org.

CHAPTER 4

Interviews with a wide range of executives and experts in green buildings and energy efficiency constituted the bulk of research for this chapter. They include Andy Ruben, Wal-Mart; Tom Hicks, U.S. Green Building Council; Jon Livingston, PG&E; Ralph Cavanagh and Barbara Finamore, NRDC; Amory Lovins, Rocky Mountain Institute; Eric Martinot, Tsinghua University, Zhang Zhong Chen, Shanghai Energy Conservation Supervision Center; Chris James, Cree; and Aaron Nitzkin, Clarum Homes. Key reports cited were the 2005 Turner Construction *Market Barometer Survey*, the 2005 Ren21 report on global clean-energy development, Interface Engineering's *Green Building Breakthrough: Engineering a Sustainable World,* and Ed Mazria's "It's the Architecture, Stupid!" (*Solar Today* magazine, May/June 2003). Useful Web sites for this chapter and for further research include those of the U.S. Green Building Council (www.usgbc.org), the National Association of Home Builders (www.nahb.org), the WGBC (www.worldgbc.org), Climate Solutions (www.climatesolutions.org), and the Rocky Mountain Institute (www.rmi.org).

CHAPTER 5

Interviews or conference presentations by a number of key industry principals provided significant material for this chapter. Among them are Tony Posawatz, General Motors; Niel Golightly, formerly of Ford; Loren Beard, DaimlerChrysler; Celeste Migliore, Toyota; Gunnar Lindstrom, Honda; Martin Eberhard, Tesla Motors; Felix Kramer and Ron Gremban, CalCars; Bill Rankin, UQM Technologies; Jim Motavalli, *E—The Environmental Magazine,* and Christopher Flavin, Worldwatch Institute. Several reports provided important data points and insight. These include *Mileage from Megawatts*, Pacific Northwest National

Laboratory, U.S. Department of Energy, December 2006; *The Emergence of Hybrid Vehicles: A Game-Changing Technology with Big Implications*, by Amy Raskin and Saurin Shah, Alliance Bernstein, June 2006; and *Emissions, Global Warming, and Energy Security*, by Mark Duvall, Electric Power Research Institute, PHEV Workshop, Nov. 15, 2003. News and magazine articles referenced include "An Interview with Bill Ford and Alan Mulally," by David Kiley, *Business Week*, September 7, 2006; "Boeing's Plastic Dream Machine," *Business Week*, June 20, 2005; "2004 Car of the Year," *Motor Trend*, December 2003; "More Hybrids to Enter Chinese Market by Year's End," *Xinhua*, February 13, 2006; "Carbon Fiber Cars Could Put U.S. on Highway to Efficiency," *Clean Edge News*, March 8, 2006; and "Honda Hypes Hydrogen for Homes," by Tyler Hamilton, *Clean Break*, November 22, 2005.

CHAPTER 6

Insight and background for this chapter came from conversations and interviews with Chuck McDermott, Rockport Capital Partners and the GridWise Alliance; Peter Corsell, GridPoint; Leroy Nosbaum, Itron; Dr. Wade Adams, the Richard E. Smalley Institute for Nanoscale Science and Technology; Nancy Floyd, Nth Power; Jesse Berst, Center for Smart Energy; Bill Kingsley, EnerTech Capital; Steve Hauser, Pacific Northwest National Laboratory (PNNL), and Adam Bergman, Jefferies & Company. Articles and reports cited in this chapter include "Smart Grids and the American Way," by Roger Anderson and Albert Boulanger, *Mechanical Engineering "Power & Energy"* magazine, March 2004; "The Emerging Smart Grid," by Global Environment Fund and Center for Smart Energy, October 2005; "INTELLIGRID: A Smart Network of Power," by Paul Haase, *EPRI Journal*, fall 2005; and "The Information Factories," by George Gilder, *Wired*, October 2006. Recommended Web sites and newsletters, which supported the research of this chapter, include www.worldchanging.com, the *Smart Grid Newsletter* by the Center for Smart Energy (www.smartgridnews.com), and www.energypriorities.com.

CHAPTER 7

Material for this chapter drew heavily on a number of reports from market researchers, consultants, and industry experts in the United States and Europe. Sources included *Fuel Cell Market Survey: Military Applications*, Fuel Cell Today, 2005; *Focus on Batteries*, Freedonia Group, September 2006; *World Emerging Battery Markets*, Frost & Sullivan, May 2006; *The Defense Industry in the 21st Century: Thinking Global or Thinking American?* PricewaterhouseCoopers, 2005; and *Energy Security and Emergency Preparedness: How Clean Energy Can Deliver More Reliable Power for Critical Infrastructure and Emergency Response Missions*, Clean Energy Group, October 2005. Key industry principals whom we interviewed included Jean-Louis "Dutch" DeGay, equipment specialist and outreach program coordinator for the U.S. Army's Future Force Warrior Technology Program Office; Joseph Edwards, vice president of new ventures for AeroVironment; Scott Sklar, vice president of SkyBuilt Power and former president of the Solar Electric Industries Association; and Howard Berke, founder, chairman, and CEO of Konarka.

A number of articles provided important information. These included "In the Iraqi War Zone, U.S. Army Calls for 'Green' Power," by Mark Clayton, *Christian Science Monitor*, September 7, 2006; "Venture Firms Chase Battery Makers," by Jonathan Shieber, *Wall Street Journal,* November 29, 2006; "3M: A Safe Play in Lithium Ion Batteries," by Jack Uldrich, www.themotleyfool.com, October 31, 2006; "The Ultra Battery," by Kevin Bullis, *MIT Technology Review,* February 13, 2006; "The New Electric Lamp," by Jeremy Caplan, *Time,* May 29, 2006; and "The Katrina Crisis" (op-ed) by Daniel Yergin, *Wall Street Journal,* September 2, 2005.

CHAPTER 8

Information and insight for this chapter came from a range of interviews with water and technology industry leaders, including Tralance Addy, WaterHealth International; Laura Shenkar, water-tech consultant; Doug Brown, DFJ Element; Abe Shear, Aqua Sciences; Steve Maxwell, TechKNOWLEDGEy; Ira Ehrenpreis, Technology Partners; Evan Lovell, Texas Pacific Group Ventures; Ray Doane, Water Security; Scott Mize, nanotech consultant; Scott Livingston, Livingston Group; and Mathew Nordon, Lux Research. Source materials included the following reports and articles: "The World Health Report 2002," World Health Organization, 2002; "Dirty Water: Estimated Deaths from Water-Related Diseases 2000–2020," a Pacific Institute Research Report by Peter H. Gleick, August 15, 2002; "Water Outperforms Oil, Luring Pickens, GE's Immelt, Guy Hands," June 26, 2006 article on Bloomberg News; "Water: Pure, Refreshing Defensive Growth," report by Deane M. Dray, the Goldman Sachs Group, Inc., August 27, 2006; "Desalination, with a Grain of Salt: A California Perspective," by Heather Cooley, Peter H. Gleick, and Gary Wolff, Pacific Institute, June 2006; "Energy Security: The Connection: Water and Energy Security," by Allan R. Hoffman, published by Institute for the Analysis of Global Security, August 13, 2004; and a radio report entitled "Water Desalination Without Emissions," December 6, 2006, ABC News, Australia. Web sites for the companies and organizations noted in this chapter, in particular NEWater, along with www.watertechonline.com, www.cnet.com, www.wired.com, and www.cleanedge.com provided additional insight and leads into global water developments.

CHAPTER 9

The majority of material in this chapter comes from personal and telephone interviews with key government figures in the regions and cities that we've spotlighted. These include Katy McGinty, Commonwealth of Pennsylvania; Ariella Rosenberg and Saul Shapiro, New York City Economic Development Corporation; Stephanie Swanson, Portland, Oregon, Office of Sustainable Development; Jim Butler, City of Austin; Sadhu Johnston, City of Chicago; and Jennifer Entine Matz, San Francisco mayor's office. Additional information and insight came from executives at companies doing business in these clean-tech cluster areas: John MacDonald of Day4 Energy, Dave Weddle of Effenergy, Paul Zimmerman of Angstrom Power, and Dali Ding in the Shanghai research and development facility of Accelergy. Other key interviews were Rich Amato of Austin's Clean Energy Incubator, Warren Karlenzig of SustainLane, Rhys Roth and Barry Pfundt of Climate Solutions, Zhang Zhong Cheng of the Shanghai Energy Resource Center, and Ashley Henry of law firm Stoel Rives in Portland.

Several reports provided important data. These include *San Francisco's Clean Tech Future*, by Ron Pernick, Joel Makower, and Arthur DeCordova (Clean Edge, 2004 and updated in 2005; www.cleanedge.com/reports-SF_cleantech2005.php); *The Impact of State Clean Energy Fund Support for Utility-Scale Renewable Projects*, by Mark Bolinger and Ryan Wiser, Lawrence Berkeley National Laboratory, 2006 (www.cleanenergystates.org); SustainLane's *2006 U.S. City Sustainability Ranking* (www.sustainlane.org/overview.jsp); *Creating Clean Companies: White Paper on Incubation*, New Energy Finance, 2006 (www.newenergyfinance.com); *Creating Cleantech Clusters: 2006 Update—How Innovation and Investment Can Promote Job Growth and a Healthy Environment*, by Patrick R. Burtis, Bob Epstein, and Nicholas Parker, Environmental Entrepreneurs (E2) and NRDC, 2006 (www.e2.org); and *Race to the Top: The Expanding Role of State Renewable Energy Policy*, by Barry Rabe, University of Michigan, for Pew Center on Global Climate Change, 2006.

CHAPTER 10

This chapter is modeled after a green-marketing course developed by Ron Pernick for the New College Green MBA program (spring 2004), along with conversations with a range of green-marketing experts and professionals, including Joel Makower, GreenBiz and Clean Edge; Jordan Harris and Roo Rogers, OZOcar; Aaron Nitzkin, Clarum Homes; Brian Keane, SmartPower; Terry Swack, formerly of the Beam; Andrew Shapiro, GreenOrder; Christine Biondi, formerly of Ford Motor Company; Tom Arnold, TerraPass. Other source material came from attendance at LOHAS Forum 2006, in particular a talk by Steve Case, former CEO of AOL and founder of Revolution LLC.

CONCLUSION

Much of the conclusion draws on our research and reports at Clean Edge, all available for download at www.cleanedge.com. These include *Clean Tech: Profits and Potential, Clean Energy Trends 2005, Clean Energy Trends 2006,* and *Clean Energy Trends 2007*. The interviews, research reports, and conferences noted throughout the book were influential in the conclusion.

ACKNOWLEDGMENTS

Any book is a journey, and there are so many people along the way whom we would like to collectively thank. While we cannot name everyone, we would like to acknowledge a number of people who have particularly helped, inspired, and enlightened us. At the top of the list is Genoveva Llosa, our editor at Collins, whose spirit and indefatigable good nature eased a sometimes demanding process and whose intellect and instinct kept us on track to remember that it's all about the reader. We also owe a debt of gratitude to our first editor, Leah Spiro, whose early enthusiasm and guidance got these first-time authors off in the right direction from the beginning. And to our agent, Jonathan Harris of Analogue Arts Agency, who has been our clever, insightful, and much-needed guide to the publishing business.

We'd like to thank the hundreds of people and organizations around the world that we interviewed or chronicled in the book. It is these pioneers who are leading the way in the growth and development of the clean-tech sector. They are the cast of characters profiled throughout the book who not only provided the landscape and template for the book itself but who also inspired us to write *The Clean Tech Revolution* in the first place because of their passion, creativity, intelligence, energy, and dedication.

As part of the research for the book, we went on numerous journeys to get a close-up look at the clean tech revolution in action and to garner inspiration. We'd like to thank all of our gracious hosts in Beijing and Shanghai, but a particularly heartfelt thank-you goes out to Kyle Wang, who made so many valuable introductions and helped us navigate the intricacies of the Chinese utility and business landscapes. We are grateful to our friends Leslie Danziger, Joel Goldblatt, and their dog Solaria, for opening up their solar-powered New Mexico haven to us for a weeklong writing retreat. And to Suzanne and Jonathan Hansche, owners of the Blue Plum Inn in Portland, Oregon, who've contributed lodging, friendship, support, and inspiration (not to mention great food) to our journey all along the way.

A special thanks goes out to all of our colleagues at Clean Edge who have supported and guided us during the journey of writing this book. First and foremost, to our colleague Joel Makower, who's an inspiration not only to us, but to all those working in the fields of green business, clean technology, and sustainability. We would also like to thank all current and former Clean Edge colleagues, consultants, and interns, including Dexter Gauntlett, Tim Miller, Alison Wise, Andrew Beebe, Andrew Friendly, Zach Nobel, Kelly Costa, Nick Brod, and Mariève Gauthier.

Ron Pernick would like to thank his parents, Stuart and Edie, for conveying so many wonderful messages to him as a youth: key among them, the inspiration to follow his dreams. I also owe a deep debt of gratitude to my sister, Karen, and brother, Craig, who, respectively, taught me the art of creativity, love, and emotions and the value of integrity, business, and commitment. Inspiration for the book also came from my summers spent at Camp Tamakwa in Algonquin Park as a child—where I could drink the ice-cold water straight out of the lake. This simple act, which came to an abrupt end with the advent of acid rain, is one of the greatest inspirations for my work in the clean-tech field and for the writing of this book. Special thanks go out to friends Billy Fenster, Alan Caplan, and George Gundrey, and all of my other friends who have supported me and inspired me throughout my life. I also wish to thank Hitomi Maeda, and all the other hiking buddies, who spent hours traversing the hills of the Bay Area with me in the early and mid-1990s—patiently listening to and encouraging my dreams of working in the world of clean tech before the world seemed prepared for such a shift. I have had the privilege of working in three major technological transformations during my life: first the rise of Asia, telecommunications, and consumer electronics during the 1980s, then the Internet and World Wide Web during the 1990s, and now clean technologies during the 2000s. I owe a debt of gratitude to all the amazing people I've met along the way who have influenced and shaped me both personally and in business. I don't have words to describe my appreciation for coauthor Clint Wilder—who at times felt as much like a brother as a coauthor. Finally, and most important, I thank my wife, Dena, for all of her support, assistance, and understanding during the sometimes arduous task of writing this book. I couldn't have done it without you . . .

Clint Wilder would like to thank his sister, Rachel, and brother, Rob, and their wonderful families for their support, interest, love, and laughs that are beyond measure. Thanks go out to my extended family of in-laws, all of the Barretts, Lokitzes, and Knapps, and spouses and significant others, whose love and encouragement are both invaluable and unforgettable. And to my late parents, Anne and Bob Wilder, who encouraged me to take up professional writing at age 16 and became my biggest fans for the rest of their lives.

I have a very long list of friends and professional colleagues who inspired and supported the writing of this book in ways obvious and not. In a very random order, they include John Mejia, Joe Khirallah and Diane Rezendes, Bob Howe, Steve Abt, Mike Bradley and Noreen Doyle, Sam Teeple, Allen Rivers, Susan Gubernat, Kelly Fitzgerald, Pam Preston, Jim and Kim Nash, Jeff Angus, Amy Cortese, Jim Daly, Don St. John, Gary Rieschel, Sahn Tolbert, Steven Herrmann, Julie Sheetz, Brian Beaudoin, Jordan Harris, Charles McGlashan, Robin Raj, Trip Allen, Kyle Datta, Nancy McCauley, Donna Miller, David Weckler, Aimee Silver, Kristen Steck, Amy Poftak, Erin Hartman, Barbara Knox, Sarah Lammert, Mark Tovey, Ed Nelson, Helen Gilhooly, Nancy Hernandez-Black, Angela Amado, Bunny and Dick Blattner, Judy Manza and Ethan Allen, Linda Marousek, Scott Marousek, Judy Louie, Sunny Smith, Brad and Kim Fisher, Amy and Steve Snyder, Tom and Jane Becker, David and Ellen Rosi, Bob and Pam Bowers, Ben Benedict, Pete Pedersen, Holly Egan, Flo Shields and Paul Richardson, Jennifer and Dave Mittereder, Anne Flanagan, Pam Lanza and Glenn Hirsch, and Scott Taylor. And to my coauthor, dear friend, and "partner in crime," Ron Pernick—thanks for your amazing knowledge, energy, talent, and drive for the success of this book and for clean tech across the world that we've now traveled together. The journey wouldn't have happened without you.

Finally, to my wife and best friend, Ellie Barrett Wilder—for your boundless love, guidance, patience, and support—thank you for truly making this book possible for me.

Portland, Oregon, and Sausalito, California
March 7, 2007

INDEX